STATUS SINGLE

THE TRUTH ABOUT BEING A SINGLE WOMAN IN INDIA

SREEMOYEE PIU KUNDU

AMARYLLIS

AMARYLLIS

An imprint of Manjul Publishing House Pvt. Ltd.
7/32, Ansari Road, Daryaganj, New Delhi 110 002
Website: www.manjulindia.com
Registered Office:
10, Nishat Colony, Bhopal 462 003 - India
Distribution Centres:
Ahmedabad, Bengaluru, Bhopal, Kolkata, Chennai,
Hyderabad, Mumbai, New Delhi, Pune

Copyright © Sreemoyee Piu Kundu, 2018

The views and opinions expressed in this book are the author's own and the facts are as reported by her which have been verified to the extent possible, and the publishers are not in any way liable for the same.

ISBN 978-93-81506-90-5

This edition first published in 2018

Printed and bound in India by
Thomson Press (India) Ltd.

All rights reserved. No part of this book may be used or reproduced, stored in or introduced into a retrieval system, or transmitted, in any form, or by any means (electronic, mechanical, photocopying, recording or otherwise) without the prior written permission of the Publisher. Any person who does any unauthorized act in relation to this publication may be liable to criminal

To
Sreelekha (Geru)
My lover, my sister, my friend.

Contents

Prologue / ix

Turning 30—Transition from Bechari to Bitch / 1

Is What You See, What You Get? / 27

Baby-making Factories or Baanjh? / 46

Motherhood in My Own Hands / 68

Bultu, Biye and Bachelorettes / 91

Sex in the City / 114

Parents, Privacy and Protectiveness / 140

The New Singles / 162

Friend vs. Unfriend / 185

From 'I Quit' to 'I Do' / 200

Epilogue: Single, Not Sorry / 218

Acknowledgments / 231

Prologue

'Not married? Single, huh?'

I was recently on a holiday to Sri Lanka with my parents and during the immigration process, something uncalled for happened. The immigration officer was a swarthy man, possibly in his late 30s, like I was. (I'm 39, by the way.) He looked me up and down, staring sheepishly at my passport and visa papers, even as the rest of my family breezily completed their immigration formalities. After a few seconds of anxious waiting, I leaned closer and questioned why I was being made to wait. The officer narrowed his eyes and asked, 'So, first time here?'

I nodded.

'Staying where?'

'Hilton, Colombo.'

'Alone?'

I shrugged my shoulders, gesturing to my mother that she should proceed to collect our baggage, with Dad, sensing from the corner of my eyes that she was beginning to get anxious about the unforeseen delay.

'What do you do?' he continued, checking me out, in a fashion that I now think every Indian girl is accustomed to. Invasive, lustful, open-mouthed, stares that we resist, revoke and retaliate, daily—

in crowded buses, in shared autos, in swarming bazaars, swanky boardrooms, in long-winded wedding processions.

'I write, I'm a novelist.' I took a deep breath, wondering whether this line of questioning was more personal than professional.

'What kind of novels?' he chewed on the top of his ballpoint pen. My parents were nowhere in sight. I speculated if mentioning that my second book, *Sita's Curse*, had been touted India's first feminist erotic novel would help my case or further fuel this persistent Q&A.

'Fiction,' I decided to keep it simple.

The man smiled. A slanted, slimy, half smile. Then scratching his ears, he asked, 'So you like travelling to places alone? Having fun?'

I stared at him—directly for the first time.

'Actually, I happen to be here with family, who've finished their immigration well before me, and are now probably through with their luggage collection as well. And if I may ask, how does my travelling alone or with them have anything to do with this delay? Don't Sri Lankan women travel alone? And just what do you mean by "fun", as in, what does fun mean in your country for such women?' I tried hard to keep my temper in check.

The man appeared startled, some fellow passengers—mostly women, carrying bawling babies; others accompanied by their doting husbands, looked equally alarmed.

'Okay, Miss... Miss, right?' the man tried making light of the moment.

I grabbed my passport and other documents back.

'Sreemoyee Piu Kundu. Yes, Miss. Anything else?' I spoke loudly on purpose.

There was a minute or two of awkward silence.

'Have a nice holiday,' the man said, adding cheekily, 'with your parents.'

The last part of the line caught my attention, and has stayed with me for the longest time. The manner in which his words were unduly patronising—first interrogate a woman on her unmarried status, and then to save face, and the embarrassment of being handed over the pervert card, sneak in the parents bit. Like actually implying, who on earth travels with mummy and daddy, that too at this age? Like a report card, a personal marksheet, a social judgment...

As I recollect this incident, my thoughts veer to a similar experience, exactly a year back. This time on home turf. The same line of jarring questions...

'Are you married?'

'What? Still single?'

'Parents not looking?'

'Not found anyone yet?'

'You must be the picky sort, huh? Too choosy... nothing is good enough for you ever.'

'Tell the universe you need a husband. Visualise your dream wedding... the babies you want. What jewellery you will wear. You want a son? What! Fat son?'

'You need a good husband, a man. Healthy body. Your body needs it...'

Picture this scene that happened a year prior to my trip to Sri Lanka. I am standing butt naked in a large hospital room, miles away from my home in Delhi. My face is bluish green because of three consecutive respiratory attacks in a span of three days. I was wheeled into emergency by a bunch of friends. My hands are swollen with unwieldy blood clots from continuous IV drips and steroid injections. My eyes are puffy from lack of sleep. My breathing is intermittent. The doctors don't have a freaking clue what caused this, or what is the next test I should be prescribed. All I get is vague answers on my diagnosis.

Sponging me are two women—a frumpy ayah in her mid-fifties who has a veritable moustache, and a nurse, a twenty-something

Malayali, in a pale olive green uniform, who chatters on relentlessly on how she can't wait to join her spouse in Saudi. I listen in, my limbs aching every time I am pushed and prodded, as I ponder on the unfortunate fate of many women from her native state who are married off to men they hardly ever see. Except on holidays—if they're lucky.

The ayah, on the other hand, is a native Kannadiga—her husband is a drunkard, who occasionally lives with a younger woman. The ayah is childless. She and her husband have tried. *She* has failed, according to him. She curses the 'other' woman, rolling her eyes, her lips quivering with an impotent rage.

And yet, as these two women wipe my privates using a warm sponge, the room reeking of the nauseating smell of antiseptic, they constantly express a singular disbelief at how I am still single at 38! Going on to suggest I consult a good astrologer at the earliest, alarmed at how at a critical time like this, I land up all by myself in a hospital. Muttering how I require a husband—and that it's unfair to have my greying father fly down to firefight a looming health crisis.

As I slip into a knee-length, pink-striped gown, I watch the two women converse in a tongue not mine, till the ayah blurts out bluntly in broken Hindi, 'You don't look your age, but a woman's body is known to lie. Don't delay things further. Having a child will inevitably get tough soon and then no man will ever touch you. What can you possibly give him then?'

Like in her case, will my man also desert me within days of our marriage? This is the unspoken question on my tongue. I wonder if that is the real fear that haunts millions of childless women, or those trapped in mute marriages—afraid of not being able to procreate timely, failing the highest duty of a wife and the ultimate benchmark of the average Indian family: producing a bunch of noisy children. Images of cheerful families shown on television commercials drift past my fatigued mind: Ageing grandparents. Picnic baskets. Matching T-shirts and Bangkok holidays.

Thoughts form and melt.

I check my phone to see if my father has checked in at the airport, and if he has texted confirming his flight is on time. Logging on to Facebook, I read the status I had shared way past midnight, confessing that I was living my greatest nightmare, and how, for the first time in my life, my aloneness had stared me in my face, literally knocking me over. The way my heart skipped a beat when I filled out the following—Status: Single. The same hollowness returning as I now scanned through the virtual concern pouring out on my timeline, providing, in a sense, a passive sort of reassurance. Except one of the comments that said, 'Sucks being single, right? Your poor dad.'

My room is eerily empty. And so, as I stare at the two women conversing amongst themselves, I wonder if I am actually living out my worst nightmare—sick in the city. A place where I hardly have any direct family or really close, old friends—the kinds who take the suffering away. A city where I came to teach in a media school, wanting a break from the monotonous rigmarole of my life back in Delhi—an alternate career, maybe?

I was tired of waiting for the editing to begin on my third novel, and had a massive fight with my mother, just before I left home. As it happens in the case of mothers, it was her that I missed the most that day. My so-called rebellion and wanting to strike out on my own, to live and work solo, sort of sounded vacuous under the present circumstances.

'So what if he's away? But to society I am married. My parents are relieved too. I have someone to look after me, especially on days such as this. See, you don't even have a single visitor at present. Who will come and be with you, that too, on a working day? As it is, no one likes to serve time here!' the nurse defensively interrupts when I try and make a joke that she is as good as a single woman like me then—meaning, she does not have an active sex life. The way she had earlier implied.

An uneasy silence descends upon us. The three of us saddled with our own thoughts and concerns, have a lot to mull over.

A couple of months later, I am sick again, demonstrating the same symptoms: retching and breathlessness. This time, I am subjected to the same patronising condescension from a reputed and young gastroenterologist in the city of my birth, Kolkata, just after he's prescribed tests ranging from an MRI to endoscopy to squeezing my stomach in every possible spot, nodding morosely as I writhe in pain to suggest that I could be critically ill. After we pay him a whopping ₹2000, he frowns, looks at my mother, and probes, 'How come you never thought of getting her married? She's what...38... will be 40 in 2 years? A single child, that too!'

I grimace. It's literally like a blast from the past. I've been sick off and on with a mystery ailment that has seen me on a bumpy medical rollercoaster from ERs at midnight, pulmonologists, heart specialists, ENT surgeons, gastroenterologists down to psychiatrists who prescribed sleeping pills and anti-depressants, while suggesting personality disorder tests to ascertain what, according to them, may just as well all be stress-related, in the absence of a real diagnosis. And now, if that wasn't enough, to top it all, my single status was suddenly back into the screeching limelight. My mother glances away, says nothing. She has nothing to say.

'It's not good...' the surgeon shakes his head from side to side, looking like an astrologer who's just declared my chances of finding a man are slim, thanks to my newly discovered and severely debilitating 'Manglik' status, which, loosely translated means I am better off marrying a tree first, like Aishwarya Rai did before she became Rai Bachchan. I want to bash him up right then, scream that my singlehood is frankly none of his bloody business, that as a medical practitioner he needs to focus on my complaints as a patient. I want to walk out after kicking him hard in his privates. I am also fighting a gnawing sense of guilt for brainwashing my mother to take me to see him, after we had been introduced by a common doctor friend, in the same city—after I had accepted his Facebook friend request and even liked a couple of his pictures.

I wondered if he viewed me as desperate? Why would he mock me then? Even picking on my poor mother, blaming her, in some measure for my single status. I pondered about why there wasn't a line of protocol for a doctor, just as there should be in any other profession—meaning, if he crossed the line of decency or professional conduct, how, as a woman, I had every right to complain to a consumer forum, for instance? How sexual harassment should also cover undue nosiness?

That's when it first struck me—what if I were to write on what it meant to be single in this country? To speak with and record the no-holds-barred truth of women like me and many others—girls from urban, educated, middle-class India who work for a living and constantly fall in and out of the marriage market, who believe in dream dates and Mr Rights and have craved children at some point, who have been insulted or insensitively dismissed by landlords, bosses, relatives and gynaecologists and suffered the indignity of being a single, unmarried Indian woman, past a certain age that society has chalked out for us—a legit *Lakshman Rekha* of sorts. What makes us a community—a demography sans a definition, and why does popular culture prefer to most often showcase the brighter side: the 'happily unmarried' label? Is being a 'happily single' woman a myth in a nation that places the highest premium on marriage or motherhood, or is it a safe defense?

As I collect my thoughts on shaping my own experiences as a single woman, with those of others who may have been in a similar life situation, feeling alienated and anguished—just as I have—whose singlehood is criticised and not celebrated, I think of a brilliant book, *All the Single Ladies: Unmarried Women and the Rise of an Independent Nation* by Rebecca Traister, that I had incidentally picked up before my Sri Lankan vacation. The book claims that single women in the US, instead of grieving the absence of a wedding ring, were seen exulting in their single status, in what was seen as a mindset shift from the compulsive soulmate-search of a Carrie Bradshaw or the pining away for reciprocity and sexual acceptance by Bridget Jones.

For instance, in 2009, for the first time in American history, unmarried women outnumbered married women. By 2012, they constituted almost a quarter (23% of the electorate, occupying every class, region, and racial group in America), with their numbers surging ahead every year.

In 2014, there were 3.9 million more single adult women than in 2010. Marriage rates have also dropped steeply among young adults in the age group of 25 to 34, according to Population Reference Bureau's analysis of new data from the U.S. Census Bureau's 2009 American Community Survey (ACS) and 2010 Current Population Survey (CPS). The data suggests that more young couples are delaying marriage or foregoing matrimony altogether, allegedly as an adaptive response to the economic downturn and decline in the housing market. In a dramatic reversal, the proportion of young adults in the United States who have never been married now exceeds those who are married. 'We are a new republic, with a new category of citizens,' Traister nonchalantly declares.

Closer home, according to the 2011 census data, single women form 21% of India's population and are close to 73 million in number. These include unmarried, divorced, separated and widowed women. Recently, taking a step towards recognising and treating single women as independent entities, the government's draft national policy on women has suggested several enabling factors such as legislation, economic reform and other measures to facilitate the process. The Ministry of Women and Child Development under Maneka Gandhi was slated to revise the policy for the first time since 2001 to address concerns such as taboos that surround single women, including social ostracisation and institutional indifference. There was a stupendous growth in this sector with a 40% increase in the population of single women in India between 2001 and 2011. The ministry officials claimed that government policy must prepare for this evolution by empowering single women through skill development and economic incentives. The policy was also slated to address concerns related to widows and universal health benefits for all women.

And yet, despite the social relevance of the subject, when I actually discuss the idea of a book on single women within my existing circle of single women friends, I sense a somewhat stubborn reluctance to freely talk about what being single really means in India—how some of them, post 40, shyly admit that they've just created their nth profile on a matrimonial site, making me swear I won't tell anyone else. Others clandestinely confess to flings with married or younger men. There is a lot of struggle I sense in basic things like getting a flat on rent or being taken seriously as a start-up entrepreneur, along with a gnawing sense of loneliness and fear, especially with the eventual onset of old age, health issues and losing parents and friends over time.

'Every time I shop for jewellery, or attend a funeral these days, I feel a tug at my own heart… what when it's my own time? Things like inheritance and blood lines are suddenly important, or maybe, the arrogance of youth is wearing away, chipped off by life's blows… the failure of romantic liaisons over time, professional setbacks, health woes, watching young people perish from cancer and heart ailments and the death of parents, most friends who are now happily married, have gotten busier with kids, their school and college plans, nannies and in-laws, the exhaustion of constantly proving you are "happily unmarried", a successful banker in her 49th year, pens as her status message on social media, a week before her 50th birthday, a sense of poignancy soaking her last words.

I react to this post with a sense of familiarity, knowing that while personal space is critical to single women as we age and nurture fixated habits and idiosyncrasies, the constant off and on search for a soulmate and the primal need for companionship results in a feeling of fatigue setting in, mostly post our 30s, as we are beleaguered of the age-old formula of having to kiss many frogs first. Dating is liberating, dating apps convenient, as is the significance of empowerment associated with casual sex and no-strings attached hooking up that is abundantly commonplace today—but in its wake breathes a deep-seated sense of passive anger and what a single friend, about to turn 45 next month, calls 'a process of internal hardening. All the bullshit over the years makes you this way... cynical, cold...'

Over time, I start thinking of my own single life—when did I begin to realise it wasn't so much of a choice, but a circumstantial culmination that I had to eventually get used to and learn to adapt, despite the occasional speed-breaks. I wondered if being single was purely relationship-centric, or, if it simultaneously also covered domains like physical and mental health, living with parents vis-a-vis living alone in another city, the never-ending pressure of marriage, the need to have sex (a friend insists on calling it 'internal servicing'), the desire to have one's own children, coupled with a general all-round pressure to conform to the larger majority—married people, who seem to be swallowing you up and swarming in population, be it virtually or for real.

I looked back at how my college bestie had also turned an alien to me ever since she started lecturing me on the 'need for a man for companionship,' using the word like a crutch, a quick-fix, or something. She would talk about how some men assumed I was frigid when I refused casual sex, how I was constantly probed even by my so-called liberated girlfriends about what I do to get laid, and how my life was constantly being compared and measured up to something that was probably considered normal and safe—marriage.

I spent the next few weeks wondering if turning 40 next year had something to do with this urgent self-introspection, and that's when it struck me that maybe it was turning 30 that had kick-started the whole process of internalisation—when being single started sticking out from being an upbeat, celebratory moment to being more real, something that I was stuck with and confronted daily, that I would have to fight hard for, and even defend occasionally. That isn't always all hunky dory, or peaceful and pretty.

'Turning 30 is a life lesson,' a girlfriend had scribbled in a birthday message to me, almost a decade ago. She was a year older than me, and joked that at least finally being 30 was better than being politely referred to as 'in your late 20s.' Another friend, who had recently turned 30 herself, asked me one night if she should be afraid of this decade. Like me, she, too, is still single. I smiled thinking how she made it a point to reiterate every time we chatted that she gets asked out on dates—a lot. Was she secretly petrified of turning into me then—a sexless spinster living with her ageing parents? Successful, maybe, but not quite in the way women have been conditioned to measure their self-worth?

'Do you lie about your age? Sometimes?' she whispers to me.

'Actually, I do. I did once or twice, especially if there was a really hot younger guy in question!' I laugh, making light of a midnight conversation.

'But you don't even look 39,' she cuts me short.

I shrug my shoulders.

I want to ask her if looking younger helps score brownie points on your single resume. For instance, would it count when a guy interested in me, discovered I have endometriosis, a gynecological condition that could hamper my chances of natural motherhood? Does looking younger actually count when you are butt naked with a man? I mean, is anyone actually looking? Or is age synonymous with attraction—with the opposite sex, that is. Why we rarely find single women role models in their 60s on billboards and in magazines? Why sexuality is akin to a jar of imported mayonnaise—with an expiry date firmly attached on it.

'Are you scared you may never find someone?' my friend breaks my thoughts.

'There are bigger fears—more real ones—like being an unemployed author with no steady income, my parents' health deteriorating rapidly all of a sudden, being an only child...' I trail, trying to rationalise my viewpoint.

'Are you lonely, Sree?' my friend is relentless.

I decide it's time to cut the sweet talk and confess, 'Yes, terrifyingly at times.'

'So, turning 30 will start to suck a lot more if you remain single... if you pass another decade all by yourself?' she sighs slowly.

'It's a big deal, I won't lie, but if you're lucky, chances are one day you'll wake up and won't remember a thing,' I hope to ease the tension.

'You make it sound like a relationship, dude,' she remarks wryly.

I take a deep breath and then exhale. 'It *is* a relationship—just with yourself, maybe mostly with yourself, with good and bad days thrown in.'

'Bad?' she interrupts in a sharp tone, sounding a trifle anxious.

'Turning 30 isn't the life lesson,' I resume. 'Surviving the 30s is. The decade is a full-blown, fucking war. You either become a seasoned war veteran or a hapless martyr,' I hope to reason, optimistic that I have made some sense at least.

'You know, I don't want to be still single at 40. It's daunting and dangerous when I think of it,' she retorts after a stifling pause.

'Dangerous?' I repeat, surprised at the sudden change in her pitch.

'Because, in reality, no one wants to be single forever, and in India, you will be crucified socially. This may be perceived as a deliberate choice you made, and this is a country where a woman's choices are never quite hers to begin with,' she hangs up in a huff.

This is what makes me say yes to this book. I want to know more. I am convinced that singlehood is as much societal as it's deeply personal, not to mention determined by destiny. I am convinced I am not hearing the full truth—the uninterrupted voices of women whose single status is more than just a standardised stereotype. I want to celebrate their successes, the same way I want to dig deeper into their sadness and life struggles. I am sure I will discover something in there—something that turning 30 hadn't prepared me for. Something that being single has…

I simultaneously decide to christen the book *Status Single* when it shapes up, giving myself a year to reach out to as many women as I can, because anything else will be a half truth, and because *Status Single* is a personal testament, as much as I want it to become an impersonal recording of urban, successful, single women's voices. Sans the sugar coating and the rose-tinted lenses. Without the double standards or the moral preaching.

Some of the names of the 2,800 women I have interviewed between 2016 and 2017 have been changed on request. But, not their stories.

This is *our* voice.

Sreemoyee Piu Kundu
March 2016

Chapter One

Turning 30—Transition from Bechari to Bitch

I TURN 40 BY THE end of 2017, and I honestly have no clue what the big deal about turning 30 was, and what were the life lessons I was supposed to learn—or unlearn—or the exact reason why such a hullabaloo was created about the last decade. Frankly, all I remember was just before my 30th birthday, when almost everyone I knew seemed eager to offer unsolicited advice on what to expect—I impulsively dumped a man, who I suspected to be yet another commitment-phobic. I was head over heels in love with him. I also remember what a single friend, a couple of years older, wrote as a reply to a gut-wrenchingly lengthy mail where I'd basically dissected my decision to walk away from the love of my life. Her single, embarrassingly pithy sentence read: 'You turn 30. Soon you'll have to drop the bechari tag of a woman who can't seem to find a man to settle down, and transition into the bitch who's single on her own terms, because honestly, it's what the 30s will boil down to—the clash of the two B words.'

Back then, I didn't have the faintest inkling what my newfound single status and my impending birthday had in common or why I had to choose either of the two B words. Which is why it's probably taken me these many years to figure out that my friend was so darn right. Because the 'Status Single' spiel pretty much commences from a woman's 30th birthday—but since you are usually so caught up in turning 30 and uploading ecstatic pictures on social media, or getting sloshed or losing your virginity that you are pressured into believing defines your sexual emancipation that you hardly notice the change in the way you will be viewed and bracketed henceforth.

Let's face it—turning 30 in India is made out to be this life-altering, inner-goddess-awakening sort of experience for most women, similar to how it's the world over. 'Thirty is the New Twenty!' glossy fashion magazine covers scream, while sassy internet pieces declare exuberantly how the 30s are supposed to be the most liberating years of our lives—overflowing with the promise of daring adventures and unapologetic rejuvenation!

The 30s are often thus labelled the new 20s—and why not? Our 20s could desperately do with an image rehaul and serious rebranding, being as they are, for most of us, a rollercoaster ride from hell. Not knowing what we wanted, wild, unstable relationships that could have been avoided, most often deeply regrettable, vacillating career dilemmas and lousy job decisions, raging rebellions and teary tantrums with parents and lovers. The banging of the front door and walking out, promising never to look back. Whew!

Our tumultuous 20s pretty much double up as a waiting room of sorts, a transitory phase, where time seems to be on our side. Where women are not yet singled out and suffocatingly boxed as unmarried/divorced/widowed/childless/with child, or pressured to enroll on a million matrimonial websites, where heartbreaks don't turn you distrustful and distant and when making babies seems like a cakewalk. Where you are forgiven easily if you screw up in romantic relationships because you have the all-empowering 30s to look forward to, and 'find yourself.'

And yet, when we actually dissect the 30s, mostly in hindsight, it's practically baffling how most people who either occupy or have crossed this decade, women especially, won't tell you what to realistically expect after the last candle is blown out and the last glass of champagne guzzled down. About what it *actually* entails in terms of peer pressure and 'performance' anxiety.

Which is why, later, when you are well into your 30s and still single as I am, you start noticing an almost serial pattern to patronising sermons about women being able to bear kids at 40 these days, tech-savvy friends suggesting you immediately download the latest dating apps along with 'keeping an open mind' with the word 'companionship' cropping up in almost every girl talk. Some will even ask you to enroll in singles communities that meet over the weekend and go on vacations together, while others will send you useful medical information about freezing your eggs. Like every single woman must love children, and crave her own, someday. Like you are a bad person if you reject the notion that there is more to your womb than reproduction.

The Big O: Deceptively Packaged Or Life-Altering?

Being 39 and still single, I can't help but wonder if the idea of being alone as a woman is an anomaly that Indian society thinks we need to be constantly cured of. And if that is the real reason why turning 30 is almost always deceptively packaged and marketed as 'transformative' to conveniently camouflage the darker shadows and uneasy secrets it guards?

Run any random Google search with the search phrase 'single women in India + turning 30' and you are sure to be bombarded with a zillion articles offering reams of superficial advice—ranging mostly between 10 and 30 things to do before one hits the magical figure. One of them titled *10 Things Single Women Should Do Before Turning 30* makes the most inane, generalised suggestions: go on a road trip with pals, live alone/with roommates, get a tattoo, learn how to cook, join a new hobby, get a dream job, go through heartbreak. Like we can't do or haven't done any or all of this before or after. Duh!

Having been there and done that, I can safely claim there are largely two versions of singlehood for an unattached woman post her 30s. The categorisation of the two Bs, as my friend had pointed out, is determined to a large extent by your marital status and which side of the fence you prefer to sit on. Which probably explains the general panic that one also associates with the figure 30. So much so that a woman's sexuality, too, isn't spared. Along with finger-pointing at parents and an invasive curiosity about how she's still allowed to be unattached, and her life choices, including the quintessential blame game for choosing professionally demanding careers, especially ones that involve late nights and frequent touring, or a doze of glamour and free mixing between the sexes, often painted as a 'fast' lifestyle that doesn't conform with the ideal of a *pativrata, Karwa-Chauth*-observing, *abla Bharatiya nari*.

Delhi-based 37-year-old Aditee Biswas, an alumnus of the National School of Drama (NSD), is like me—an only child who resides with her parents in South Delhi. Aditee manages her time looking after her family, emotionally and financially, besides teaching full time at the British School, Delhi, apart from being visiting faculty for theatre at the B. El. Ed. Program, Lady Shri Ram College and NSD. She also runs her own theatre company, Ilhaam Collective, with one of her ex-students from NSD. It's a busy and full life, and yet she's not spared the periodic taunts, as her retired father and garment-designer mother face scathing comments such as, 'Of course, you people are not interested in getting your daughter settled, as you can't do without her income.' Apart from societal curiosity that hounds a single woman, Aditee's work in the domain of gender and identity politics has often also come under the scanner and unfairly held responsible for her singlehood. Aditee specifically recalls how she was once directing plays that examined bisexuality in women, when a professor asked her point blank if she was a bisexual herself and hence still single at her age. There are also numerous inquisitive probes within her extended family. A male relative, close to her, once patronisingly asked if she was a lesbian and needed help to come out of the closet.

Having borne the brunt of this incessant witch hunt and constant, unwanted match-making, she says, 'Since I also suffer from Leucoderma, a lot of people assume that no one will marry me because of my appearance, some of them even going on to allege that it's a result of some *paap* my parents must have done, marks of which I'm bearing on my skin.'

Aditee, who maintains an 'I don't care' attitude, admits that she may be seen as 'over the hill' by Indian standards, since by her age, most women are mothers to teenagers! She adds tongue in cheek: 'Turning 30 for most single women is deliberately built up as larger than life because we need milestones to celebrate and validate our freedom and personal space in India. But, beginning from 30, a single woman starts attracting an almost familiar condescension, either reducing her to a pitiable creature or a selfish, ambitious slut. Single in your 30s, while projected as "sexy and special", isn't quite.'

Listening to Aditee makes me wonder whether a single woman's 30s are a staunch societal benchmark, by which time she ideally should have sown all her wild oats and settled down to docile domesticity and delivered one child, at least? If there is a standard operating procedure, a book of set rules, for a single woman and does life actually get harder, if she doesn't conform to this all-encompassing 30s code of moral conduct? So, while for men, the 'settled-at-30' checklist includes a stable job, material possessions like a car, a home EMI, savings, etc., for women, it's pretty much a lopsided formula that sums it up in two words: marriage and motherhood.

And, honestly, the men pool—as I call it—begins to steadily deplete as you scale up the 30s ladder, as we grapple with the painfully practical realisation that most eligible bachelors are either hitched or gay or frankly, only seek a bit of fun on the side, and not a lasting, long-term commitment. In reality, our 30s mark the beginning of a certain lingering aloneness, despite being touted as the high point of personal discovery.

The fear of the 30s is, thus, directly proportionate to its fun and feisty projection—a two-pronged sword that one can't seem to run away from. 'Turning 30 is terrifying if you're still single, because on the one hand you're supposed to feel more empowered and all there, and finally taking charge of your life. While, on the other hand, there is this persistent nagging to settle down,' confesses 27-year-old Somdatta Ray, pursuing her Ph.D in Biology from the University of Alabama. 'Personally too, it's difficult to find a guy, because whether you admit it or not, the stigma of a single woman in her 30s, being "too" educated for her own good, still exists beneath the glimmering surface of women's lib and all the feminist freedom talk.'

Somdatta's family, based in Durgapur in West Bengal, is a well-educated, upper middle-class family and while they are supportive of their only daughter's choices of pursing higher education overseas, she isn't spared the concerned questions, by her mother mostly, during their routine Skype chats that inevitably culminate by harping on marriage and men. *'Ekta chhele dekhna'* (just find a boy, please) or 'How is it possible, *je tor kauke bhalo lagena?*' (how come you like no one?) being the usual refrain. The same way one of my maternal uncles back home in Kolkata, under the guise of being a 'genuine well-wisher,' whose only dream was to see me settled, literally goaded my retired-school-teacher mother to cough up a whopping 1.5 lakhs and get registered on a new, premium matrimonial website that promised 'high-flying CEOs and managing directors' as prospective grooms, with the words 'well-settled' and 'mature' as key search words. This was the year I touched 30.

'He's done the same thing for his son,' my mother retorted defensively, when I accused her of plotting behind my back, reprimanding her at the same time for wasting her hard-earned money.

'Your daughter is a journalist, they are "fast", sleeping around, don't believe in having children,' a mother of a prospective suitor told my mother to her face on one occasion, while another man I met over coffee, asked me point-blank whether I was a virgin, adding that he was suspicious how a 'pretty girl' like me hadn't been able to find a man to marry by now. The word 'pretty' almost akin to a punishment. A penalty for being an independent, career woman. Also, 30. At about the same time, I started hearing the adjective 'choosy' a lot. Like I was wrong in knowing my mind, and not be overtly desperate to sport vermillion on my forehead. Marriage is a rat race, even amongst well-meaning friends. A social media spectacle. A sign that a woman is healthy, and all is well.

Now, while parental pressure may sometimes be simpler to manipulate and distance yourself from, it's the parallel peer pressure that often adds to the gnawing insecurity and questioning of an uncertain future that may not include a significant other by your side. Reasons Somdatta: 'My "attached, not-so-single" friends tend to joke that I may end up being an old lady with lots of cats. Maybe their leg-pulling originates from a deeper uncertainty every woman nurses somewhere of ending up just by herself. So, while today I may be cool being in and out of casual relationships and occasionally saying yes to the concept of "friends with benefits", but as I approach my 30s, I suddenly feel this compelling need to settle down, especially with most of my friends getting married and distanced, thanks to their newfound familial responsibilities.'

Finding commitment when one needs it most is also harder in an age of speed dating and casual sex—a road block Somdatta, too, agrees, prevails in her inner circle. 'In the Indian community overseas (mostly grad students), the majority of guys desperately want to get into your pants. Then there is another section of the desi crowd that judge whenever they see a single woman past her so-called prime hanging out with a bunch of men and drinking and smoking uninhibitedly. Immediately, she gets branded as a woman with loose morals and whispers run down the corridors that she's sleeping around. This crucification of a woman's character is inevitable post 30, if she is single!'

If age is just a number, like women's magazines and pop culture icons would have us believe, why are we still trapped voiceless in it? Why should we have pre-fixed Mrs. and mother to our names in this day and age? Why is looking younger after you turn 30 such a monstrous deal for the average single Indian woman? Is preservation of our youth an almost direct reference to our marriage market value, the way an aunt in Kolkata keeps eying me suspiciously, announcing that I possess childbearing hips, before rolling her eyes and lecturing my mother on finding me a boy at the earliest, claiming and probably rightly so, that I am already way too late for an arranged marriage. 'Especially with most men in this country desiring a virginal, young bride, you must maintain yourself, Sreemoyee. You have as it is a round face,' she comments sternly, the same way she always told me I was fat as an adolescent—a jarring, judgemental tone ringing in her voice.

What's So Scary About Being Single, And 30?

What to me is simultaneously surprising and sad is how this persecution of a single woman and her projection as a dried-up spinster seems to haunt even educated, upper-middle-class women who face the same sexist battles on a daily basis.

Namrata Deka, HR coordinator with a financial consulting firm in Bengaluru, turned 30 last year and is already dreading the journey ahead. 'Most women are petrified of being 30 and single in India. While it's exciting to be stepping into your 30s as it pushes a woman to a more mature category, the skyrocketing pressure of getting married is like a noose tightening around your neck, 24/7. Even my own mother who happens to be a gynaecologist tells me indirectly that I have to settle soon as it might get difficult to have kids or find the right guy, post my 30s. In office, too, these days I am tagged as the "oldie". Looks like I am being seen as a boring spinster who sticks out like a sore thumb,' she rues.

Mumbai-based Riya Mitra, head of Content and Development with Vishesh Films, with 17 years of experience in brand communication, points out to the film industry as a glaring example of all that's wrong. 'No matter how much we talk about coming of age of Hindi cinema and with a few exceptions like Sridevi in *English Vinglish* or *Mom* or Madhuri Dixit in *Dedh Ishqiya* and *Gulaab Gang*, in the film industry, the 30s pretty much mark the shelf life of a leading lady. How many roles are specifically written for mature women, who can act *and* look their biological age, on-screen? The rat race is so back-breaking that everything is skewed to preserving one's youth—naturally symbolic with glamour and thus longevity in the trade. I mean, why can't a heroine be 40 and not be typecast to simply playing glamorous-looking yummy mummies in water purifier or diaper ads or family-oriented commercials? Or become judges on talent contests and reality shows? Feminism is mostly made to appear apologetic in Bollywood because we are constantly catering to the masses and our social fabric is constructed to fit women into a cookie-cutter mould.'

Having faced the scathing pressure of singlehood in her 30s, Riya recalls how, when she turned 30, all around her in the organisation she was then working in, people would keep asking her if this was going to be the 'big' marriage year? 'Simultaneously, the pressure of motherhood acts as another huge detriment. In fact, I was once told by a man that the only reason he's agreeing to marriage is wanting to father children, otherwise he has no interest in matrimony. Personally, I've never wanted kids, and I've realised how that can act as a major deal-breaker, because for Indian men conservatively brought up, craving their own progeny is almost seen as a fundamental right—a control mechanism, in other words,' Riya analyses.

As I recount the conversations I've had with various women—all independent, successful professionals—I'm forced to ask myself again: what is it about the 30s that make us equally desirable and dreaded? Why do women constantly hear the refrain, *'Tees ki ho gayi ho,'* like a primitive death knell? How do we silently consume on a daily basis, serials packaged as 'bold and women-oriented' that primarily revolve around a woman who hasn't yet found a suitable life partner, even though she is in her 30s. Her professional success is always projected as second hand. Or maybe she's the darker or more daring one of two sisters. Single women who're shown portraying on-screen *mardangi* need to beat up the bad guys, cuss and act tough physically, to prove their sexual and emotional independence.

Does Professional Success Really Count If You Haven't Prefixed 'Mrs' Yet?

What does our professional status and success mean if we are still single post 30? Does it act like a deterrent to keep out the wagging tongues, or will it only confer on us a secondary sort of citizenship that is comfortable, maybe, but not entirely safe from criticism?

Kolkata-based PR consultant Supreeta Singh, who quit her job as a five-star chain PR head to start her own events company, is set to turn 35 soon. And yet, Supreeta admits how being successful and single isn't quite the socially and morally palatable combination, drawing on an interesting comparison to prove her point. 'Look at the way a girl's marriage is celebrated in this nation, the sheer expenditure and hoopla it attracts! On the other hand, being single and into our 30s is viewed as either *phuti kismat* or aspersions are cast on the woman's character.'

Supreeta usually takes on her detractors when they pry as to why she's still single by pointing to the sad state of modern marriages that either end up in messy divorces with ugly custody battles or rampant cheating and open arrangements. She feels we are constantly weighing the success ratio of a single woman's life based on her relationship status, and not her professional milestones. According to her, 'A lot of women love flaunting men just to prove they are in demand and available and getting enough sex. If I am single and in my mid-30s, it could be as much of a choice, as plain circumstance. I don't need to flash my identity like a placard before others, and as for the proverbial loneliness, aren't married women sometimes equally, if not more, lonely? No wonder Tinder is flooded with married housewives desperate for sex on the side and married men scouting for easy hook ups. Most families in India want to get rid of the societal liability of their daughters living with them, so that they don't face these embarrassing questions. There is a sense of failure that parents are often thrust with, which is another reason the majority of Indian parents show zilch support for their daughter when her marriage is breaking down. This is the reason why scores of women swallow disrespect and abuse and carry on becoming shadows of themselves, pretending to save their marriages for the sake of their child.

'And why women alone? What about men who are single? Why are *they* not questioned and pulled up in the same manner? If a man is single, then it is usually felt that it's fine, his biological clock is not ticking and therefore he is good to do whatever he wants. A woman, her marriage and her body are somehow a time bomb, ticking for the society,' Supreeta strongly states.

Perhaps it is this constant nagging and the need to defend our life choices that lead to a natural transition of single women in their 30s from being vulnerable to learning not to care a damn and becoming more emotionally guarded. An inner reorientation of sorts that comes with its own set of trials and tribulations and most often involves also losing your old friend circle. A personal, painful evolution of sorts, as most single women end up losing more married female friends by their mid-30s.

'Just because I am 37 and single, and I bought myself a new home, and because I love to travel solo, there is an innate judgement and suspicion about my lifestyle—how can I have the money to invest in my own living space *and* fulfill my wanderlust? I must admit here, women are women's worst enemies and bad-mouth them much more than men!' sums up Ayandrali Dutta, travel and food blogger and ex-editor of a digital platform in New Delhi.

She shares a rather poignant, personal experience. 'A friend getting married told me just before her *mehendi* that I must attend but ensure I didn't chatter away like I usually do. The image of a 30-plus woman is pre-constructed and a lot of married women are threatened by the idea of a bold, independent, headstrong, single woman just the way men are intimidated. Most assume we will seduce their husbands and lovers... as we are unfairly typecast as "fast" and promiscuous. And god help you if you dress provocatively and happen to be free-spirited! It's the same way with men who, when they realise I am living alone, suggest they want to come to my place for dinner, knowing I am a good cook and love entertaining guests. Why not lunch and why not at their residence?' Ayandrali questions sarcastically. 'It's either the available slot or perhaps I'm seen as high-maintenance and so why do I even need a man? Name tags come as part and parcel of being single in your 30s! Also, being comfortable in my own skin is a source of discomfort for others and it's possibly the same reason why I'm labelled "selfish". My singleton status doesn't bother me, which is why I don't care to look for validation outside of myself. Thankfully, from my immediate family there is no pressure to conform to the traditional social narrative of marriage. The "baby clock" may perhaps be ticking, but I choose to nurture my relationship with myself, above all, today.'

Marriage-Crazy To Marriage-Cynic: The Single In My 30s State Of Mind

The *bechari* to bitch journey isn't a cake walk, and not without its share of personal heartburn and inner realisations. I personally cringe every time my 60-plus, anxious mother brings up, yet again, the prospect of giving another matrimonial ad or when she stores the Sunday newspaper's matrimonial supplement stealthily. And while I own up to extreme loneliness and the occasional craving to freeze my eggs or think of adoption, I am internally wary every time I think of this. The sense of personal failure, synonymous with finding a companion to settle down with, seems a road I'd rather not travel down again.

Once 'marriage-crazy' by her own admission, 35-year-old Poulami Ghosh, who works with a technology conglomerate in Bengaluru, calls herself, just like me, a 'marriage-cynic and cynical workaholic'. She shuns the very idea of being 'set up'. Recounting her role reversal, she reminisces, 'We advertised in practically all the newspapers, enrolled on almost every conceivable matrimonial website, visited hordes of astrologers and did just about everything a woman does to get married by the "right" age. But all I got were ugly rejections, left, right and centre. Sometimes for being fat, at times, for my elder sister being divorced and a victim of domestic violence, on other occasions, for my pay package not being up to the mark, and with each negative response, heartbreaks were the mandate. Even now, relatives or neighbours bring up references of some guy who stays abroad or in my city and praise his family just to lure us into matchmaking. But I have become very strict nowadays, no meeting strangers and wasting my time. Even my maid once tried to fix me with an extremely *forsha* (fair-complexioned) guy. My answer was a polite NO.'

Having been the victim of sabotaged arranged-marriage setups, false hopes and shattered dreams, Poulami is today clearer about her priorities, 'I don't want my mother to suffer any more than she has. To mail my latest photo "no later than tomorrow" to some prospective who wants to basically check out my physical attributes and then turn me down randomly on the basis of my skin colour or waist size, for her to run to the nearest astrologer and source information on the NRI guy's dad's demands at the earliest, then match *kundlis* obsessively, wear stones and rings on practically all my fingers, maintain staunch *vraths*, travel cross-country to sip coffee with strangers who think they have a right to run me down and objectify my womanhood. So no more of this circus for me!' Her vehemence strangely familiar...

Why Unmarried And 30-Plus
Is A Cruel Character Certificate

As if being single wasn't bad enough, the bigger shocks come not just from prospective grooms and their families, but are reflected in the grim, everyday battles a single woman faces in the real world. Getting an apartment on rent, for instance, even in so-called cosmopolitan cities like Mumbai and Bengaluru, where women are regularly asked invasive questions on their personal life and suspected of being divorced, even if they've never tied the knot!

'*Sabh bin bihaye ladkiyan, tees se ooper ho gayi hain, tumhare mata pita kya kuch nahin karte? Aise hi padha-likhake choddh diye hain—akeli Mumbai jaise seher mein—sabh sex ki bhuki, gandi harkaton wali…*' a buxom landlady in her 50s screams at a perplexed broker in Mumbai, for bringing her yet another single woman in her late 30s, even as the tenant to be, a successful HR professional, insists that she's even ready to produce a company lease to prove her legitimacy.

'*Kya guarantee hain, yeh* divorcee *nahin hain*? Marriage annulment *ka koi* certificate *hain isske paas*?' the landlady rants, citing an example of her last tenant who worked in an ad agency and apparently had a married man as her boyfriend. '*Phir ek din, uski biwi aa tapki.* Till then she used to say, "*woh mera bhai hain*, from Jalandhar!"' she curses under her breath, insisting on the need to talk to the girl's parents and boss first, to ascertain the authenticity about her single status.

A psychology graduate from Delhi University, former radio jockey and theatre artiste, Shikha Makan, now in her mid-30s, faced a similar distressing experience when she moved to Mumbai to become a filmmaker a decade ago. 'I was very gung-ho, the way it is when you leave your roots, and set foot to claim your independence,' looks back Shikha, whose opinion of the city as cosmopolitan, migrant-friendly, and a bed of opportunities was soon to be tried and tested. 'In Mumbai, every residential complex has a housing society headed by a chairman, with the usual nomenclatures like treasurer, secretary, etc. While they are supposed to supervise mundane things like monthly maintenance, installation of new lifts and the upkeep of water pipes, in most cases, they are a voluntary unit comprising mostly elderly men who do nothing better than moral policing, and whether you want to rent or buy, the broker will inevitably present you before this ten- or eleven-member board.

'It's baffling the kind of deep-seated biases that exist in a so-called progressive city like Mumbai on narrow lines of religion, caste, food preferences, marital status, pets, sexuality, etc. And each of these committee members bring their own discriminatory attitudes to the table, as a means of exercising control. As a single woman I have found it very hard to raise my voice against this because, essentially you are battling a deep-seated assumption that a woman who hasn't married past a certain age is 'characterless'. It's humiliating to sit across this board and not feel an uncomfortable gaze, which doesn't even spare not-so-taboo professions like teaching, banking or education. And while single men, too, face the pressure of not finding a pad here, they don't carry the baggage of patriarchy. So in many ways the gender gaze is much more demeaning for a woman,' she pauses to catch her breath.

Shikha goes on to share an episode that left her scared. 'After much searching, my sister and I located a flat which fit our budget and we moved in. But from the first day, we were uncomfortable, because of the way the watchman, in so many ways a bastion of morality, who guarded our entry and exit, considered himself to be an authority to question us on our whereabouts. He would keep staring open-mouthed, as if he wanted to find out what we were up to. I worked in advertising, so kept late hours. Once when I returned home at 2 am, a male colleague accompanied me, since I mentioned being uncomfortable with the way the watchman looked at me. But as soon as we reached the gate, he stopped us and called the society chairman who started alleging that I was running a brothel. Both my friend and I were in shock!

'The chairman even threatened to throw my sister and me out. I called my father, who gave him a piece of his mind and we continued to stay there. But we still felt extremely uncomfortable. And then, the harassment started—someone would ring our doorbell at 3 a.m. or write nasty things about us on the walls. We decided to leave.'

Ironically, the same chairman changed his attitude after Shikha's father appeared on the scene. The association with a respectable man turned the so-called 'slut' into a *'sanskaari beti'* overnight! However, Shikha's nightmares were far from over. 'Housing brokers claimed, "*Aap bachelor girls ho, aapko compromise karna padega.*" Your choices start shrinking as a "bachelor girl". You either have to take up residence in a subpar building or you have to be so rich that you can afford a penthouse in a gated community,' she adds matter-of-factly.

The common refrain found in most girls sharing their stories of finding apartments in Mumbai irked Shikha enough to direct her first documentary feature, *Bachelor Girls,* a compilation of interviews of urban, upwardly mobile, English-speaking single women who have come all the way to Mumbai from various small towns. Presented as seething testimonies from bankers, students, a former UN employee, someone who works at the French consulate, etc., *Bachelor Girls* attempts to capture the real experiences of life in a big city for women in the workforce. 'The subtext of my film is that in India the feminist battle is now 3 or 4 decades old and we have an ideology on women empowerment, *beti bachao, beti padhao.* There is so much of emphasis on arriving at a liberated version of a woman who is educated, financially independent and can survive on her own. But when this version of a woman comes to your doorstep, we slam the door on her face. We are living in spaces where people tell us that it's not safe, we have to wear *"dhangke kapde"*, we have to work doubly hard to be taken half as seriously at work and then landlords tend to also lord over us.'

Shikha's powerful premise personally resonates with me when I visit a friend, single and in her 40s, at a plush apartment complex in New Town, supposed to be Kolkata's new-age residential address inhabited by high-flying corporates with pots of disposable income and a fast-moving lifestyle. As my rented car enters through her imposing iron gates, a burlesque lady security officer asks me which apartment I wish to visit. I rattle off my friend's address and her name, to which she retorts sarcastically: 'Oh, the madam who lives all by herself? *Eka*? Unmarried?'

I am taken aback by the sting in her words and her rather putting off body language, and the way a single woman is brandished by another woman. I wonder if married couples in the same plush complex are also identified as those who live with families—perhaps marked mentally as 'safer', in other words. Upstairs, at the get together, two other ladies present also mention that the same security officer had referred to my friend in the same manner—when they had asked for her address. My friend, a divorcee, then admits how there's a great deal of curiosity about her living alone in her expansive apartment, and how a married neighbour is often desperate to offer his 'services' at any given hour of the day and night.

A lot of single women I know, who have parents living in the same city, including quite a few friends even in Kolkata, prefer living alone. After a certain age, space becomes vital, as is having the freedom to enjoy a certain lifestyle that perhaps an older generation cannot quite understand or support—parties that go on past midnight, married lovers, live-ins with a person of the same/opposite sex depending on what one's sexual orientation is, and a life not bound by a strict timetable that hasn't changed since when you were 10. Then there are others like my friend, who stay alone, in company-provided accommodations. I ask, why is a single woman living alone such duress on society? Why is her life a constant source of scrutiny for others? What will it take before a single woman is not painted either as a slut or a sexless saint?

Before her personal choices are not weighed by someone else's searing value judgement? And when can she afford rent and stay on her own, sans this pervasive intervention? When her aloneness isn't seen as physical and emotional desperation?

What's odd is that women are sometimes the most insensitive. On the same trip, a well-meaning, married girlfriend asked me over for a party at her home, promising she'd introduce me to a bachelor friend of her spouse, based in the US, also on the lookout. Her text akin to a bait—like telling a child: study and then you get to watch TV; or getting a man at 39 a veritable reward; or even a retribution for being single all this while—a reformative social pattern.

At the core of these myriad threads is an overwhelming presumption that I am 'looking for marriage since I am way past my 30 goalpost'—and that it is just about everyone's moral responsibility to either advice me on the need to find a good husband/benefits of companionship in old age, suggest men that are then, more often than not, never introduced properly by the well-intentioned friends/relatives in question with zero follow-up, or assume that I am in some way unhappy/unfulfilled. I didn't even exchange a word with the prospective suitor at the party and when I asked my friend what happened to the grand promise, she messaged back casually saying, 'I thought you would introduce yourself!'

The battles may differ, even though the war is the same...

A single girlfriend I was speaking with recently in New Delhi while researching for this book, asking her to connect me to more single women she may know, named a 36-year-old journalist colleague, before hesitantly saying, 'I don't know whether she will talk though. She's closed about her being single and over 30. See, it's like a failure, right?'

From Finding The Right Man To Finding The Right Health Insurance: Regrouping Life Goals

Despite all that's written about the empowerment and emancipation of the single-woman tribe and the economic liberty that fuels our independence—all the women-only holiday companies, vibrant online communities formed on Facebook and a flurry of pictures of singles socialising with their own sex on social media—is being single *and* in your 30s nothing short of a shrouded silence we often shy away from admitting and accepting as the sordid truth? A decade of shedding our old skin, in a way, and preparing for the years ahead.

Mumbai-based consultant and digital entrepreneur Tanya Sen (*name changed on request*), now in her early 40s, refers to her 'turning 30' moment as the big leap into actual adulthood. Married in her early 20s and battling a fractured marriage, Tanya ended up as the primary breadwinner—being financially responsible helping her come to terms with her otherwise dysfunctional relationship. 'Being a breadwinner was never a problem. In fact, I saw this as being an equal: if a man can, so can I. But, being denied marital rights, including an attempt to have a child along with mental abuse is when I decided I had to close the chapter. I didn't ask for alimony. My main aim was to build my life again with my will power and mental strength. The truth is I have never been able to trust people again, and I feel it's very hard for a woman with a mind of her own to find a companion of her choice.'

Having broken free from the shackles of a faulty marriage, while consciously opting for the single-again tag, Tanya today feels: 'Thankfully, these days, despite the larger societal loopholes, there's much less pressure on modern women to conform and get hitched by a certain age. And that's what makes single and in your 30s empowering. In fact, I returned from a big, fat Bong wedding in Kolkata where I was petrified of being asked offensive questions on my being single, but much to my surprise I found everyone advising me on getting a health insurance instead. To me, staying single is soothing, and while emotional intimacy is certainly going to be harder to find, post 30, women should rather get rid of the soppy bullshit and claim their own space!'

Like Tanya, 45-year-old Anuradha Varma, an editorial consultant in New Delhi, recently found herself taking on an additional HDFC Cancer Life Insurance, that added to her financial responsibilities, including a whopping ₹40,000 EMI home loan and an earlier Apollo Munich Health Insurance. 'I think turning 30 is like a coming of age for a single woman because suddenly you start developing health problems, since most of us are lax on exercise and have a sedentary lifestyle. Also, everywhere you look, you read and hear of women succumbing to cancer. Even social media often throws up friends of friends battling the life-threatening disease. And given the fluctuating nature of the current job market, with people being fired at the drop of a hat, and the economic upheavals in India, as one gets older, you realise the value of increasing the insurance cover you may already have, the way I hiked up mine from ₹10 to 15 lakh, and maybe even getting a special cancer policy.'

Anuradha's words echo in my mind when recently, I went through a nerve-wracking experience. I was spending a weekend with a single girlfriend just a month before this book went to press, and while getting a massage by her house help, I grimaced when she pressed under my right breast.

'Didi, come here, look,' she called out urgently to my friend.

Together, we discovered a swelling. A frantic call to my mother, a rushed appointment with my gynaecologist and an urgent breast ultra sound later, I discovered that the black spot under my breast and the niggling pain that I had ascribed to wearing underwire bras was actually a cyst.

And so, 20 odd years after I lost my maternal grandmother to oesophageal cancer, I sat confronting my worst fear of facing an oncologist in a top super-specialty hospital in Kolkata. As I filled up a lengthy form, searched for a seat for my mother to sit in a swarming oncology department and waited endlessly for my consult, I found myself in a sea of women. Some, with wigs. Some, flat-chested. Some with hands swollen from painful IV drips. Some too weak to stand or walk. Accompanied mostly by women—daughters, sisters, mothers, sisters-in-law, aunts, friends—a nameless community of caregivers. Huddling heavy files and medical reports, carrying plastic water bottles, their gaze, restive.

Next to me sat two women.

'Patient?' one of them asked. She was middle-aged, clad in a modest salwar kameez. Her hands barren, her right wrist bandaged.

'I'm waiting to find out. You?' I leaned in closer.

'I am waiting for my chemotherapy schedule. I lost my mother to 4th-stage cancer. I was diagnosed last year. Terminal stage. I have had both my breasts operated. I had 15 cycles of chemo… then radiation… my hand… it's undergone plastic surgery…' she paused, biting her lower lip.

I looked away.

'You are alone today?' I resumed after a while.

'I have been alone all my life practically. My husband cheated on me… and was abusive… I almost lost my daughter. He hit me with a rod. I walked out. Alone. Took up a job in a Montessori school, to keep myself going, staying with my mother. My father, too, had abandoned us, after my mother birthed three daughters in succession. Today I teach in a reputed school, and give tuitions. I have bought a home of my own. My daughter will soon be in college…' her words trailed.

I moved closer.

'Are you scared?' I looked into her eyes.

'I only wish I had come to the doctor sooner, you know. I kept waiting for my daughter to finish her twelfth... thinking why spend money on a doctor's visit? I was almost ashamed of my nipples... the way the puss oozed...' she looked down at her hands.

I think of the lady who had performed my ultrasound a couple of days earlier and had asked me pointedly, if I touched myself and how I took a while to answer her.

'All you young women spend so much on your faces, figures and hair and skin, but don't prioritise your health. Hardly coming for annual checkups, getting regular mammograms and pap smears... self-examining your breasts,' she had scoffed.

'Go on... you will be fine. I know you will. You have so much life left to live. Didn't you say you were a writer? So many stories waiting...' the lady sitting beside me said, bringing my thoughts back to the present.

It was my turn to enter the oncologist's chamber. I nodded urgently. Looking back over my shoulders, all I could see were members of my own sex. Strong, scared, scarred, surreal.

'You too,' I raised my voice.

Our eyes met.

'You will live, too. I know you will. Okay? You will be well, okay?' I clasped her hands tight, walking back, almost choking.

'You too,' I heard a flurry of voices almost say together.

'You too,' I repeated to myself, pushing open a heavy door...

In the next few weeks, as I grappled with multiple visits to my oncologist, I also realised how common breast cancer was, and how callous we women, even those of us who are educated and enlightened, are when it comes to our own body. My condition is not life-threatening but I have to be careful, starting now, and may even require surgery later to remove my sebaceous cyst. A study published in August 2017, examining breast cancer awareness in India, found that more than 70,000 Indian women died of breast cancer in 2012, and predicted that the number of deaths was likely to increase to 76,000 in 2020. Younger women are also more likely to develop breast cancer with the average age of incidence shifting from 50 years to 30 years. The Indian Council of Medical Research finds that India is likely to have more than 17.3 lakh new cases of cancer and over 8.8 lakh deaths due to the disease by 2020. Breast cancer is the most common of the types of cancers occurring in India followed by lung cancer and cervical cancer. The Council estimates that there were 1.5 lakh new cases of breast cancer in 2016—that is more than 10% of all new cancer cases in 2016.

We spend so much time fretting on whether our breasts are too large or too small and therefore an object of sexual titillation for the opposite sex, splurging on push-up bras and breast enhancement surgeries. And yet, we often delay treatment when confronted with pain, discomfort, discharge, discolouration or can feel a swelling of any sorts. As my oncologist Dr Tapti Sen, head of the department at the Medica Institute of Breast Diseases, Kolkata, said on my last visit. 'Instead of Mother's Day, Rose Day, Sister's Day, if we as mothers and sisters and colleagues and friends can actively encourage and support each other, in our existing communities and influence groups, breast cancer will not be the life-threatening epidemic it is now. Prioritise your personal health. Be breast empowered.'

Commercials about women's beauty famously proclaim a woman's body is not the same after she turns 30. So, what if it were true? What if instead of focussing on the external, a single woman in her 30s tunes in? Reclaims her physical and emotional health, and instead of the dull skin and spot-reduction regime, is unapologetic about her body and mind, and places herself first, whether or not she ever gets married.

And so, I can't help thinking, are single women in their 30s trapped in two opposite ends of the two-B theory—either the staid spinster or the 'fast', sexy chick who's out partying every night? Who is the single woman of today, when her greasepaint is off and she's back home at her apartment after a long day of work? What makes her sad? Is she lonely? Tired of mechanical dating apps and casual sex that leads nowhere? Does she dread popping the pill the morning after the guy from the bar leaves, sans even a goodbye kiss? Are we going to be bracketed as old-fashioned if we expect romance? Does craving for a child and a normal, well-sorted partner, make her no less a feminist for wanting it all? Is she tired of gynae visits and petrified to grow old alone, of losing her parents? If like me, she, too, is an only child, this will no doubt add to her list of worries.

'Everywhere I go people are asking why I'm not married at 39? It's like a grim reminder that the 40s are staring at us. Like it's *my* fault that I found no one. But where are the guys? I'd rather buy a vibrator than invest in yet another newly launched matrimonial site or install my nth dating app…' a single friend, the same age as me, laughs. I laugh along, though it's a question that haunts me personally. Isn't so much of why we are single solely attributed to the absence of a male life partner? Ironical though, how first society expects us to not settle for less, and then lectures us on setting impossible personal relationship standards? Perhaps, hypocritical, too, at some level? Maybe that's what makes singlehood easier to glorify than own up to? Or perhaps starting at 30, it's time we stood up for our status—single and unapologetically so!

STATUS SINGLE: *The 30s aren't exactly the new 20s, because every decade is about moving forward and gaining a fresh perspective in life and is different from the past decade. So treat the next 10 years like a life lesson and be prepared for the self-discovery, struggle, potential loneliness, letting go of relationships and friendships, and the tough survival that they bring in its wake. Also, in India, 30 is usually viewed*

as the final marker for marriage, so be prepared to be lectured on the topic and hooked up randomly by all and sundry and to feel the peer pressure that naturally builds all around us—be it by your well-meaning neighbour, your married friends constantly bombarding social media with happy-couple pictures or the grim-faced family astrologer. And you are likely to hear the phrase 'biological clock' a lot more now that you are in your 30s, along with being made to feel you are already late for motherhood, which is assumed to be an instinct all women are supposed to be born with!

Best to filter out the unnecessary noise and treat your 30s as a hardening process where you learn to stand up for your singlehood and not be apologetic for your life circumstances—and look at the next 10 years more as an elimination process—to discard people, jobs and experiences that bring nothing to your self-evolution as an individual. Embrace that you are no longer 20-something, and that part of your personality also may have changed along the way. Stop lying about your age—and become who you are today.

Chapter Two

Is What You See, What You Get?

On one particular family trip to Kolkata I broke out into a severe facial rash that needed urgent medical intervention. After much reluctance, I decided to ditch the local chemist and my tried and tested Betnovate-and-Lacto Calamine regime for a pit stop at a swanky new skin and hair clinic that had opened doors in my otherwise staid South Kolkata residential neighbourhood. The clinic had polished glass doors and wall-to-wall posters of a popular Tollywood actress flashing her pearlies and her luscious, waist-long curls. I had, in the past, always joked while passing the outlet about how misplaced the location was, demonstrating the naïve arrogance of a Kolkatan who had left the city more than 19 years ago—assuming that it would be underpopulated, perhaps to be predictably soon replaced with a beauty parlour or a popular pizza outlet, or something. However, I was in for a shock when I walked in one evening: the plush purple lounge area teeming with patients, mostly young women accompanied by their grim-looking parents, some only with their ageing fathers, all waiting or asking for an appointment with the dermatologist.

There were hardly any male patients.

'Are you here for the skin lightening and chemical peeling? Platinum package? Getting married in August, right? Third session? Cash or card?' a distracted lady sporting the same garish purple uniform with the insignia of the clinic looked up absent-mindedly and quizzed, studying me carelessly from the corner of her eye.

I shrugged as a mark of protest, saying, 'No. I just have a rash. See…'

The lady stopped typing on her laptop, and stared me straight in the eye this time. 'First time here? You'll have to wait then, ma'am. There are many appointments today. Would you like to see our brochure until then? Also, I think your hair is thinning. May I recommend some packages for that as well…there's a joint hair and skin offer going on presently…wedding season is coming soon, and before that Durga Pujas.'

There was an awkward silence.

'Are most of these women getting married?' I leaned in closer and probed all of a sudden, my words short of a whisper.

The lady looked a tad perplexed. Chewing for a few seconds on the tip of a ballpoint pen, she smiled. 'You must look beautiful, ma'am, to get a boy. If your forehead is, say, too broad, and hair scanty, there are greater chances of being turned down.'

Her comments took me by surprise. I mean, was this the new form of dowry? Fair, slim, convent-educated, working, and clinically manufactured—a blemish-free bride?

'I was very fat, you know. That's why I wasn't getting married. These days, of course, there is also bariatric surgery to take care of obesity. In fact, we are soon opening a branch for weight reduction, liposuction and cosmetic surgery. Now even housewives dream to have Priyanka Chopra's thick, pouted, collagen-pumped lips. How old are you, ma'am?' she had fished out a form by then. Some sort of preliminary paperwork, I guessed.

'39,' I retorted curtly, her words still ringing in my ears.

'Maybe Sir can recommend a good skin-rejuvenation package… you have spots too and a deep mark on your nose,' she resumed politely, before I walked away. Finally, I flopped down beside a young woman, possibly in her mid-20s, her cheeks flushed from the sweltering heat outside. Filling up the same form.

'Status: Single', it read.

What was she here for, I wondered.

'Seema Biswas, skin lightening. Seema? Please proceed to the first floor…' a loud voice interrupted my thoughts, as the girl next to me arose with a spring in her step.

'Go on, I'll pay and wait here for you,' her father mumbled in Bengali, fiddling in his crumpled kurta pocket.

As I watched the girl named Seema go, I grappled with a familiar pang of regret. Remembering the numerous instances I myself had been at the receiving end of a cruel arranged-marriage market where women are auctioned through elaborate ads via portals, apps and relationship managers—scrutinised and surveyed physically, first, and most often rejected for not meeting the lop-sided standards set by Indian society for a woman to qualify as 'marriage worthy'. With an immense and unending pressure to get married by a certain age—one of the biggest banes of remaining single post 30, I couldn't help but think, are the body issues the average Indian woman nurses, doubled and directly proportionate to her unmarried status? The way she is cruelly singled out as being imperfect for men, marriage, and motherhood, consequently. Constantly.

The way I was once. The way I still feel about myself. Somewhere…

I'm going to be completely honest. I'm a fat person. I mean, inside. Which when translated implies I feel fat, most of the times. Ever since I can recall, I've struggled with my weight. Ever since I was born. In fact, I was probably born with most of it. The fat part,

I mean. I weighed 10 pounds at birth. My mother was constantly teased about the possibility of bearing triplets. Her mother, my maternal grandmother, legendary as one of Kolkata's most sought after Kayastha beauties and a fitness freak herself, constantly screamed instructions, asking my very pregnant and very rotund mother to exercise. Eat right. Do what the hell it takes.

As a chubby and buck-toothed teenager, I remained at the receiving end of second-class treatment, my grandmom perennially suggesting diets and marching me onwards to swimming and Bharatnatyam classes. I was still obese, though. Boys treated me as though I were invisible, and anyone I remotely liked, or nursed a crush on, turned his face away, as if I were untouchable. I had no boyfriends till college when post my first gynaecological surgery (that too was blamed on my excess weight) I joined a gym and began—what can be best described in hindsight as—an almost self-destructive regime of losing weight drastically. My instructor, too, seemed hell-bent, often pumping his fist and screaming, *'roga kore charbo'* (I *will* make you thin). Like it was his personal target achievement mission!

It was easy to believe him, I suppose. And so, I ran like a maniac on the treadmill, did more than a hundred crunches, performed lunges and squats with athletic precision, and revelled at the shape of my newfound abs, fitting into clothes I had till then only eyed suspiciously, bunking classes to focus instead on my gruelling aerobics and gym regime that became more of a lifeline.

The compliments flowed in. Women checked me out and everywhere I went, relatives complimented me on my looks, their tone suddenly more than passingly sympathetic. The boyfriend I had made finally, was hornier and constantly sought to make out, touching me in places I was scared of even looking myself, and before I knew it I was more imminently alive than I had ever felt before. But, what I didn't know at 19 was that the weight would soon return to haunt me—the moment I thought it was lost forever. As would the irregular period problems, sombre gynaes steadily replacing interested suitors, attacking my flab, the tyres around my tummy, my single status, especially after I had stepped into my 30s. Before I knew it, I was up for rejection again—this time around by prospective mothers-in-law and to-be grooms who sized me up shamelessly, demanded full-length photographs, told me I was already on the wrong side of 30 and blamed my weight and short height as a mismatched criteria for the alliances never clicking, along with of course my profession as a lifestyle journalist which loosely translated meant promiscuous.

Clearly, not homely enough!

Why Is A Single Woman's Physical Appearance Her Meal Ticket?

The humiliation a single woman faces for the sake of marriage is a scathing commentary on not just our skewed social structure, but also the looming darkness that prevails in popular mindsets—where mothers persecute their own daughters and instill in them a shallow sense of self that is fragile, false, and in constant need of a higher male validation and moral acceptance.

32-year-old Ishita Priyadarshini, a successful corporate marketing professional, lives and works out of Mumbai. And yet, her fancy postgraduate degree in advertising and marketing, attained from one of the top-notch management institutes of the country, can't seem to take away the reality of her conservative Bihari upbringing where her mother, a Jamshedpur housewife, strictly prohibited her from consuming sweets and stopped relatives from pampering her with the same, while she was growing up. Picked on since childhood for her dark complexion and chubbiness, Ishita, who is still single, remains an anomaly in her community where girls her age are mothers already. Ishita also carries ugly personal scars of a broken engagement in 2013, where following an elaborate ring ceremony, the boy's family unexpectedly retracted from formalising the relationship, the very next day, alleging that a girl like Ishita wouldn't quite be acceptable to their extended family who wouldn't settle for anything other than a fair and thin bride.

Battling a nervous breakdown, Ishita sought counselling to gather the broken pieces of her dreams, and while she has made peace with her singlehood now, she admits rather matter-of-factly, 'My guy friends who also are into dating are basically looking for skinny hot women who they can basically flaunt as arm candy. I've personally dated a guy sometime back who seldom went out with me to public places… and sadly, much later did I realise that he didn't want to be seen with a fat chick.'

Ishita travels back home only once a year, for Diwali, for a maximum period of two weeks—calling her home visit 'torture enough'. 'I will never forget how my mother once yelled at me saying her biggest disappointment was that I'm dark, fat *and* 31!'

The pressure to become a plus one, almost a socially conditioned requirement, coupled with one's personal struggle with physical perfection, makes remaining single in your own skin an uphill task—a battle that becomes daunting, particularly when you belong to a conservative business family where marriage is considered the greatest goal of women, and, therefore, looking good, their biggest criterion. Sonali Dave (*name changed on request*), 30, a lifestyle writer from a Mumbai-based Marwari family, recalls how one of her aunt's brothers actually wrote in her matrimonial CV that she was 'white'! Sonali confesses to always being made to feel ugly, since she was dark and plump and grew up constantly being compared to her older sister who was thin and fair-complexioned. Comments like, '*Itni sundar thi! Kya ho gaya, dekho?*' have stalked Sonali as an awkward adolescent and contributed to her severe eating disorder at

21, where she literally yo-yoed from binging to absolute starvation, ultimately shattering her self-worth. What adds to her tumultuous personal struggle even now is that within the family, most of her younger cousins, too, are all married and with kids.

'Though I've knocked off most of my earlier weight, I still can't seem to take a compliment, and have deliberately created filters in romantic relationships, including being unable to enjoy sex with the lights on,' Sonali confesses, even dreading her subsequent weight loss. 'The very second I shed a few extra kilos, my aunts are after me to remove my old snaps from Facebook, and get a professional photo shoot done so that this time around, at least, they can get what they refer to as a *pukka rishta*. They are probably dreading the stigma of me soon hitting 30 and still being single. What will they blame then, apart from my below average looks? We talk about men in India being superficial… what about families of women like me whose daughters still haven't got lucky in the marriage department?' she questions.

Pressure to get married timely, constant harassment from family, especially the persistent criticism from one's own sex, and painful matrimonial rejections, all add up to a single woman's sense of alienation in a society, which normatively believes a woman's highest purpose is in adding the prefix, Mrs, to her name. In fact, I've always speculated how popular TV wedding shows perennially dangle the big, fat, Indian dream *shaadi* card to aspirational brides by offering them a chance of a lifetime for a fully sponsored cosmetic makeover that transforms them into physically flawless creatures—free skin lightening, hair straightening, teeth and jaw resetting and fancy cosmetic surgeries, which while promoting the expertise of doctors, upmarket parlours and fitness gurus on prime time—add to the age-old adage of Indian marriages being largely founded on a woman's physicality.

So, is what you see what you get?

Virgin, Not Vamp:
What A Single Woman Does To Win A Suitable Match

Born and raised in an unwieldy conservative UP-ite family, and having grown up watching her mother face the painful ostracism for not being able to deliver a son, including her paternal grandmother trying to fix her father's marriage to a younger woman, I meet 34-year-old marketing professional Nita Mathur (*name changed on request*) in an upscale South Delhi café. She is barely a month away from her wedding, meticulously arranged by a family astrologer based in Kanpur, her hometown, who also organised elaborate *havans* and performed a ceremony called *kumbhvivah*, in which Nita had to marry a peepal tree symbolic of the Hindu God Vishnu, to remove the cursed *Mangal Dosha* from her birth chart, believed to be unfavourable for conjugal relationships, feared to be responsible for the untimely death of the husband.

But we are not here to discuss Indian astrology.

'I grew up with a deep-seated guilt that I was born a girl. My father is the oldest in a business family that had always prayed for a boy, so as to secure the line of inheritance. At times, I wished I'd died at birth itself, because all I heard were curses, never quite receiving the affection that an older grandchild is supposed to get in a joint family. I just wanted to get out of Kanpur, at any cost. I fought with my father and uncles so that they let me come to Delhi to get an MBA degree, and even then I was subject to snide remarks as to how my ambition would cost my two younger sisters, my cousins, adding that there would be no money for my dowry and theirs, and that I would only possess a tree as my husband.

'I didn't care initially. In Delhi, my years in a hostel and later working and living alone in a PG meant I could live on my own terms and was earning my own keep. I also started dating off and on, and sex with men felt hugely liberating. It was, in some strange manner, also a way to get back at the closeted patriarchy that I dealt with as a child. That always asked me to cover up and not come back home late. My father had even beaten me one evening with his walking stick, on seeing me head back with my cousin brother's best friend who I tied Rakhi to, calling me *randi*. I was 16. He was quick to blame my mother immediately. He screamed, "*Tumne hi use chhooth deke chora hain.*"'

Nita takes a minute to compose herself before adding, 'Turning 30 and still being single, working in a big city, and living alone was proving to be a stigma for my parents, because now my sisters also sought the same freedom. So they started pressurising me for marriage. My mother always wept on the phone, warning me that life as a single woman, though seemingly attractive presently, would return to haunt me later. She'd always bring up how my irreverent behaviour was going to affect my sisters' future, and honestly, it was more for them that I agreed to an arranged alliance. I'd created enough controversy, and worried if its impact would mean a lifelong imprisonment for my siblings.'

There is a brief spell of silence before Nita returns to the topic that has brought us here this evening. 'I didn't really care about it, but as I belonged to a severely orthodox, small-town UP-ite family, I couldn't confess to my parents and my would-be that I wasn't a virgin and that I was sexually active. It also happened to be the first question my to-be *dulha* asked me when we were granted half an hour to ourselves, after our parents had met and liked each other, and my *kundli* had matched his. We had seen close to 25 boys by then and probably my profile existed on every matrimonial site there is, with my family hell-bent on getting me married before I turned 35. Maybe, somewhere I, too, was tired of dressing up like a bride and serving sherbet and answering asinine questions like if I could cook, what time I got back from my job and if I loved children. The same way I felt soulless after my flings fizzled out after a while, without a commitment or a significant promise. Almost all my friends were hitched, even my roommate was moving out soon, her parents having found her a boy.

'The parents of my prospective were going to allow me to work after marriage and also because I would be moving abroad, it felt like a breath of fresh air. But I could sense that they wanted to know if I had any past relationships as I'd lived alone in Delhi until then, and I remember reading how these days even in family-arranged alliances, a private detective is hired to ascertain the past of a guy/girl. At approximately the same time, I learnt about this surgery in a leading woman's magazine, and read up on the internet extensively, before I finally opted to get it done in the hope that my marriage would at least begin on a positive note with no suspicion about my past or sex life. I had no intention of telling my husband about my ex-boyfriends either, one in business school, and the other a colleague from work with whom I had also been in a live-in—what was the point, anyway? Both had left me because of the same caste and background issues… all men are the same… in the end… spineless cowards!' Nita's daring decision to go under the knife in a West Delhi clinic burnt a hole in her pocket as she shelved almost ₹60,000 for a half-an-hour procedure that promised to restore her hymen to its immaculate condition.

Ironical, huh, for a professionally qualified woman whose biggest, lifelong battle against misogyny had turned her into a mute victim herself? Has Nita, who now aspires to settle down with her techie husband in the US, shortly after the completion of her nuptials, paid the painful price for wanting to be set free from her fate? Is the deeply prejudiced Indian mentality, when it comes to singlehood in women, the real reason behind the rise of such corrective cosmetic surgeries? Will Nita's two younger sisters, now studying, also follow suit? Their womb, their destiny…

Our cultural vigilance on perfection, fairness, slimness, etc., that is ultimately connected at a much deeper level to the value of virginity rampant in the marriage market has in the recent past consequently led to a veritable surge in the Indian cosmetic surgery industry. Single women today opt not just for lip tucks, breast enhancement and rhinoplasty, but also for hush-hush hymen reconstruction surgeries that are steadily on the rise.

In an April 2015 report in *Indiatimes.com*, Dr Anup Dhir, leading cosmetologist at Apollo Hospital claims, 'There has been an increase of 20-30% in these surgeries annually. Majority of women who opt for this surgery belong to the age group 20 and 30.' Anita Kant, head of obstetrics at the Asian Institute of Medical Sciences, Faridabad, is quoted in the same piece as saying, 'Hymen reconstruction surgery has become an emerging trend over the past 3 to 4 years.' The main reason, experts assert in the same piece, is the prevalent conservative mindset.

The surge in the demand of genital cosmetic surgery has naturally resulted in a sudden burgeoning of aesthetic genital surgery clinics in India, with some doctors also uploading rate cards for procedures packaged as of 'vaginal rejuvenation'.

'You desire to look beautiful from the outside,' Mumbai-based Dr Sejal Desai's website declares, 'Now you can choose to look beautiful from the inside too.' One whole wall of her consulting room in Sarla Hospital, in the Mumbai suburb of Santacruz, is plastered with photographs of vaginas. Each one carries a tag: 'before' or 'after'.

Recently separated herself and presently single, 44-year-old Dr Desai identified a great demand for such procedures around 5 years ago, when patients started asking her if she would carry out labiaplasty, performed to improve the 'look of the area' by trimming the labia minora and majora. Subsequently, in 2012, she signed up for surgical training in Los Angeles, and today performs two or three procedures a month. 'Where single women go, there are two distinct categories: one, unmarried, mostly in the 20-30 age group who usually seek hymen reconstruction as they insist that they have to "bleed on the first night", as they are unwilling to arouse the suspicion in their newly wed spouse's mind of having led a sexually active life, that they now fear could be a matter of life and death post marriage. Secondly, divorced women who are newly single, again, mostly opt for vaginal rejuvenation/vaginoplasty or breast lifts to augment and remedy sagging breasts, common, especially after breastfeeding, that is priced anywhere between ₹80,000 to a lakh. Vaginal tightening procedure ranges anywhere between ₹80,000 to ₹1,20,000. Though these days we're also recommending a non-surgical ThermiVa treatment using radio frequency to deliver heat into the female genital region. This causes increased blood flow, increased sensitivity, increased tissue tightening, and improved moisture balance. The outer genital region benefits when the tissues are tightened. This is painless, and needs 3 to 4 sittings, 3 to 4 weeks apart, costing approximately a lakh.'

Potential clients look at these photos and feel comfortable opening up about their sex lives and their inner desire to have 'designer vaginas' depicted on the wall and on Dr Desai's website. 'I have also opened an Academy of Vaginal Aesthetics offering a training course to doctors on vaginal aesthetic surgeries,' adds Dr Desai, who calls herself India's first 'aesthetic vaginal surgeon,' performing complicated surgeries to unhood the clitoris and remove or trim the vaginal labia. She surgically reshapes the labia majora—the externally visible portions of the vulva—to create a single-creased vagina free of wrinkles, besides tightening vaginas 'for increased sexual arousal and pleasure or to correct age-related sagging and wrinkles that need to be lifted and filled'. Some vaginal surgeries allow women to achieve what she brands a 'Barbie look,' described as 'possessing the vagina of a newborn.'

Reacting to the ethical concerns of vaginal surgeries that on the lines of fairness creams and wrinkle reduction lotions, sell a shortsighted and superficial idea of beauty, especially in a country where there is no candid conversation about sex, Dr Desai feels that the word 'aesthetic' falsely denotes a sense of vanity, when it is actually a necessity, since having a fulfilling sex life is as important as striving towards a healthy heart. Also, as a counter argument to the notion of virginity in a new bride, she throws up instances of women clients who want to 'bleed for their husbands', after many years of being together, as a gift on a birthday/anniversary!

With every feature of a woman—a single woman, arguably even more so—being scrutinised at surface value, it's not surprising how all our stereotypes with regards to being a conformist society ultimately boil down to the salability of the female sex. And very often, this incessant quest to be flawless so as to be prime bait for marriage, turns out to be a lonely road of personal suffering and financial losses.

30-plus content writer Shikha Singh (*name changed on request*), suffers from a rare skin condition that leads to freckles and uneven pigmentation on sun-exposed areas of her body—mainly on the face, neck, arms, and slightly on the legs, due to excess melanin formation—a disorder that commenced 10 months after her birth. Doctors were clueless about Shikha's ailment since it wasn't genetic. Her parents are spotless, as is her brother. However, her sister, 4 years her junior, also happens to suffer from the same skin problem.

Growing up in a joint family teeming with cousins, uncles, aunts and grandparents, Shikha sensed their uneasy concern about her peculiar skin illness—an apathy usually reflected in the way they would talk highly of her to their relatives, praising her on her educational achievements and life choices, but always making it a point to add that she just lacked in one thing—her outer appearance.

Even her parents were forced to deal with countless sniggers and mean jibes over the past three decades.

Sadly, since a flawless complexion seems to be the highest premium of a woman's self-worth at times, Shikha's struggle has been ridden with scathing self-realisations. Engaged at 25 to a fair-complexioned guy, a week before their engagement, the boy's *bhabhi* rang Shikha asking if she could attach net sleeves to her blouse so that her freckles were not visible. Shikha flatly refused. Within the next week, the boy's mother, too, started giving Shikha stern instructions on using home remedies and fairness creams to lighten her freckles. And soon paraded her to a quack in Tilak Nagar, New Delhi, who provided the lamest of explanations about Shikha's skin condition, alleging that her mother had possibly eaten something wrong during her pregnancy, which had led to the freckles on her skin. Shikha could only laugh it off: 'Oh, so you mean she ate the same thing during her second pregnancy, and forgot to eat it again while she was pregnant with my brother? Crap!' Within the next month itself, Shikha called off the engagement and has remained single ever since.

Acclimatised to being viewed and treated like a freak, Shikha is constantly the object of curiosity and probes, especially on her travels using public transport in New Delhi. A lot of women approach her to question her on her peculiar skin condition and even lend unsolicited advice on a random home remedy or recommend a doctor. Shikha says, 'Sometimes it gets suffocating when a stranger randomly asks, "Do you have birth marks all over your face?"... "What happened to your skin?"... "Is this just an allergy?"... I mean, must I really answer all the people I know?'

Shikha has also undergone various medical treatments (Ayurvedic, allopathic, homeopathic) to cure her skin condition, and the after-effects, she confesses, have been more damaging. In 2009 after watching a cosmetic surgery show on a popular television channel, she decided to visit one of India's leading cosmetologists. After examining Shikha's skin, the cosmetologist suggested chemical peeling (mild to begin with, that gradually became stronger), and though he didn't commit to the number of sittings initially, or any concrete deliverables, he provided her family a glimmer of hope, saying that if not removed, his treatment would at least help in lightening the freckles and spots.

After shelving out ₹30,000, Shikha underwent around 8-10 sittings over a span of 6 months. Initially, she was told that there would be a downtime of 3 days, after which she could resume office work. Yet, when her treatment actually commenced, she discovered that she would take as much as a fortnight to recover, since the wounds would peel off and by the time her skin would actually heal, it would be time for the next sitting.

Soon, Shikha opted for work from home for 5 months, and was eventually forced to resign from her job in July 2009. During those 6 months of her treatment, her life turned into a living hell. The pain was excruciating, since her skin got burnt after every sitting and it took a good half-hour to calm her down with wet towels and lotions. She couldn't even move her arms or neck and lay on the bed straight, simply surviving on just juices and liquids. 'I missed the normal life I had led until then and often felt suicidal. One midnight, I remember sitting with a blade in my hand, wanting so bad to give up, before I finally told myself, "Shikha, you are this close to death. Why don't you try living for a change?"' she recalls emotionally. After 6 months, Shikha's family finally decided to stop this line of treatment as it wasn't displaying any concrete results. But her trauma was far from over as the side effects soon reared their ugly heads with painful blisters all over her arms and back. Unwillingly, Shikha had no choice but to visit the same doctor again to seek a solution, and was in for another shock when he charged her an extra ₹5,000 to cure the aftermaths of his own treatment!

Shikha, by her own admission, has today met close to 30 guys via the arranged-marriage route, on various matrimonial websites, and despite some stimulating conversations, she concludes, 'I don't even need to rack my brains as to why it never works out finally for me. No matter how perfectly I dress, how well I converse, how impressively I carry myself, my professional expertise—physical beauty, outer appearance is all this fuck-all, a so-called modern society seeks in a single woman looking to settle down.'

Why Singlehood Remains Skin-Deep?

Is the grass greener on the other side for single women in love affairs that promise to be more democratic? Or is beauty a thin line, there too? 30-year-old Reeba Paul (*name changed on request*), a Mumbai-based singleton working with an online cosmetic company, claims to have been at the receiving end due to being extremely dark, in sharp contrast to her Mangalorean, light-eyed, fair-skinned, Roman Catholic family. Reeba's relationship, too, that culminated after 7 years, would often involve her skin colour being raked up. Growing up with a deep complex about her complexion, and being overweight as well, she never had any boyfriends as an adolescent. In school, since fourth standard, she was labelled '*kaaliya*'. 'It was akin to having cancer,' she confesses.

Like many single women being discriminated against for their not-so-perfect features, Reeba doesn't place the blame on the men in her life, but alleges Indian society with its unfair beauty standards pressurises women too. A case in point is her own mother who nursed an inferiority complex, deeply worried about Reeba being bullied and typecast because of her complexion. As a young girl in the fifth standard, Reeba would be constantly reminded to apply fairness creams on a daily basis. Her mother also insisted she bleach her face regularly. 'Being a part of the beauty industry, I'm aware of this deep-rooted colour bias—the majority of Indian women apply foundation at least two shades lighter. Also, how come most cosmetic giants never hire a dusky brand ambassador? All we have is Nandita Das—but she's married!' she scoffs.

Does Our Innate Need For A Significant Other Also Make Us Physically Vulnerable?

What makes it gruelling for single women to be liked just for who they are? Would our physical parameters not be so critically measured if we were not constantly being subjected to marriage pressure? Seeking companionship and completion in the form of a male partner? Smita Deshmukh, divorcee, veteran media professional who currently dabbles in sports education is single at 48 and humorously recalls how her divorced, 36-year-old doctor, who her friends dreamt of setting her up with, since she shared a warm camaraderie with him, shocked her recently by asking pointedly, 'Don't you have any younger girlfriends, huh?'

'I'm pre-menopausal,' declares Smita with an air of cold pragmatism. 'So, I am of no use to men in the marriage market who are basically looking for childbearing hips to immediately start a family with.'

Having always been plus-size, Smita was comfortable with her weight and never quite opted for desi clothes, except on her wedding. Divorced at 29 from a cheating spouse, Smita claims that in the last 17 years of living alone in Mumbai, she's never met a man who liked and accepted her for who she really was. Her body, however, has been, as expected, the easiest target for her relationship failures. After her fiancé left for the US in mid-2001 and never returned, despite countless calls and mails, it was clear to Smita that she had been dumped, unceremoniously. An emotionally shattered Smita, who plummeted to rock bottom with spiralling health issues, finally took to the gym with a vengeance, scaling down from a size 24 to a happy 14 now.

Almost naturally, she sensed a huge male interest, but points out ironically, 'Since I own a flat and am financially independent, most guys were looking for free sex and a swanky pad to hang out at. Also, at my age, they probably see a no-threat situation. No wonder a lot of younger men also hit on me claiming they fantasise about me! I think most Indian men just don't get the concept of dating someone—because they are looking to get laid as early as possible. Neither do they get that any romantic relationship is about building equal consensus, first. In the new dating apps scene, most men don't even want to see you in the morning with the anonymity of the virtual world acting like a drug. That I am an award-winning journalist means nothing. And frankly, their attitude is probably no different than my own family who blame me for my earlier failed relationships. Women above 35 are mostly considered useless, independent and problematic, and there's a slim chance of an Indian man even being remotely interested in the person you are, and your life goals and aspirations. Single women such as me are marginalised entities. So when I am told I should settle down with just about anyone, as I will be desperately lonely in my old age, I today answer that I have the money to afford a good old age home.'

Is our fragile body image finally reflective of a more deep-seated inner patriarchy that thrives on conformism to next-to-impossible standards set by popular culture, the advertising and film industries? Are men, therefore, the mouthpiece of a larger social dissent against a less-than-perfect single woman? Our biggest enemy or our last refuge?

Could we accept ourselves as we are—if our mothers had taught us how to in the first place? If they were taught the same by their mothers, maybe? Would being single be less superficial if it wasn't about its external manifestations only?

STATUS SINGLE: *Whether we like to face it or not, no matter how successful an Indian woman is professionally or whether she lives independently, she is the sum total of her sex, and her respectability hinges precariously on her marital status. In a country that lays a lofty premium on youth, where newspaper adverts still declare in the most sexist fashion—'wanted fair, good-looking, thin, working, convented bride', where mothers persecute their own daughters for their bodies and blame them for being unmarried, thanks to their physical flaws, as women are shamed and humiliated openly in the marriage market, a large part of the work of being single and in your 30s involves making peace with how you look, how you are viewed by others and what you feel within. Not everything depends on male validation, and while it's important to look after your own body, what's more important is nurturing your mind. Don't fall for the whole anti-ageing formula. Don't colour your greys if you find they make you look sexier. Tell people you are smooth at the edges. Fight the I'm-too-fat stereotype that is mostly preconditioned by popular culture and unrealistic body images. And remember: a marriage or a relationship based on looks is not just superficial, but silly in the end. Also, have you seen most Indian men after a certain age!*

Chapter Three

Baby-making Factories or Baanjh?

JUST A COUPLE OF weeks ago, over a leisurely lunch, a single girlfriend and I were discussing gynaecologists in India, especially placing our experiences in the context of single vs. married female patients. My friend then shared a recent experience of one of her married colleagues who wanted to abort an unplanned pregnancy, and the sheer harassment and invasive questions she suffered after going through a slew of gynaecologists. How she soon got tired of listening to opinionated, know-it-all women gyneas who mouthed pretty much the same thing—that since her first born was now a year and a half old, she should consider keeping the second child. How, according to them, her first-born needed companionship, in a nuclear family setting, more so. Their personal opinion on her childbirth choice akin to the unending *gyaan* that a bossy mother-in-law probably doles out—someone who thinks she knows better—just because she's been there before. The woman's husband finally had to intervene, after the couple had already changed a couple of gynaes, and convinced the doctor that they hadn't wanted children in the first place—and their presently busy careers as corporates would make it tedious to take care of more than one offspring. 'Why are women perpetually being lectured on their sex life and childbearing prerogatives, especially by married women gynaes, who one would assume should rather be more sympathetic towards their own sex, instead of acting like petty mid-wives offering unsolicited family-planning counsel? Now just imagine if it was you or I going in for an abortion? We'd be branded as cheap whores at first glance!' my friend smirked, a tinge of poignancy soaking her last words.

Most Indian Gynaecologists No Better Than Nosy, Next Door Neighbours!

Gynaecology is defined as 'the medical practice dealing with the health of the female reproductive systems—vagina, uterus, ovaries and breasts.' Literally, outside medicine, it indicates 'the science of women'. And yet, looking back, after the trauma of arranged marriages, the stigmatising body shaming and the humiliation a single woman endures for the sake of finding a life partner, possibly visiting a gynaecologist in India is her second worst nightmare. Both situations unavoidable to a large degree.

Almost every other Indian woman today suffers from disorders such as Polycystic Ovarian Syndrome (PCOS). In fact, an inclusive study to observe the trends in PCOS cases in young women in India conducted by Metropolis Healthcare Ltd shockingly revealed that 1 in 5 Indian women suffered from PCOS with east India leading the chart where 1 in 4 women suffers from PCOS. PCOS is a very prevalent reproductive disorder in women and held as the leading cause of infertility these days, with cosmetic symptoms such as facial hair, thinning of the scalp hair, and acne, and gynecological symptoms that include irregular or scanty period, usually also considered the first red flag in adolescents. I have suffered from

PCOS since I was a young girl with little or no understanding of my own body back then—and thanks to it, have remained at the harsh receiving end of much gynae high-browed judgement, almost sentenced to a life where the possibility of childbearing seems bleak and distant. With my single status and age the softest, easiest targets to attack my womb.

To begin with, let's consider this line of questioning that most women are bombarded with:

Why are you still single?

By when do you intend to get married?

Virgin?

When was the last time you had sex?

When do you wish to start a family since you are already above 30?

Is your sex life very active?

Do you have a high-stress job?

How many times do you have sex in a week?

What do you mean you don't want kids? Want or can't?

Have you ever had an abortion?

Have you always been this overweight?

Do you use protection?

Work out?

Have you tried any of these marriage websites? Shaadi.com?

Why haven't your parents got you settled down yet?

Like me, possibly every single woman in India, at some point or the other, may have faced this line of staunch questioning while staring at another woman, probably the same age as her older sister or mother, seated on a high-backed, rexine chair at a stuffy hospital OPD or a cramped diagnostic center. Meeting a pair of deep-set eyes that literally peer into your face, a thick blob of vermillion conspicuous between her tresses or a slim *mangalsutra* dangling around her neck—as the battle lines are clearly demarcated.

There is barely time to come up with smart answers before your legs are yanked open, ankles callously pushed through two stirrups. A greasy gel smeared over your privates.

You're wet. Smarting.

Slowly, a pair of gloved hands are shoved inside your vagina—tearing through some of the coarse pubic hair you haven't trimmed in a while. Dispassionately, sans a care. An expressionless nurse watches the mute spectacle—as the patient squirms uncomfortably, writhing in a dull, throbbing pain, as a mechanical plastic probe, with a condom stretched over its length, is shoved further up.

All your life lessons are likely to flash before your eyes in that defining moment—the first time you started your periods; the way you were told not to wear shorts anymore and show your '*taange*'; the age when you called it 'chums'; how you stained your pristine white school uniform and were laughed at by your classmates; the afternoon you had sex; the clumsiness of losing your virginity to a boy who never looked back; the same pain returning now in short waves, the way you have remained sexless for so long, hoping to find love again, the ache of watching younger cousins and friends from the same school and college boast of marriage dates and sport baby bumps soon enough. The spate of happy and complete family albums on social media. The rawness. The reactions. The reality of being a woman, who failed to make the cut.

Even in here. In a place where you thought you would just be treated. That would take away some of your pain. That wouldn't remind of your of your single status and link it to your sexual health—like a penalty or a punishment. That would explain the excruciating pain that ripped through your insides every month or the emptiness and panic you feel when you don't menstruate on a date circled in red on a flimsy paper calendar pasted on your toilet door or on a smartphone app. That wouldn't remind you of your failed romantic relationships, the constant attempts at dating and the embarrassing newspaper, matrimonial ads. The numerous rejections. That wouldn't blame your ambition or career or sex life… that wouldn't castigate you as fat, again. That would make the acne, hair fall, extreme mood swings, blood clots disappear—that would give you hope, and reassure you that you could be a mother, some day. That would treat you the same as a married woman. Or just a patient, who wanted her insides to be well…

At 32, Kolkata-based author Sudesna Ghosh is like any other single woman who dreams of marrying Mr Right and lives a life complete with her parents, cats and books. And yet, one can't help but overlook the fleeting pain in her eyes, when she shares her personal ordeal with Indian gynaecologists who sadly reflect the same suffocating Indian mindset that places marriage and motherhood on a pedestal—easily and insensitively linking every gynecological complication to a woman's singlehood, her being above 30 and childless, and almost announcing like a death warrant that childbirth will be next to impossible. Ironical in a country that has an IVF clinic at almost every street corner with surrogacy and donor sperms being an open secret—even resorted to publically by stars like Aamir Khan and Shahrukh Khan.

Sudesna's story, however, began at the age of 10 when she fell grievously ill and bled non-stop. With most women in her mother's family, like mine, having nursed gynecological problems and undergoing hysterectomy by 50, what she didn't know back then was that she had inherited the same medical condition.

At school, soon enough, classmates teased Sudesna mercilessly, as she had no choice but to change her sanitary napkin every 45 minutes. With hardly any concrete and comprehensive sex education or proper awareness about a woman's bodily/hormonal changes post her period or her sexual and mental health thereafter, integrated into the school curriculum, an impressionable Sudesna became the butt of many speculations and weird stares. As weight gain is another scathing side effect of this disorder, soon she bloated up, and that became another reason for becoming a victim to incessant teenage bullying. At 14, Sudesna went through her first major surgery to remove a polyp. Being prescribed Novelon from the age of 13, a hormonal oral birth-control pill most commonly prescribed for PCOS by doctors here, she soon spiralled into manic depression—another major side-effect of the disorder that is seldom discussed openly, as mental and sexual health are considered taboo topics, almost on the verge of being sacrilege and dirty. Rendered completely dysfunctional, Sudesna was soon forced to seek serious medical intervention. She still has trouble sleeping.

'30 years have passed and I can't even recall the countless gynaes I have changed in Kolkata, because honestly, they are no better than those gossipy, middle-aged women, who scan every young woman in their housing society, judging the length of her skirt. They are the ones who roll their eyes disbelievingly when you pick up a packet of condoms at the local supermarket. All of them picked on my obesity and singlehood instead of showing a mature understanding in trying to treat PCOS, which is a medical condition and not a curse that affects only unmarried women. Being a woman I naturally gravitated more towards women gynaes, but the way a woman puts down another here is unfortunate.'

Constant degrading of her self-image alongside years of coping with depression and unforeseen weight gain coerced Sudesna to stop the pill 9 years back. 'My periods wouldn't stop—so I was forced to go back on it again. In the last 3 years, I've deliberately avoided gynaes as I'm sick of them constantly warning me of barrenness or ridiculing me over my body, instead of sharing positive feedback or connecting me with dieticians or fitness specialists.'

Sudesna, who does in fact follow a regular gym and diet plan, says the biggest shock is reserved for the moment when she declares that she has no interest in bearing kids. 'Being committed to animal welfare, my rescued pets mean more than the idea of having my biological kids. So whether I am at a high risk for infertility is of no consequence. But in our country, a woman rejecting motherhood, and by assumption therefore also marriage is perceived as a pure biological disaster.'

Recently, a dermatologist treating her for a skin cyst asked her pointedly if she was overtly sexually active, since the condition he alleged was common in women having a lot of sex. The accusation, the tonality of which was laced with patriarchal judgement, was immediately and vehemently refuted by Sudesna, since her last relationship was years ago. 'Having lots of sex—who qualifies that for us? Parents? Lovers? Society?' she questions stoically, adding in the same breath, 'Ever since I was a little girl, I was told everything would become okay with marriage. Were they implying with sex? That is, sex within the normative boundaries of a legal man-woman, socially sanctified marital relationship? And just who decides the timing of this so-called biological clock which gets allegedly ticking furiously post 30? Nature or doctors?'

As I find a resonance in Sudesna's pain with my own, I wonder why women's health, despite being such a high-risk and sensitive subject, is shunned to a silent, scary corner, even medically. I think of a cousin sister, a year younger, and still single at 38, who recently underwent breast removal surgery, barely a couple of years after having lost her mother to the same disease. I think of genes, and if we've ever thought about breast or ovarian cancer as being hereditary in the female population? How my mother suffered a miscarriage before conceiving me, and my grandmother always had trouble with her menstrual cycle, is never really studied as family history. Gynaes rarely ever have the time to understand the source of pain, and are always more interested in doling out marriage advice or informing me how I may not be able to conceive at my age, given the complications. Breast cancer, for instance, is now said to be the most common cancer in most cities in India, and second most common in rural areas. For every two women newly diagnosed with breast cancer, one woman dies of it here.

One woman perishes of cervical cancer every 8 minutes in India. Cervical cancer, mainly caused by Human Papillomavirus (HPV) infection, is said to be the leading cancer in Indian women and the second most common cancer in women worldwide. HPV transmission is influenced by sexual activity and age. According to the Indian Journal of Medical and Paediatric Oncology, Vol. 33, No. 1, January-March, 2012, almost 75% of all sexually active adults are likely to be infected with at least one HPV type. Though there are several methods of prevention of cervical cancer, prevention by vaccination is emerging as the most effective option, with the availability of two vaccines. And yet, how many single women walking into a gynae's clinic are advised to take a routine Pap smear test, a mammogram, or given adequate information on the vaccine available? Isn't prevention of cancer a more telling topic than dissecting pregnancy and contrived marriage counselling? I mean, why are we always assuming a woman must crave children?

Are doctors who treat a woman's insides actually tuned into the woman's innermost feelings? Or does calling the profession 'woman's science' invariably discount the above? Making most gynaes callous, clinical, calculating... every woman a project, a prognosis, a prescription? Giving them the absolute right to ask a woman about something as private as her sex life? Counsel and coax her into seeing the perks of timely marriage since she's still single, automatically making it synonymous with childbirth? The highest justification of our lives—both the patient, and the doctor's—sans which the science wouldn't sell the way it does, maybe. Making the Indian gynae a perennial outsider.

'Get her uterus removed,' my third female gynae at one of Delhi's prestigious hospitals announced 3 years ago, without batting as much as an eyelid. When I kept going back to her every Wednesday at 4 pm, waiting patiently on the claustrophobic ground floor, complaining how my menstrual pain had gotten extremely severe in the last few cycles, I think I used the word unbearable a lot. My mother accompanied me on most occasions, also vouching for the same, a lingering sadness in her eyes. Perhaps she was just as fragile. Somewhere.

'But she's so young, what is mid-30s these days?' was all she could stutter.

Meanwhile, the doctor in question conversed with the nurse, asking about a woman she'd just induced into labor. Making so little of the ones who didn't qualify—in her estimation. Those, like me, who kept coming back—same complaint, same pain, same marital status.

'Why don't you find a boy soon? With her history... first PCOS... now endometriosis...' was the last thing she uttered, before I pushed my chair back impatiently, fighting back tears.

'Shall we try *Ananda Bazaar*? They have a "Cosmopolitan" section... more your type,' Ma whispered on our way back, as I looked away.

Beleaguered. Belittled. Barren?

What is it about our power to procreate that gives a complete stranger the license to dent our self-worth? Attack it, using one casual caustic remark. What gives the right to a gynae to take a decision on my uterus? To ask me to remove it when I didn't even have a tumor? Just a condition she can't fix? Make any more money out of? Scaring me once after a Pap smear, speculating how I could have cervical cancer. Why don't we sue such medical practioners serving in swish hospitals? Isn't invading my womb a service I have paid for? Why shouldn't I want logical answers? Slowness? Sensitivity? What if my uterus had a voice? What would it say in response? Why couldn't my clitoris be a consumer? Pissed off?

Advocate Sujata Lal (*name changed on request*) has a similar story to tell. She says, 'Mine is the fifth gynae in Delhi. The search never ends. I've always had a history of irregular periods and have had to undergo hormonal therapy and regular scans from time to time. I lose weight. Put it back on, despite the gruelling workouts. I am constantly on medication, and always getting blood tests done. Despite never being detected with sugar or thyroid, I'm perennially asked to get tested for the same, just in case. Sometimes I just want to get my damn uterus and ovaries, or whatever else that's inside, removed. I'm so tired of being asked why I am still single at 43. That too by a female doctor, who typically then turns to my mother or married younger sister usually accompanying me, asking what they are doing to get me settled. As if they are responsible for my relationship status or sex life! I am constantly warned I may never conceive, implying I have missed the bus, and that with my present medical condition, I may miscarry, too, later.

'I sink into depression thinking of my gynae and the way she always frowns while examining my insides. Like she disapproves of my lifestyle, my career as a high-profile, successful professional. It's thoroughly humiliating when she told me once after I shared the news of the birth of my niece with her that perhaps I should think of adopting her. "Your sister will have another child, I am certain. Age is on her side. What will you do with what you earn? All these diamonds you wear, this travelling you say you do, fancy clothes… who will look after you when you are old? All you single women are the same these days—too choosy, prefer dating over marriage, freedom-loving…don't want any responsibility…" the gynae nodded disapprovingly,' recalls Sujata. She then added slowly, 'One of my married clients, who has had her third miscarriage, once broke down telling me how her gynaecologist blamed her career as an air hostess and late marriage at 39, for her losses, no better than her mother-in-law who was scheming to get her son remarried, alleging that her family was cursed and thus she kept losing her child repeatedly—maybe the fate of a barren woman labelled cruelly as *"baanjh"* is the same as a single woman in India. We are both easy to attack and crucify.'

The War Against Our Wombs

Supreme Court advocate on record, 43-year-old Amrita Swaarup has borne the brunt of endometriosis for the past 25 years since being diagnosed with the disease at 18 while she was in her first year at Delhi's Lady Shri Ram College. 'I suffered 104 degree fever for a year and finally when I was taken to Mumbai for treatment, the doctor told me that I should get married quickly and have two kids at the earliest. She also suggested I be taken home instead of living alone in the hostel since the disease is also emotionally draining. But my mother staunchly refused and said that it should be my call entirely, as she always wished that my sister and I should move away from home and see the world. I decided to persevere, struggle and finish college, living alone. Also, being the quintessential *"gori"*, it was assumed naturally that I'd get married off at an early age. My then boyfriend who was enormously supportive of my illness, immediately volunteered marriage, but I refused to say yes simply fearing being childless in the future,' strongly states Amrita, who underwent her first surgery at 19, followed by another one at the age of 24, again at 30 and finally a full hysterectomy at the age of 41.

'All the hormonal injections I was taking over the years had depleted my bone density and I underwent a slipped disc and was wheelchair bound for a while. Having suffered intestinal adhesions, I have practically lived in writhing pain most of my life, on painkillers daily, thanks to which my digestion is also severely affected. After my hysterectomy, I plummeted into depression for a few months as knowing that I can't be a biological mother dealt a major emotional blow, as I craved children all my life. But soon, I decided to snap out of it. I have changed my gynaecologist whenever I found them too preachy and delivering lectures on early/quick marriage and children, instead of simply dealing with the medical situation. I was determined that my womb will not define me, and used my will power to not feel the blame,' she grittily adds.

Amrita, who has had nurturing romantic relationships, insists she will never opt for surrogacy and once turned down a marriage proposal post her hysterectomy from a man she was seeing, simply because she didn't want to make her disease her crutch. 'I told him, "What's so great in our genes that we need to extend our own bloodline? I'd rather provide a home to a homeless child",' she asserts.

'I collapsed in court on 20 May last year and was bleeding internally and had to be hospitalised. I had my exams to qualify me as an advocate on record in the Supreme Court, and I knew that having prepared for it I must appear for the same. So even as the doctors grumbled and made me sign an undertaking that I was risking my own health and they bore no responsibility, I still cleared the exam!'

Amrita has recently also completed an arduous trek to the highest Shiva temple in India at Tunganath, made it onwards to Deorital Lake, before opting for a solo helicopter ride to Kedarnath. 'The night before, my anxious dad said, "*Agle saal kisike saath chaali jaana,*" when I interrupted him asking, who will I come back again with next year and also, since I am going to remain single, why make my single non-marital status an impediment to my travel plans?' she adds in a carefree spirit.

When I ask Amrita what can we do legally to shame and put in place some of the obnoxiously callous and intrusive gynaecologists that most Indian women suffer at the hands of, she raises a pertinent argument. 'In the Consumer Protection Act there is a provision to sue any person for mental harassment and agony, but how will one evaluate and categorise this mental torment becomes a sticky area as the court can always say a gynae advising you on early marriage and timely childbirth is only giving sound medical counsel. As in, how will we claim, say, 2 lakh in damages for mental agony, unless we establish a sound correlation? Also, most courts are protective of doctors and give a lot of benefit of doubt to human error, so segregating the negligence from error is key,' answers Amrita.

Why aren't we, as women, taught to fight for our womb by women who rear and nurture us? Not just when we are pushing out a child or preparing for one. But when we wait? Why can't we stand up to defend its emptiness, its plight, its pain, its losses? Give it a legitimacy that does not constantly require male validation or clinical authoritarianism? Why are our greatest enemies, sometimes the closest?

Battling endometriosis—a disease in which the tissue that normally grows inside the uterus grows outside leading to excruciating pelvic spasms, painful intercourse and is also linked to infertility—content writer from Delhi, 37-year-old Priya Bhaglani's *(name changed on request)* journey has been agonisingly painful, and personal. Priya was forced to resign from various jobs, as the pain grew unbearable, and she wasn't even able to wear clothes. At home, a different and deeper darkness haunted her, as she was constantly pressurised to get married, with her mother accusing her of having unlicensed, premarital sex with her then partner, that she presumed had caused this disease. Priya was made to feel she deserved the trauma she suffered monthly.

Immediately after her first surgery, with the stitches still not removed, she was forced to meet a potential groom, sternly instructed not to tell him a thing about her operation or that she was battling endometriosis. 'The guy wanted to just walk and talk, and I had no other choice but to walk for almost 40 minutes with my stitches smarting. I came down with high fever the very next day,' she recalls, being bedridden thereafter, her recovery naturally slowing down. Having been through severe character assassination, Priya feels it's the people around a single woman who compound her gynaecological problems—leaving her with no choice but to compromise on marriage, just to prove a point of normalcy to society.

The unsolicited advice that single women dread and the lack of empathy from the medical fraternity is therefore responsible for a digital revolution that has shaped up in the women's health space with The Crowdsourced List of Gynaecologists We Trust, for instance, that was an initiative by lawyer Amba Azad and her team in search of non-judgemental and non-moralistic doctors.

Tired of every visit turning into an evaluation of their life choices, the team decided to invite women like them from across the country to list and rank their gynaecs on a total of 40 parameters, including how they reacted to alternative sexual lifestyles, to a patient being accompanied by an unrelated man, or even discussing sexuality among the physically challenged. The list that exists now covers 200 doctors across 23 cities, including Mumbai, Delhi, Bangalore, Thrissur and Indore. The city-specific list also carries comments from users. 'Not trans-friendly but woman-friendly,' one claims. Other parameters compiled in the list are: Will they keep your information private, even from your parents or partner? Will they treat you as autonomous, not demanding permission/consent from parents or partner? Will they positively and non-judgementally respect your choice to be accompanied by someone who is not a biological parent or husband?

OoWomaniya, too, is another online network platform for women's health and wellness, similar to the more recently unveiled Lybrate that seeks neutral medical advice, where a woman can post anonymous queries on subjects she may be hesitant to discuss with so-called 'family physicians', and even sign up for e-consultations. Lybrate's goal is to bridge the doctor-patient gap digitally and it receives 20,000 queries from women, a 70% to 80% jump from what the user traffic was when it started in January 2015. All these new websites boast of certified doctors, counselors, dietitians and nutritionists across categories such as menstruation, breast care, pregnancy, sex, relationships and fitness.

'We wanted to be able to answer any question a woman may have about her health, and provide her with a safe and anonymous platform to get them answered,' says OoWomaniya co-founder Sneh Bhavsar, 30, a business analyst, in an interview published in *Hindustan Times*. Based on the nature of the query, a notification is sent out to a specific doctor or specialist, who typically responds in 4 to 8 hours. The anonymity of discussing a medical condition without an immediate cross reference to one's sex life and the patronising moral fibre of the gyane makes these virtual platforms a safer bet.

Whose Vagina Is It, Anyway?

Despite these forward-thinking initiatives, a single woman's worst nightmare sometimes occurs in the form of an unwarranted pregnancy or the risk of a sexually contracted infection, inviting much of the same ire. Something that singleton, 27-year-old, Greeshma M, originally from Bengaluru, and presently pursuing her Ph.D in humanities from a reputed national university, discovered quite by surprise. Incidentally, Greeshma's mother happens to be a gynaecologist back home—someone she calls 'selectively conservative'. 'I was 23, and in a long-distance affair, when I skipped my chums and got totally paranoid,' she recalls matter-of-factly. Deliberately going through the campus hospital panel and opting for a woman gynae who she assumed would be more sensitive, Greeshma was curtly told to consult her mother, instead of wasting time at the hospital she had chosen. 'My cycle had already touched 35 days, instead of the usual 28, and naturally, I was being defensive with my guard on as I distinctly felt as if the female gynaecologist was having fun at my expense,' she alleges.

Recently when she acquired a vaginal infection, Greeshma wasn't keen on the campus doctor, so she rang her mother instead, who started bombarding her with all sorts of suspicious questions about her personal life, when all she wanted was some professional expertise and a sound opinion on the next course of medical action. Another gynae in her hometown wanted to get Greeshma tested for HIV, Syphilus, and other sexually transmitted diseases, but added that she should also get a blood test for thyroid done, so as to avoid any inferences that she may have had unprotected casual sex. 'There's a clear chasm between what cinema and popular culture depict about a single Indian woman, and on-ground reality. Pop culture prefers to project this saleable image of a liberal woman, financially empowered, completely comfortable with her sexuality, unafraid to have sex on her terms, exercising her right to sexual pleasure, who demands sexual satisfaction. But what it fails to account for is the insecurity and shaming that most single women undergo at the hands of their gynaecologists, almost daily. As a woman, when I visit my gynaecologist, I want to be reassured, listened to with the promise of confidentiality and perhaps even advised about the choices available to me in terms of birth control pills, abortion timings and safe procedures. Instead, the doctor's chamber is replete with an air of hostility, with single women given lengthy lectures in morality, made to feel guilty about having premarital sex.'

Greeshma's account echoes the hypocrisy of Indian society that remains cagey about sex even as dating apps like Tinder offer a world of promiscuous pleasure and the rates of teenage pregnancy skyrocket. And it's not just the gynae herself and her moral high-handedness that is to blame—but the entire medical paraphernalia around them that is deeply conservative and closeted. 'It's the same weird looks you attract walking into a medical store, alone and unaccompanied by a man, and asking for a condom or an i.pill. Having been on the pill myself, I realise how little we single Indian women actually know about safe sex—what our birth control options are, except the condom, which we all know most Indian guys abhor claiming that it's uncomfortable, since it probably dents their masculinity and need for sexual dominance,' says Greeshma.

She adds, 'There is a hormonal injection I have read about that women can take every 3 months, or insert a diaphragm, or even basic things like what one should do to keep the vagina infection-free, or what are the signs of a vaginal infection and is it necessarily sex-related or can also be contracted from using unclean public toilets. Why not talk to us about these topics frankly, instead of probing about my boyfriend, why I broke up and if he was cheating on me. Let's face it, young India is getting laid and how. Apps like Tinder are intended primarily for sexual hook ups. But what if a woman does get pregnant? The guy in most cases washes his hands off and the gynae will be like the parent—shocked and desensitised to the point of humiliation.'

On the face of it, abortion is legalised in India by the Medical Termination of Pregnancy (MTP) Act, passed by Parliament in 1971, and came into effect in 1972. The Act permits abortion if the doctor believes 'in good faith' that '…the continuance of the pregnancy would involve a risk to the life of the pregnant woman or of grave injury to her physical or mental health; or there is a substantial risk that if the child were born, it would suffer from such physical or mental abnormalities as to be seriously handicapped'. As a result of this focus on maternal health, the responsibility rests largely on the woman to explain or prove how it could harm her physically or mentally. So, like married women blaming contraceptive failure, single women are left with barely any choice but to state coercion or rape, or betrayal as a reason for pregnancy.

The Nightmare Of Getting An Abortion As A Single Woman

Though abortion is indeed legal in India—unlike in a number of Western countries—women here have hardly any control over their reproductive future. Statistics collated by Mumbai's International Institute for Population Sciences (IIPS), a public health organisation, claims that about 21% of males and 4% of females in rural areas admitted to premarital sex against an urban figure of 11% of males and 2% of females. The age range is 15-29. Another study by IIPS, claims 76% of the women who come for first-time abortions are single. In a piece compiled for Firstpost.com in 2013 titled *Shamed and Scarred: Stories of 'Legal' Abortions in India*, journalist Neha Dixit writes, 'Studies show that a considerable proportion—one-fifth—of young abortion-seekers delayed the termination of pregnancy until the second trimester. The unmarried ones were significantly more likely to have done so than the married: one-quarter of the unmarried, compared to 9% of the married, delayed abortion until beyond 12 weeks of pregnancy.'

39-year-old legal professional, Divya Bhandari (*name changed on request*), who resides in Hyderabad, conceived accidentally last year after a night of casual, unprotected sex with a younger man she had met for the second time, via a dating app. 'We had hit it off and were attracted to each other physically, and after a few drinks, decided to check into a hotel. The man made it clear it was just a hook up, and that marriage or commitment wasn't on the cards. I was game, having done the rigorous rounds of arranged marriage for years, and tired of waiting for the proverbial knight in shining armor. I craved sex—and we had a night of passion,' says Divya whose fun one-night stand never quite culminated into the third date. She adds unemotionally, 'He had withdrawn before his orgasm, so I never suspected that something may be amiss, till I skipped my period. Having always had an irregular cycle, I shrugged off my doubts till I missed another month. On a work trip to Mumbai, I took a pregnancy test and my doubts were confirmed. I was never into kids and pretty clear I wanted to get rid of this unwanted pregnancy.'

However, Divya's tribulations had only just begun. 'My own gynae in Hyderabad, from one of the top hospitals, looked shocked when I told her about my decision and asked me if this was my first abortion. I assumed it was routine Q&A, till she suggested I talk to the father of the child and think of this as an opportunity to settle down. When I came clean about how I had conceived, her body language and tonality transformed, as she kept probing further on my personal life, often using the word "reckless". I was extremely uncomfortable with her line of investigation, since I am well aware that as a single woman I have every right to have sex and abort the child if I am not interested in motherhood.'

Changing her gynae didn't provide much respite as some of them insisted she come accompanied by her father or brother, one of them calling Divya too 'fast' and way too westernised. Another doctor, a man, threatened to ring her mother and have a talk with her and even suggested she seek spiritual counselling to 'calm' her hormones.

'Married or not, having a child is not my only mission in life! My married friends also frowned on my decision—some instantly withdrawing from me and bitching behind my back that being sexless for so long had turned me desperate. One friend's husband, in his late 40s, on the pretext of helping me, started sending me lewd messages and mails complaining about his dull sex life and how his wife was a "fat, boring, pre-menopausal hag who snored". I was labelled a 'dirty' woman just because I had an abortion. Once when I told my married best friend that even she had once contemplated aborting her second child, born a year after her first, she answered,

"That's different. I am someone's wife and the child wasn't going to be a bastard. Here you are sleeping around and having fun in cheap hotel rooms, since you are horny at your age. You think any decent man will ever touch you after this?" It was the last time we spoke…' Divya's words trail.

In an article published in *The Ladies Finger* in June 2015, writer Zenisha Gonsalves relived a similar horror story of Disha *(name changed on request)*, who conceived at 19 and sought an abortion in a Pune clinic, accompanied by her boyfriend. 'Before the procedure, when I tried asking the doctor and the nurses questions, they were dismissive of my worries. They looked at me like I was unworthy of information, and the only thing that would have made me less anxious that week, would have been to know what was happening, and what would happen. I couldn't tell my parents about the abortion, so I really needed the gynae to answer my questions,' Disha is quoted in the piece.

After the procedure, when Disha asked the doctor if it had been successful, the doctor brusquely replied, 'Wait for the report.'

'I was in a lot of pain after the abortion, and I tried calling the doctor on her mobile. When she finally picked up, she yelled at me for disturbing her and hung up.' The report came a full, excruciating four days later. In retrospect, Disha adds, 'The strangest thing was that the gynae was so hesitant to look at me. She seemed as scared of nudity as an ENT would be! And she's a gynaecologist!'

Zenisha claims that most medical students she spoke to for her article—from colleges in Belgaum, Goa, Mangalore, Hyderabad, and Manipal—said that they are taught to ask women whether they're married or unmarried, and not whether they're sexually active. She says, 'In the same breath, they all say that they're also taught not to distinguish between married and unmarried women, in their treatment. However, as many women were quick to observe, "Are you married?" is the Indian stand-in for, "Are you sexually active?"'

Civic planning expert, 34-year-old Suhasini (*name changed on request*), another victim of insensitive gynaecologists, puts across an idea worth execution: 'I wish there was some kind of public rating system that we can have for medical services too, the way we rate and criticize restaurants in Zomato, for instance, because way too often, a woman's marital status is the base line for the medical responsiveness she receives, even when her health is at peril. There should be a way to shame these doctors and institutions on a public platform so that other women can stay away from these sexually repressed and sadistic practioners,' she asserts, the anger evident.

With a rapidly changing social and cultural milieu, and with sex and marriage becoming disparate entities, one can't help but wonder when will a single woman be spared the shoddy second-hand treatment? When abortion will be a legal right she can exercise at will, when common medical conditions like PCOS and endometriosis will be understood in totality, and not remain narrow reasons of persecution and shame? When all the advancements in medicine can actually make a single woman's life and sexual choices simpler? Instead of being what they are now...

A sentence? A trial? A decision? Fate?

STATUS SINGLE: *From timely mammograms to pap smears, to heart, sugar and thyroid check-ups, don't take your health for granted, especially after 30. There is nothing embarrassing in asking for more information on the recently introduced cervical cancer vaccine or seeking counseling if you are feeling unusually depressed. Most doctors in India, especially gynaecologists and counselors lack the sensitivity and sometimes demonstrate the lowest possible respect towards a single woman—no different than the rest of society. So don't be afraid to give it back to them and make complaints to the consumer forum if need be. Walking*

into a hospital is the scariest thing possible and one of the times when being single hits you the hardest—but don't pay with your health, both physical and mental. The greatest sufferers of silent heart disease happen to be women—and while you'd rather splurge on a Zara dress or take a short spa vacation than invest in a complete health package, weigh the odds and make your well-being top priority. You have only yourself!

Chapter Four

Motherhood In My Own Hands

𝒜LMOST EVERY SINGLE WOMAN has at some point grappled with motherhood, especially since turning 30 makes the phrase 'biological clock' the most commonly used refrain—whether you are facing your grim, female gynaecologist (my gynae at present, since I change them very often, makes it a point to show me the complete wedding album of her only daughter on a slick smartphone, before describing in abject detail what jewellery she invested in, the price of gold, how the boy is not as fair or good-looking as her daughter, but happens to be from IIT and studied in an Ivy League college), or listening to a well-meaning married friend dole out unwarranted *gyaan* on how childbearing gets tougher as you scale the 30-plus wall, with the quality of a woman's eggs supposedly rapidly deteriorating.

Motherhood Isn't Male-Reliant

Separating motherhood from marriage isn't easy in India, since they are socio-culturally suffixed, but a lot of single women are gutsily taking on the system on their own steam, with adoption being the most preferred avenue to provide a child with a dream, and a home of their own.

45-year-old Malini Parmar, an ex-IT professional turned waste warrior, who also operates a social enterprise promoting sustainable living in Bengaluru, stands as an exception to the rule that one needs a man to have and rear a child, with not one, but two daughters: biological sisters, 12-year-old Tara and 10-year-old Lila, whom she adopted when she was 36.

'Sometimes,' Malini says, 'we live the dreams of our parents.' Her mother, Maya, wasn't allowed to study beyond Class 10 and was taunted for producing girls before birthing a son, her third child. It was then that she decided her daughters should be given every opportunity that boys get. Consequently, Malini grew up with a mother talking about education and not being proficient in housework, and was told to focus on working towards standing on her own feet than luring a suitable husband. Never the 'settling down' sorts, Malini began dating while pursuing her engineering degree. Several men even proposed marriage in the past, but each time, Malini claims, she asked herself if she'd be happy married to them or remain single. And the answer was always single. Perhaps bitter memories of her parents' failed relationship further convinced her that staying single was better off.

'I've never heard the words "biological clock ticking" or felt lonely—the two most common reasons a lot of my women friends preferred settling down by a certain age. My mother taught me to think and not do things just to please society,' Malini adds, justifying her decision to remain unmarried.

Inspired by Bollywood actor Sushmita Sen's decision, Malini began considering the option of being an adoptive mother at the age of 26—an idea further cemented by her charity work for Child Rights and You (CRY) and the books she read, especially those authored by Father Flanagan. Soon, however, Malini was transferred to the US by her then employer and almost felt her new professional stint would inevitably throw back her personal ambition to be a mother, as she was supposed to be posted overseas for a minimum period of 3 years. Ironically, once overseas, Malini would meditate every week with her siblings, both of whom were also in the US then, and this brought her the clarity that there was so much more to life than spending $500 for a night in New York or climbing the greasy corporate ladder.

Malini spent a lot of her time also researching on single moms which made her realise that children of single parents like her wouldn't start with a disadvantage, as the generic research reports seemed to suggest. That's because single moms by choice start with an advantage as finances were typically in order and adoption a conscious, well-thought-through decision. Malini even concluded that 99% of those who adopted were looking to adopt an infant, though she knew that she'd unconsciously been selecting books that spoke about attachment with older children. Soon enough, she began talking to her mother and sister and working through their resistant objections, and within 2 years she found them on her side, fully supportive of her decision.

'Thankfully, my finances were sorted and being very close to my sister, I knew somewhere that I wanted to adopt siblings and that too from a slightly older age bracket, instead of being fixated on an infant like most single women are,' says Malini, adding that in India, 95% of people desire a child less than a year, and 99% less than 3 years—a fixation that probably also explains the frustratingly long wait and the dismal figures in the current adoption scenario. Finally, in December 2008, during a deep meditation session, Malini claims to have had a vision of a child saying, 'Mom, come quickly.'

By April 2009, Malini had relocated back to India opting for a sabbatical for at least 6-8 months. During this time she applied for her papers, and got in touch with the adoption coordinating agency in her hometown of Bengaluru, using her 'me time' to speak to over 25 couples who had adopted kids to understand what it really took to go down this path. Finally, one day, Malini received a call from Orissa informing her about two sisters as young as 2 and 4 who were available for adoption. 'I boarded the next available flight to meet them in person, and honestly, I didn't need a picture to confirm their presence, as I was feeling divine guidance,' recalls Malini.

On reaching Cuttack, Malini was informed that the kids she had been told about were already being adopted by someone else, but there were two other children, aged 4.5 and 2.5 that were available for adoption in an orphanage in Bhubaneswar and was sent there instead. Malini was soon introduced to two small children, Kumi, the older sister, and Gulli, the younger one. 'I felt an instant emotional connection with the elder one. The younger one actually just adopted me.' 2 months later, on 2 July 2009, all the paperwork finally came through in Bhubaneswar. A milestone for Malini and her newfound karmic family, she still celebrates this day as their family day when she brought her daughters home.

'I think a lot of single women fear adoption as they worry about the poop-and-pee stage of an infant, but I can vouch for the benefits of adopting an older child, including health reasons, since by a certain age you already know if there is any physical or mental deformity, etc., and are also sure the child isn't stolen, but genuinely an orphan,' Malini reasons.

Initially, Malini's mother was away in Himachal taking care of her 95-year-old grandmother, and her sister was still stationed in the US. 'Books, the internet, friends, sister on Skype daily and mom on phone—day and night. That's how I learnt how to be a mom. It takes a village to raise a child and thankfully my village was and has been very supportive,' says Malini. The journey to motherhood slowly smoothened out when after 4 months she was joined in by her sister, who stayed on for a year, after which her mother moved in permanently in August 2010.

Today, Malini leaves her kids with them and takes as long as a month to indulge in a vacation to let her hair down, every once in a while. Her daughters are aware that they are adopted. On Lila's birthday once, one of her friends quizzed her if it was true that she didn't have a father, to which she replied that she had come from Malini's heart and not her tummy. Yet, despite such positive reaffirmations, Lila has been called to her computer centre to inform them the name of her father. Malini also used to receive school emails addressed to Mr. Not Applicable. Therefore, Malini also makes it a point to tell her daughters imaginary stories about fairies, mermaids and previous births—always explaining how the trio are connected at a deeper level.

Malini firmly believes she was destined to be a mother. 'From grades 1 to 5 usually the teaching revolves around the family unit and ours is different. It has Nani, Mummy and two, little sisters. We also wove stories starting not with the proverbial "Once upon a time," but "In previous to previous to previous life, there were..."' Malini smiles wistfully.

Based in the same city of Bengaluru, Srobona Das, with her partner Swarna, has initiated an 844-member-strong online community on Facebook called *For & Of Heart Babies* (https://www.facebook.com/groups/ForOfHeartBabies/). It comprises adoptive parents and prospective adoptive parents who are allowed to become part of the group only after a strict screening process.

Das, however, claims the number of single women becoming adoptive mothers is still miniscule in comparison to childless couples, and adds that despite a lot of positive support and encouragement for unmarried women, the scrutiny and verification process is largely tilted in favour of couples.

'There is a detailed questionnaire one has to fill to join our group, as we don't want any government, social agency or adoption firm to be a part of this community. Our aim is to create a unique space for safe parenting—a platform to listen and share genuine parenting queries and dilemmas. We already have 3 single mothers and another 2/3 soon-to-be single moms who have started the documentation phase and are in the application mode. Like I was "happily married" when I adopted, and 5 years down the line, my marriage ended, so while my status as a woman changed, my role as an adoptive parent stayed constant. I don't see too many divorced/separated women opting to adopt, but I definitely see an increase in single women aspiring to be mothers, and opting for adoption, without hankering for marriage. Most single women make the decision to be mothers by their mid-30s and I think they are symbolic of a more progressive societal order where women are taking full control of the decision to be a parent,' says Srobona.

Silver Lining For Single Mothers?

According to a recent decision taken by the The Ministry of Women and Child Development (WCD), single Indian women over the age of 40, and with the financial resources to bring up an adopted child, will be given preference in the adoption process. The resolution passed in July 2017 by the steering committee of Central Adoption Resource Authority (CARA), a statutory body of the WCD ministry, took cognizance of the rising trend of single women who were keen to adopt and raise a child on their own. The adoption rules also specify the age of prospective parents. Single women and men up to the age of 45 can adopt a child under the age of 4; those up to 50 years will be given children between 5-8 and those up to 55 years can adopt children in the age group of 9 to 18. Adoption is not allowed for anyone above the age of 55.

The decision in favour of older single women signifies that they would get to jump the long queues of those who have registered for adoption with CARA. This is significant as there are only 2,000-odd children who are legally available for adoption, 50% of them with special needs. In comparison, the number of wait-listed couples and individuals who have registered for adopting a child is 16,000.

Indian society with its innate, male-controlled roots remains culturally coloured with common phrases like '*bacche ka baap kaun hain?*' and 'man of the house'. Personally, being raised by a young, widowed, single mother, I can also vouch for the way she was deliberately singled out—especially at family functions like weddings and *godhbharais*—and how in school I was constantly interrogated on my father's inconspicuous absence at parent-teacher meetings and annual day functions, so much so that I created a make-believe father who lived and worked in London, just to ward off the suffocating curiosity.

'While there are success stories and happy ones too, Indian society is still cold to a single mother and she *has* to confront a deep-seated stigma where her character is doubly scrutinised, an undertone of prejudice that one has no choice but to get accustomed to. Akin to the odd, invasive stares in a public transport system when you wear a backless blouse,' observes 41-year-old Mrinalini Dave from Mumbai. Two schools placed Mrinalini's adopted son on the waiting list, and one simply refused to admit him, despite her son clearing the admission test with flying colours. When she was called in for an interview with the principal, the kind of intrusive questions asked made her feel a complete lack of privacy and respect. The principal insisted on wanting to know why she had adopted a child and if there was any family problem, practically refusing to believe she could be single. At Parent Teacher Association meetings, Mrinalini regularly faces a stiff upperlip attitude—especially the condescension of married couples with more than one kid, who pretend to know all the parenting rules, and dole out unsolicited *gyaan* having reached there first. Mrinalini calls this upper hand they exude a 'victory lap'. Like many other single women without kids, Mrinalini also faced a rough time getting a house in Mumbai, and recalls how it's usually the landladies who pose uncouth questions. One of them even went on to ask in front of Mrinalini's 7-year-old boy, *'Kitne mein liya?'* Another one sniggered at her ageing father accompanying them with the standard peeve, *'Isski shaadi kyun nahin huyi?'*

'Having kids or wanting motherhood minus marriage is a social anomaly. One has to own up to the fact that it does exist,' adds Mrinalini, shrugging her shoulders.

Apart from societal pressure, there is also the discomfort the decision of becoming a single mother elicits from one's immediate family. 31-year-old Tanya Choudhury, a marketing professional with a private university based in New Delhi, claims the idea of adoption first came to her back in college, around 2003, a 'feminist' thought that was immediately brushed off within her close friends circle as a passing whim, and perhaps just a cool thing to say and do. 'I had my first romantic relationship while pursuing my MBA and I did discuss adoption with my then partner, who was kicked about it. However, the failure of that relationship and the ones that followed, and me approaching the proverbial age of 30 made me reassess my priorities, given that I hadn't dated since 2012 and wasn't actively seeking out prospects. I was also clear that I wasn't interested in the traditional arranged-marriage setup. Soon enough, my thoughts veered back to my college phase where I always envisaged a full house with lots of children, but not necessarily involving a man as a husband and a provider. I had a great role model in my own father who always encouraged my independence. So at some point, I did deliberate on whether I was going to deprive the child of a father figure, but the more I studied and explored alternate families, saw brave gay couples bringing up children, I decided while I am open to partnerships, I will not make child-rearing and seeking companionship synonymous,' asserts Tanya, who is awaiting her home study.

Tanya's parents, who reside in Kolkata, are not pleased with her decision of motherhood minus a man, being 'still hopeful that I will opt for the conventional model of marriage first, child later.'

Tanya remarks, 'While the whole structure of adoption is now more centralised and everything is done online, the social workers tend to ask more grilling questions of a single woman on matters such as having live-in help, whether I intend to give up my day job and/if I can avail of work-from-home facilities, basically trying to ascertain whether the living environment is conducive for bringing up a child.'

To this end, Tanya recently moved out of an apartment she shared with three other women where there was regular partying and alcohol flowed freely. 'Social workers are open to shared setups, but I personally felt I wanted an independent space to raise my child,' says Tanya, who isn't daunted by her family not sharing this critical life moment with her. 'Even if I had biological children, I wouldn't like to impose their care on my ageing parents as having a child is solely a woman's decision. I intend to take time off work, as per the new maternity laws in the country and finally seek out a professional day-care centre and hope that my professional organisation allows me to return home at a reasonable time. It's important that a child grows up seeing the reality of the world we live in today—and grows accustomed to a working, financially independent mother figure.'

Eager to hold her baby in her own hands soon, Tanya shares that she has opted for a baby girl in the 0-2 years age bracket. 'My mother is very fond of children, and I think it's a matter of time before she will come around,' she signs off with bittersweet expectation.

When Sperms Don't Count

Even as the journey to single parenthood remains as challenging as the choice to remain single, stories of everyday heroism and ditching the patriarchal bogey trap continue to inspire women to shatter the male bastion. Kolkata-based filmmaker Anindita Sarbadhicari always nursed a natural maternal instinct, being a mother first to her pets. During her student years at Delhi's prestigious National School of Drama or Pune's Film and Television Institute of India, she would always adopt strays or abandoned dogs and wryly feels that somewhere she even mothered the men in her life.

Engaged to a German man when she lived and backpacked in Europe, Anindita's friend circle included many brave single moms, as she also read up many a feminist short story celebrating the victory of single motherhood. After her break-up, Anindita returned to her roots in Kolkata, at the age of 29-30 and soon co-founded a wine club with a doctor friend. By then, single motherhood was already her Plan B.

On the personal front, Anindita was having flings off and on but none of her affairs lasted beyond a few months, since Bengali men, she claims, either found her too bossy or way too independent to settle down to mundane domesticity. Marriage as an institution also didn't quite hold supreme importance for Anindita who felt that love and the commitment that was synonymous with settling down could occur anytime in life. She was acutely aware that while marriage could wait till the right companion surfaced, motherhood couldn't till eternity, since her body was advancing in years.

With enough savings, Anindita soon decided on a break from filmmaking and following her own heart, grew clearer in her resolve to bear a child. 'I had travelled alone to Maoist-infested areas with my camera as my only weapon. Courage was never an issue. But before bringing another life into this world, I asked myself if I was strong enough for the uphill road ahead and how the world would receive my child in the near future'.

Much to her surprise, when she broke the news to her parents, they were very excited, with her mother even suggesting that instead of subjecting her body to the rigours of an IVF, why not simply go for a vacation with a man and impregnate herself. 'In fact, she was the major driving force on this journey, collecting information, egging me on. My father was also super-charged, suggesting he organise a press conference to announce this decision,' Anindita proudly claims. She did everything on her own, including driving herself back and forth to the fertility clinic—going to the sperm bank, buying the donor sperm, etc. On 1 December 2012, the transfer happened smoothly and Anindita soon discovered she was pregnant. But in February, on a day she was alone at home, Anindita experienced an excruciating pain in her lower abdomen; she drove herself to the clinic, only to discover she had miscarried.

Shattered emotionally, Anindita was unable to share this failure with anyone, including her supportive parents who were simultaneously grieving in their own way. 'I lived alone in my apartment, away from my family, and skydived into a black hole of clinical depression. I ran away to Delhi, finally to be with actor Adil Hussain, who happens to be my *moohbola bhai*, and his wife Kristen, and they inducted me into meditation. Finally, I decided I'd try one more IVF and if that, too, failed, I would just adopt,' says Anindita, who underwent an embryo transfer and in November 2013, her son Aarush was born, two months prematurely.

Taking a conscious decision, Anindita chose to spend the first two years of her motherhood, detached from her profession, despite battling financial issues that stemmed from bearing the cost of IVF and her subsequent medications. 'My career naturally took a backseat, but my focus was Aarush and his growth.' She adds enthusiastically, 'And now that I'm getting back to work, I'm finding a lot of positive support. It's ironical because you think for a woman with a child, the film industry hardly offers any choices.'

Having recently lost her mother, her biggest support system, Anindita doesn't even have time for a coffee date with a man today, let alone a relationship. 'I can't recall the last time I had sex!' she laughs out loud, adding with a pinch of salt, 'Also, I have to be careful. The choices I make will directly affect my son. Till date we haven't faced a single raised eyebrow or negative vibe. Instead, I always feel we are spoilt since I am a single mother by choice. But when it comes to a man in my life, it will have to be someone who is emancipated enough to embrace and celebrate my decision. Honestly, I hardly meet eligible men. Maybe my need is also to maximise time with my son and prioritise my career, while being there for my father, and my doggie son, Dushtu, at the same time. So, men ... well, they can wait!'

Anindita, who is in the throes of writing a script for her next feature, says when she tells people she'd love to adopt a girl child next, as her son Aarush is keen on a sibling, she's severely admonished. 'There are married couples, women in their forties who accidentally conceive and decide to keep the kid, or have their second child, late, and no one raises a single eyebrow on that personal choice to become a mother, or put their age under the scanner. While in my case, in a single woman's life, her intent to become a mother for the second time is always measured using the word "*sahosh*" like it's a heroic dare or something,' Anindita puts forth matter-of-factly.

An article in *The Times of India* in 2013 titled 'More single women now prefer artificial insemination' reported that while many single women these days are opting for conception through sperm donation, they rarely come out in the open about it, like Anindita. The article also held that the demands of single women opting for artificial insemination are quite different from those of couples. Quoting Dr A. Patil from the piece, 'Single women often ask for sperms from highly qualified donors since they wish to have smart babies. However, one needs to understand that higher qualification doesn't always boil down to intelligence. They also demand a healthy sperm, with the stress being on the eye colour and skin tone.' The trend, restricted mainly to foreigners till the last few years, the article claims, has now caught on with Indian women.

'Earlier, many foreigners would come for designer babies, asking for a certain type of eye colour and skin tone. But now, many single Indian women, too, have come forward,' added Dr Sourav Prasad, an infertility expert.

The piece further mentions a Jharkhand-based sperm donor, Aslam Khan (*name changed*) who says, 'I get around four queries each month from single women who want to start a family of their own. The only thing I keep in mind before donating my sperm to any such women is to be sure about her steady income to ensure a healthy lifestyle for the baby. The final exchange is done through registered medical practitioners.'

The news in January 2016 about former beauty queen, 42-year-old Diana Hayden's daughter being born from her eggs frozen almost 8 years ago has also refocused our attention on egg-freezing in India, another booming industry. Compared to more propagated reproductive technologies like surrogacy and sperm donation, egg-freezing, which was relatively lesser-known earlier, is now being commonly labelled as a type of 'insurance' for single women—a sort of family planning that enables her to make decisions regarding her body without interrupting her career, in case she wants to start a family later in life.

Hayden, who was 32 when she read about egg-freezing for the first time in 2005, froze 16 eggs between October 2007 and March 2008, with infertility specialist Dr Nandita Palshetkar. 'I froze my eggs for two reasons: I was busy with my career at that time and, more important, I was very clear that I was going to wait to fall in love and marry before having a baby,' she said at the time of the announcement. Freezing her eggs proved to be a blessing in disguise for the model-actor who at 40 fell in love and married American, Collin Dick. She soon discovered she was battling endometriosis. That is when the couple decided to thaw Diana's frozen-eggs and attempt a test-tube baby. Considered a poster girl for egg-freezing today, Diana was probably the first single woman to use it for 'lifestyle reasons' and not just as a medical necessity.

With fertility experts swiftly replacing marriage brokers, are we headed to an era when it will finally be redundant for a woman who wants a child of her own to depend on marriage? Can a single mother overthrow the age-old, top-heavy male stronghold? What if she decides to mother a love child, for instance?

Why The Father's Surname Remains The Last Word In Child Legitimacy

Blame it on popular culture or our conservative desi mindset that idealises marriage as the ultimate validation for women, there is a general tendency to, therefore, attach guilt and shame to those who choose to get involved in a relationship with a married man. Exactly the reason why 46-year-old telecom professional Amita Arya's personal saga is as complex as it is courageous.

A single mother, with a 20-year-old daughter whom she bore with her now-divorced husband, Amita also has a 9-year-old son, technically an illegitimate child, whom she chose to bear after a prolonged, intense affair with a married man, a father to 2 children himself. Soon, however, her married lover refused to acknowledge their son or leave his wife as he had initially promised, a decision that has led to Amita fighting an arduous paternity suit in court and claiming a DNA test. 'I'm not desperate for marriage or money. I just want Sunil *(her lover, name changed on request)* to accept he's the father of my son. According to the court, every child you bear is an equal son. My son knows the truth and even in school he tells his teachers before they can ask, that his father doesn't live with us. I am open with both children.

'My husband wasn't working and had zero bank balance. He hated reading, while I was into literature; the difference between us was a rude shock. I was the main breadwinner. After our daughter was born, he gained employment. I joined a reputed telecom company and was heading operations for the north. We met once in 6 months, there was no physical intimacy between us. Things changed in January 2006. I was coming out of jaundice and happened to meet an ex IIT-ian on a Yahoo chat group who also lived in Noida. We chatted for 3-4 hours and since we lived nearby, I went over to his home and even met his wife. On the fourth day of us knowing one another, he visited my house with his son. Our friendship grew slowly from there and we consummated our relationship soon after. Sunil would say: "What's there in a marriage? That is more of a duty, I want to spend the rest of my life only with you." Meanwhile, his wife got pregnant with their second son. I called her on her *godhbharai*, but he picked up the phone and said if I came clean about our relationship, she may commit suicide,' Amita looks back on her chequered affair.

'When I conceived, Sunil was determined I needed to abort the child as he feared what society will say if the kid resembled him in any way. I, however, was adamant that I wanted the child since it was the peak of our affair. He left in a huff but his friends kept calling me saying he was miserable. After the third day, Sunil returned and looking back, he was extremely supportive towards my pregnancy,' recalls Amita who, at that time, was still not divorced from her husband. She adds boldly, 'I shared with my spouse all that had happened with Sunil. He was angry but didn't know what to do since we had been estranged for years. On 19 April 2007, my son was born preterm. Sunil's were the first arms my son was cradled in. My parents arrived soon after with my husband and that's when he blurted out that we weren't together anymore.'

In 2012, Sunil's wife discovered his pictures with Amita on a Flickr account, but chose to believe his version that they were 'just friends' and that their son was born out of a night of fun when Sunil was sloshed. Sunil also requested Amita to remove some of their more intimate pictures and comments, which she obliged, even going on to meet his wife finally and divulging to her with all the details of their affair. But all she wanted to know was how many times they had sex and how many vacations they had taken!

Soon, Amita's affair soured as Sunil's friends, who were political goons, began threatening her, as he also resorted to defaming her in their IIT-alumni circles. Scared and weak, Amita bore the brunt of her decision, having to hear every conceivable kind of abuse from him, his mother, his in-laws, her own father, and losing every friend.

'My relationship with my daughter subsequently crumbled as she had got attached to Sunil. Missing him as a father figure, she took to alcohol and smoking. I was forced to refocus all my energies towards my child and sought counselling. Sunil started spreading rumours about my character and my seniors in IIT also believed I swapped men every night. The reason I had revealed everything to his wife was because I was humiliated when he would take both of us on vacations and after spending the first half of the night with her would sneak into my room. It was wrong on her too. I wasn't interested in being the quintessential second woman,' stubbornly states Amita.

'When you have an affair with a married man, you are branded a whore in our culture. My brothers don't support me, though my sisters-in-law understand. My parents also finally came around, though they always remind me how I was wrong in choosing Sunil. And are partial towards my daughter. My daughter thankfully today is close to her own father. He remarried after we divorced and funds her higher education. As a single woman living life on my own terms, I am comfortable with my personal and childbearing choices. In school, I have faced no issues with regards to my children's admission, so I believe slowly and steadily society, too, is beginning to accept women like me, and children without a father's identity. Today, on the passport, single guardianship is legally permissible. Of course, there are always married women who fear I may snatch their husbands next… but I don't care!' Amita, who has relocated to Mumbai to study women-centric social work from Tata Institute of Social Sciences, signs off brazenly.

Can Motherhood Scale Narrow Gender Boundaries?

Fighting not just regressive societal fetters, but the complex legalities of gender in India, 38-year-old Gauri Sawant, born as Ganesh, became a 'mother by accident' when she rescued a 5-year-old girl child, Gayatri, from Kamathipura, Mumbai. Their incredible journey was the subject of a popular Vicks ad that grabbed national and international headlines. Gauri recollects her transition into single motherhood, 'The child's mother had died of AIDS, and her grandmother was trying to sell her off to a dealer in Sonagachi, Kolkata, Asia's largest red-light area. There were pimps quoting varied prices, some saying ₹1,40,000, others trying to outbid the amount, yelling ₹1,90,000. I remember screaming the choicest abuses, and declaring that this child is now mine, and whoever wants to stake a claim better come talk to me. I presumed maybe an aunt or a distant relative would take her away, but no one turned up. At that time, I did not know that I'd become a mother, or that I would raise her and be narrating my story one day. I just knew that this motherless, vulnerable child needed protection and care.

'The night I got her home, we shared a slim cot where I had slept alone until that day, and we tried to share one sheet. Gayatri wrapped her tiny arms around me, her skinny, bony frame pressed against my stomach and chest. I had never felt the warmth of a child beside me; it was an experience I can never forget,' reminisces Gauri, who fed the child, cut her nails, bathed her and cleaned her up. Gayatri soon started attending school in the neighbourhood, and spent most afternoons in the little room in Malvani with her mother and a group of hijras, who were her playmates.

'We are women born without a uterus, but just as there are all kinds of flowers in nature, a mother is not a label that needs men, marriage and legal sanction. A mother is another synonym for care. It is what Gayatri, my 16-year-old daughter has taught me,' emotionally remarks Gauri, who has in the past filed a petition seeking these basic rights for the LGBT community, besides being a part of the crusade that ensured the third gender gets Aadhaar cards, as dictated by the National Legal Services Authority (NALSA) bench. Inspired by this victory, Gauri tried to legalise her arrangement with Gayatri by adopting her formally, but the government does not give custody of a child to a member of the LGBT community.

'Bringing up a girl child is like holding a glass doll,' feels Gauri while recounting a recent tour she undertook to Shirdi. 'A man was trying to touch Gayatri's hands,' she pauses, before taking a deep breath to continue, 'I am not scared of anyone, I can strip in public and scream out abuses, but I think I reacted as Gayatri's *aiyee*, when my blood turned cold as I feared for my child's safety.'

Perhaps it was the same maternal instinct that made Gauri decide to send Gayatri away to a boarding school in Pune after she got embroiled in a bitter fight with other girls from school. Within minutes, Gayatri had started clapping, and abusing like the hijras. 'I haven't done anything for her, she's given me everything—the title of "mother", which is one of the greatest manifestations of womanhood, in my journey from boy to girl,' she says emotionally.

'2 months ago, I visited Kamathipura and met two Bangladeshi sex workers. One of them offered to bring me paan. After half an hour when she had not returned, I got fidgety and started looking around. A flimsy curtain separated us. I lifted the curtain and saw the 22-year-old woman lying sprawled on the floor, her 3-month-old newborn playing with her dupatta. The woman's pajama strings were open. And over her was mounted a 70-year-old man. It was the cruelest sight I had ever witnessed in my life. I waited for the sex service to culminate and then scooped up the baby from the ground. The mother asked me if I wanted the infant, saying that she will surely become a *randi* if she continues living here in the brothel. I told her that very soon I would come back for the child. I couldn't sleep the whole night. That was a turning point in my life. I have a small farmhouse in Karjat where ageing hijras stay, and I have decided I am going to start an initiative there called 'Save the Girls', to nurture young children, after they are off the breast milk of their mothers. It will be called *Nani Ka Ghar* (which is in the fundraising stages right now).

'Day before yesterday, I was in Pune and heard about a child being thrown into a dustbin and then eaten by rats,' recounts Gauri. She adds, 'Hijras like me are viewed with contempt, because when people even see me with my daughter, say, travelling in a rickshaw, they assume I have stolen the child and that I am no better than a child snatcher. While raising Gayatri, I've seen a new sexist syndrome that I term "man-raising". Where in the absence of a father, all the men around her—neighbours, uncles, etc.—feel the need to act as primary caregivers and come with their suggestions, in spite of the fact that Gayatri still has one parent—me.'

Motherhood: A Choice, Not A Compulsion

And yet, even as singletons like Gauri, Amita and Anindita take unflinching steps in making motherhood a conscious choice, there is always a niggling doubt of raising a family without full support for an unmarried woman.

41-year-old Devi Meenakshi fought a bitter divorce and domestic violence battle for many years. She is an HR professional and a handlooms curator from Bengaluru, who confesses to having explored the option of motherhood via egg-freezing and IVF. Like Anindita, she, too, was keen to experience the joy of a child growing in her womb. But practicality intervened, with her stalling her plans, as she explains, 'Bringing up a kid needs huge support and ideally both sets of parents/an alternate support structure. I lost my dad, and my ailing mother is away in Kerala, so I lack a proper infrastructure or family support that's critical before taking the final plunge. Today, my mindset has changed and I am debating whether or not to adopt, instead of having my own biological baby, as I think there are many homeless children in this country who could do with a home. The biological clock, however, is a reality, so there's no point escaping the same!'

Craving for a child, the growing economic independence of single women making them eligible for adoption and IVF through purchased sperms, families slowly coming around and supporting their decision, along with advancements in medical science have made motherhood simpler, if not easier. And yet, 36-year-old, Pune-based lawyer Shipra Hore makes a sharp statement, 'I just wish they didn't keep dangling motherhood all the time in front of me like a carrot. Motherhood is a decision that is intensely personal, but every single woman is pressurised at some point to face it in the eye. The hard sell of motherhood is a medical construct as much as it is a social pressure and single women make for an easy bait, since most of us crave a child, and seek emotional bonding. It's the whole completion and companionship funda, force-fed to us from the time we were little girls, so much so that we all want entry into this almost privileged, women-with-child club—because, being single and childless is a curse in this country.'

'Let us not forget, motherhood through medicine comes at a huge cost because in India, infertility treatment is not covered under health insurance policies of most insurance giants across the nation. So there is no insurance cover to compensate for the bleeding, hormones and injections and rest from work required. So between maintaining my lifestyle and craving kiddie love, I finally said to hell with motherhood. I have now kept a pup!' she concludes.

To put things in perspective, infertility is not exactly considered an illness that needs to be treated; so treatment is voluntary and not necessary for the healthy survival of the individual. Most of the treatments for infertility of men and women are still in the experimental stage of their usage and implementation. Experimental treatments are not covered under health insurance in India which routinely strikes off any chance of infertility treatment for men or women, featuring on the list of genetic or contracted diseases (through sexually transmitted diseases) that are covered under health insurance policies of India.

IVF, therefore, is extremely expensive in our country, while comparatively cheaper than IVF in foreign countries like the United States from where women fly down to get operated upon in India at a lower rate. To an average Indian family, however, the amount needed for an IVF is ₹2.5 lakhs at the bare minimum. Added to this are the expenses associated with the IVF treatment, concurrent or post the treatment.

Age No Bar To Being A Natural Mother

From anxiety-mongering gynaecologists, smooth-talking fertility specialists, glib advertisers, to well-intentioned family members, as I turn 40 later this year, I am also literally bombarded and shamed into believing that post 35 a woman's eggs become less useful. In fact, given my faulty gynae karma, I may as well forget about having my own biological child. Some married girlfriends have even shared gory infertility stories that underline the risks of miscarrying or giving birth to a child with scathing birth defects. And yet, the latest research proves that popularised myths regarding women's fertility may just be another patriarchal construct. In *The Impatient Woman's Guide to Getting Pregnant*, author Jean M. Twenge challenges the prevalent belief that one in three women over 35 will fail to get pregnant after a year of trying, saying that the claim is based on an analysis of French birth records dated 1670 to 1830. In fact, about 80% of women aged 35 to 39 succeed in getting pregnant naturally today, a slight decline from the fertility rate of women aged 27 to 34.

In a 2014 study published by the Boston University School of Medicine, researchers discovered that women who are able to give birth after the age of 33 or older, sans the help of drugs, tend to live longer than those who stopped having children before age 30. An earlier study from the New England Centenarian Study discovered that women who had children after the age of 40 were 4 times more likely to live to 100 than those who had their last child at a younger age.

As women we grow up constantly hearing the adage, 'There is a right time to have a child'—as if procreation is our biggest life goal. And while being a single mother is a conscious, practical, lifelong commitment, are we wrong to assume and generalise that a woman who doesn't seek to reproduce or mother an infant might not be cut out for motherhood, at all? A woman with no heart?

While celebrating women who don't wait for the right man to have the child they craved for, let's hope as a sex, we aren't boxed and stereotyped as baby-making machines.

Motherhood is a choice. Not a challenge, after all.

STATUS SINGLE: *Having a child is like the decision to get married—it's intensely personal and while most single women crave children instinctively, I think we should be alive to the fact that having a child isn't like getting a fish bowl or a pet—it's more like getting a tattoo on your face, a full-time, 24/7 responsibility. And while today you don't need a man to give in to your child cravings, even so the final decision needs to be well thought out, supported by family and friends and backed by a strong financial contingency plan that sees the child through every phase of his/her life.*

A lot of my single friends often remark that they are tired of looking for the right man to settle down with, and would much rather focus their mind space on adoption or going to a sperm bank. However, be careful what you wish for. A child is a lifelong accountability and being a mother changes your whole life and how you can manage your time, a total life-goal-reorientation. So get the supporting framework in place and do your groundwork really well before taking the final plunge. Fortunately, today the laws in India are being altered for single mothers, with the Supreme Court also coming around and saying a mother is every bit a legitimate natural guardian—with just her name being enough on the child's passport, for instance. However, a lot of single women try to fill up the lack of a male partner with a child—and that's shortsighted, because even children eventually grow up and have lives of their own! Besides, no one is an old age insurance cover. So, don't make apologies if you love kids but don't want one of your own yet. Or would rather invest in a home for yourself than raise a child. Your singlehood is your choice.

Chapter Five

Bultu, Biye and Bachelorettes

Dear Bultu,

You may not remember me. I mean, let's face it, we just had one evening, a little over an hour maybe, and I mean, you were busy. C'mon, of course I know you were checking out my tits. You're a guy!

Oh c'mon, get over it. I've had my tits checked out before.
I'm a Bong babe, remember? We are naturally blessed.
So?
Well? I also have a sense of humour.
What?
You didn't get it.
Of course, you didn't!
You were too busy, you see. Okay, I won't bring up the boob part again. I know you are a Bong man. Sensitivity's your thing, that and poetry. But of course you can quote Satyajit Ray and PB Shelley in the same breath.
Why didn't we go there?
Umm... well, there were these delicious shammis Ma had made painstakingly, and fish fry—the bhery Bong staple. It always impresses strangers. Served with a careful dollop of Kasundi on the side.

Kasundi, silly!

Bong word for French mustard.

Didn't you study French or something? You did, right?

Of course. How dumb of me to doubt your stupendous academic achievements. You were also a light architect or something?

What the fuck does that even mean, Bultu?

Hey, and one other thing. Whoever calls their son Bultu?

Bong mothers, naturally.

Hey, Bultu, now that we are on a daaknaam (pet name) basis, why was your mum constantly asking those dumb-ass questions? Remember them?

You know, just before the time my dad asked us to go talk in private. Before your mum told my mum that you had always dreamt of a Bong wife. Before we all nodded our heads jointly. After you first smiled at me. Quickly bending down to fix your laces.

Your sneakers impressed me. Nike Air!

But… but not your hair, Bultu. I mean, let's face it, you hardly had any! Except the few stray strands billowing softly in the breeze of our new ceiling fan.

Looking back, it was rather filmy, I suppose.

The way I sat before you. My knees delicately crossed.

Your mum asking me if I liked wearing a sari…

I was in my latest Levi's Curve jeans.

I lied.

Saying it disgusts me.

The truth is, I look hottest in a sari. That, and a backless choli. I like to click a lot of selfies. I pout. I like my cleavage. My navel. My inner thighs. My—

Anyway…

Bultu. Coming back to your question of why I am opting for an arranged alliance. I have no freaking clue why. The truth is, I love being single. It makes me fearless and flirty. And I am sick of the relationship rut.

Bultu, are you a virgin?

Shut up, Bultu!

Well, I'm not. And guess what? The guy I slept with? He dumped me. Treating me like shit after we'd done it. The usual…

I was actually told our 3-year relationship had ended over an SMS. Yes, it was cruel. It sucked.

The sympathy. The sadness. The soullessness.

I mean, this coming 2.5 years or so after my college boyfriend hit me. Twisting my arms. Pressing his cigarette stub between my legs. Insisting on sex, even when I pleaded that I wasn't ready.

I had also lost a lot of weight that time.

I used to be a really fat person. Like really…

He claimed I was the most beautiful girl. It was a lot like love, actually.

Do you like sex, Bultu?

Will you ever force me into it? What if I can't bear kids? What if I want more from life than a picket fence can ever hope to give me? What if I have my own dreams? My own darknesses? The demons in my head…

Oh, but I love picket fences. Yes, I am a bit like that. I like fancy things. In books, as in, in chick lit books, that I am sure you never read. I could be labelled high maintenance. I fancy Jimmy Choos. And sometimes, I masturbate thinking of myself as a really rich woman, living in a mansion in Southhampton.

With a pair of poodles gawking.

The doggy thing?

Do you touch yourself, Bultu?

I mean, have you ever wanted to do it in an aircraft loo? Or in a public place? What are your wildest fantasies, Bultu?

Tell me everything.

Okay, fine. You come from a cultured family.

You want a son, Bultu?

What if we have a daughter instead? Have you ever considered adoption? Surrogacy? IVF? What if the stress of your high-profile career swallows the motility of your sperm or something? Will you ever tell your mum the truth about how unhappy we may end up?

Think about it, Bultu.

Because your mum categorically told me you absolutely adored children and that you wanted them to have an Indian education.

My ass!

Look around, Bultu. This country sucks. I mean, let's be frank. I was the twelfth girl you checked out. 'Sitting'—your mum coined that phrase.

Twelve unmarried ladies in one day!

Gosh, you're fast, Bultu.

And fat.

Oops. I was never meant to tell you that.

But your paunch is bigger than my dad's. And, your double chin. See, I'll be honest—I have absolutely nothing against fat people.

It's just that, I couldn't…

I, I couldn't visualise you naked, Bultu…

I'm sorry.

But I think every woman has the right to be attracted to the man she's choosing to spend the rest of her life with.

I mean, look, Bultu. I'm not going to spend my wedding night with a fancy CV.

Harvard. Gold medalist. Audi. Real estate.

Am I superficial?

Maybe.

Which is why I also didn't like the fact that your mum kept peering into our study, every few seconds, asking you to 'wrap up'.

Actually, I felt even she was checking out my tits. Which is cool. Women have equal rights to fantasise. And some women dig chicks more.

But, but, Bultu…

'Otho', (get up): whoever the hell says that to a guy sitting with a girl.

Do you know how many times she ordered you, literally screaming, 'Get up, Bultu…'

I don't, okay. I wasn't counting either.
I was busy staring at your crotch.
Wondering...
(Okay, I now sound really mean.) Whether you were impotent or something? Fearing the worst. You. Naked. On our wedding night. And she screaming.
'Otho, Bultu... otho...'
Bultu, I like you. A lot.
I mean, I think you are a genuinely well-meaning, 41-year-old, virgin NRI who needs to desperately stop meeting unwed Bengali girls in and around Chittaranjan Park, the Bong ghetto in Delhi, and chomping on oily fish fry and cholesterol-laden shammi.
Watch your scales, Bultu.
Also, you see, this arranged marriage market is very cruel. It shatters your self-image. You are nothing but a product sitting on a shelf, waiting to be picked up, before your shit rots. An advertisement. An agony, to your ageing parents. A social antithesis.
It's a dog-eat-dog world, Bultu.
You must say the right things. You must have hair. You must be fair. Slim. Non-manglik. Convented. Professional. Love kids.
But, hey, at least you're a guy.
41 is not so bad. You'll still be able to snag a girl in her late 20s. I mean, your mum did say you have a double Ph.D. Wiping her eyes.
Your mum is a widow.
My mum was too. Except, I never saw her wailing. She was a kick-ass Biology teacher. And with the help of my grandparents, she worked her butt off to raise me.
In Kolkata.
You said you hated Kolkata?
Wrong move, Bultu (read deal-breaker!).
I mean, I may not live there anymore. But it's home.
It's my Vegas, baby.

The place where my parents met.

Yes, Bultu.

Love stories do happen. Sometimes, in the unlikeliest of places. Between two people you might never imagine would end up together.

My dad. Younger than Ma. A South Indian Brahmin.

They've been together over two-and-a-half decades.

Now.

Nice story, huh?

I swear. I was about to tell you, Bultu.

If only your mum hadn't barged in on us for the nth time. Minutes after you told me it was expensive to be a writer. That you were more turned on by a professional, working woman. That in the US I'd get bored sitting 'idle'. That you were busy.

Very, very busy.

And that writing courses were bloody expensive.

'Do it on the side, like a hobby. Cornell looks good only in movies,' you made a joke, putting on an accent.

'Bulto, otho...'

I said it this time.

I also showed you the middle finger when you weren't looking, alright.

And oh, before I end this note.

My name.

My name is Sreemoyee Piu Kundu.

You never asked.

Bultu...

This cheeky column I'd penned for *Daily O*, a leading opinion website. Besides going viral, it soon transformed into something of a war cry for hundreds of faceless, nameless Indian women, most of whom I didn't know personally, frantically inboxing me on social media, claiming these were the exact same sentiments they had been wanting to scream out at their prospective suitors for the longest time ever. While some termed the piece 'bold and beautiful', others labelled it 'brutal and bitchy'. Both classifications didn't take much away from the universal truth: that every urban single woman has at some point opted for the age-old arranged marriage formula—signing up dutifully on matrimonial websites and meeting professional matchmakers, diligently filling up the groom criteria, inane specifications, like height, weight, salary package, vegetarian, non-vegetarian, eggetarian or vegan dietary choices, before going on to pen elaborate self-descriptions, family background, height, weight, age—the same rigmarole. Before racking their brains next over what pictures to upload that are likely to make the finest, quickest first cut, battling the same bunch of dilemmas we have all nursed as little girls:

Western clothes vs. Ethnic.

Docile vs. Demure.

Hot vs. Homely.

Sometimes, when I ask my fellow single friends about arranged marriages, there is undoubtedly a general consensus that it's the last resort for many, essentially because the process of selection and elimination is downright sexist and that they could at times literally murder the prospective mother-in-law, right at the outset—at least for a certain category of singletons, the ones who like to believe they can find the right guy. But when the overconfidence chips off, what is left in its place is the truth—where are the single men?

Because honestly speaking, haven't most of us confronted that awkward situation when you may just be the only solitary single girlfriend, still unmarried, and well into her early or late 30s, thereby tending to feel a tad left out if your core friend circle happens to be a sea of newly married couples/newly pregnant couples/couples with young kids. Also, as a single friend stated on her 40th birthday, rather sardonically, 'Take me to a mall where there will be no couples clicking selfies or a parlour where the woman seated next to me isn't sporting an arm clamoring with *churas*.' And while her statement may come across as agnostic and intolerant, there are actually moments a single woman feels weary of confronting couples, just about everywhere—malls, multiplexes, market places, restaurants, housewarming parties, airports, hotel lobbies, in the park adjoining your house jogging in matching track pants, in emergency rooms of hospitals!

Singled Out In A Sea Of Married Couples

I like to term what I'm currently going through as a 'men-o-pause'—a tight spot where I'm clearly looking for marriage and not just a sexual fling, even as there seems to be no target audience truly fitting my bill. Simply because everyone you knew to be once single or met socially, is now either married or seeing someone, or, as clichéd as it may sound, gay. Or if your relationship karma is half as faulty as mine, the object of your affection fits bang into the psycho, bastard, asshole, loser, sex maniac, kinky, commitment-phobic, BDSM-loving man, that you resolved at some point to have seen enough of, and just don't want to deal with ever again.

One actually becomes inwardly fatigued of watching Facebook burst at the seams with albums of women declaring their relationship status, then, before you know it, getting hitched, and posing for gooey pictures in front of a colossal historical monument or at a swish hotel poolside, wedding photography being the latest love fad, with gaudy bachelorettes soon making way for cute baby showers with constant updates on the couple's marital life, holidays, in-laws, religious festivals like *Karwa Chauth* down to baby moons, the child's messy diapers and report cards.

Extreme reactions to singlehood never cease.

'*Aapki abhi tak shaadi nahin huyi? Kyun?*' a girl with a 'May I

Help You?' badge at a mobile bill payment counter in my South Delhi neighbourhood frowns, asking me my age soon enough. When I tell her I am 39, deciding to not react to her nosiness because one is immune to this line of interrogation by now, she practically suffers a mini stroke, quickly realigning her facial muscles to claim I don't look my age. Ouch! Compassionate condescension, I remind myself, staying calm.

'*Dhund rahen hain kya aapke liye?*' she resumes awkwardly, going on to tell me how she recently got married and how her husband is also employed in the same office. That they take the metro together from West Delhi, daily. She's 26. Her parents started looking for a match when she graduated in commerce.

Lesson numero uno, I take a deep breath.

Start early.

Or as my father often likes to remind me in jest, 'When you were at the right age, you were running after the wrong guy! So many proposals had come back then. In India, 39 is ancient history, darling.' As I stubbornly defend my stand insisting that I happened to be deeply in love with the man in question, I know in my heart of hearts that it's about as close to the truth as it gets. Here.

This is the reason why so many single women give arranged marriage a shot—egged on initially by well-meaning parents, who naturally want their daughters to settle down, lest she miss the proverbial bus. With the seats fast filling up, and being limited to age and good looks, and so even as your more compassionate married friends try and convince you that being single is way more liberating than being hitched and straddled with a bunch of noisy kids and nagging in-laws, you can sense a glint of the 'been there, done that' look in their eyes that you secretly wish you didn't have to suffer any longer.

Pressure To Be Plus One, Both Peer And Parental

36-year-old marketer, Pallavi Sharma, originally from Lucknow, admits she's lost track of the number of guys she's met since she and her family started looking out for a matrimonial alliances from 2007-2008. 'Everyone in India is married by 30 and most even have kids by then,' stoically observes Pallavi while recalling the humiliation of putting herself out there with a man asking her point-blank if she was still a virgin (a common question it seems). Being a shy person, Pallavi feels her small-town conservatism may be the reason for her constant rejections. The tag of 'late for marriage' that has gotten fixed on her has been stifling, with relatives perennially prying, at any given family function, if she plans on staying single all her life? Occasionally *rishtas* of divorcees are brought to her, that Pallavi admits is pretty much standard operating procedure for a 30-plus single woman.

Pallavi is still searching for the recipe of a *shudh desi* marriage, that she deduces as, 'Men in India are looking for a *sati savitri* at home, Sunny Leone sex bomb in bed and Chanda Kocchar at the workplace, a woman bringing home a whopping six-figure salary to share home loans and other EMIs and work tirelessly in the kitchen and look after the kids. I am so wary of all these matrimonial sites. I often happen to notice married colleagues who just create profiles for casual sex and dating. Who does one trust?'

Pallavi's question haunts me since I've personally undergone a scary experience on a leading matrimonial website while working as a journalist in Bengaluru. The man I met on the site claimed to be an entrepreneur from the US, based in Delhi. We exchanged numbers and soon were chatting non-stop. The boy promised almost on each call to drop into Bengaluru where he was apparently setting up a trading firm, so that we could interact in person. I was even made to speak to a maternal uncle. Finally, on the day we were supposed to actually meet, his phone remained switched off, and he never landed up.

A tad suspicious and relying on my journalistic instincts, I ventured to the address where his company was supposed to be located, only to discover a completely different office under construction! The workers on site also had no clue of the guy in question—the so-called owner. Being contacted after a few days, the man then chose to narrate a sob story of how his mother had broken her bones after an accidental fall in the bathroom, while setting up another date on which we could catch up. By then, I had, however, put colleagues in my Delhi newspaper office on the snoop track too, and they confirmed there was no office on the location from which he would ring from, though he would always claim it to be an official landline.

I decided to just call off the friendship, saying it would work only if he met me in person—making it clear that until then, I wasn't interested in wasting time on the phone. Soon enough, the boy vanished, only to surface a couple of months later in the papers as a master fraud—arrested in Delhi for duping single women on matrimonial sites and borrowing lakhs from them for an imaginary business. The profile picture he used was of some European actor. The incident still gives me goosebumps! It was a narrow escape.

Why Successful, Educated, Single Women Fall For The Arranged-Marriage Trap?

Despite such setbacks, I continued rather reluctantly on the arranged-marriage track. Sometimes, thanks to my over-anxious mother who once paid ₹10,000 to a Bengali matchmaker in Karol Bagh, who sent us a few proposals, which, if they had clicked would translate into more commission. Needless to say, I was rejected—once for my height, and the other time for my age. One of the boys' mothers worried that since her son and I were only a year apart, it may most likely mar her chances of becoming a grandmother soon. Despite these scars, my mother chose to splurge a lakh on yet another matrimonial website—a personalised service that promised to hook you up to 'elite' CEOs and managing directors, but, again, threw up nothing. Just a bunch of fancily designated, big-buck earning, regressive-minded men—one whose mother actually told my Relationship Manager that she had Googled me and had drawn the impression that I would be too 'fast', since she thought I dressed up too much in my pictures and thus concluded I'd be spending all her son's hard-earned moolah on what she termed 'frivolous, parlour expenses.'

Another prospective asked me embarrassingly on a coffee date if I was game for an open marriage? And being a media person, if I was still a virgin since he wanted to play the field post marriage! The misogyny in arranged alliances in India is sickening and possibly the lowest common denominator of patriarchy. And yet, most single women, despite their educational qualifications and professional successes, seem to have unanimously dipped, at least once, into this unholy rut.

Perhaps to the average Indian, having a single daughter who is through with her educational degree—in most cases just a graduation certificate—is akin to a death warrant. The pursuit of a suitable match begins the minute the daughter graduates from college. From scouring website and newspaper matrimonial ads to word-of-mouth prospecting, and doling out as hefty a fee to marriage brokers (ranging between 5,000 and a million rupees), the goal of getting their child settled is undoubtedly the most crucial goal of their lives! A Reuters 2013 news report captured this parental panic perfectly. 'According to professional matchmakers, parents should start looking for a husband for their daughters as soon as they turn 22 because they may lose their innocent looks once they hit the mature age of 25. Men often get more time to play, but not much more. They are expected to marry by their late twenties. Nor is the new generation showing signs changing en masse.'

40-year-old Rimi Das, a marketing professional in Bengaluru is often told, '*Arre abhi takh koi ladka nahin phasa payi?*' 'I'm not interested in "trapping" a man simply as I seek companionship and compatibility in my relationships,' clarifies Rimi, who began losing a lot of weight in the last few years, having shed close to 16 kgs today—an achievement that was inevitably linked to her capability to hook a guy.

'"*Ab ladka milega*," I was told by one and all, as if that's why I had started focusing on my health and fitness regime—as though male validation is the sole target of a woman's fitness goals.' Rimi feels it's very hard to be single in a judgmental society, such as ours, having also tried the arranged marriage route around 6-7 years ago, wanting to give it a shot at least once. 'The same stereotypes and prejudices that plague Indian culture are worst reflected in this system and I was completely disillusioned with the extensive *janam-kundli* matching and the fair, good-looking obsessive criterion,' she remarks, recalling how she once hit it off with a prospective based in the US. 'But once I sent him my photograph, he showed it to his mother and she turned me down as I wasn't fair enough. There is a latent patriarchy in the marriage institution, connected to the larger man-woman equation here. The way a classmate at a school reunion had once smirked, "Gosh you're 31 and still unmarried!" When I retorted, "Big deal! You're single too," he bragged, "Well, I am a man." That's the standard answer of men because they can get away with anything in a country where daughters are largely seen as a liability and must be wedded by a certain age. My relatives, for instance, these days lament that since I have hit 40, "*Ekhon aar bhalo chele pabe na*". (Now you won't get a good boy.)'

Arranged Marriages Like Dating Apps Abound In Misogyny

Fed on a diet of walk-into-the-sunset fairy tales, and conditioned to family life meant to imply conjugal bliss, almost every single woman in India dreams of finding love and nurtures aspirations of having her own family—an instinct fairly natural, despite growing economic emancipation of women and their increasing social independence. Popular culture also endorses the idea of completion, via marriage, with unmarried women often projected as evil and of ill character in films and serials—the conniving, jealous spinster *bua* or the nymphomaniac *chachi* whose make-up too is very often vampish, much on purpose.

33-year-old Misha Kapoor, working in the telecom sector, is categorical that she does not want to end up alone, but feels blessed every time she can end an association with a 'demented soul,' that she claims, 'strengthens my belief in the force looking after me. It's much better to be alone, successful and happy, travel to new places than being involved with the wrong person and suffer a dysfunctional marriage, day in and day out.' Being a witness to a lot of married women (of her age) with kids, who are suffering, thanks to poor, personal choices, she adds pragmatically, 'At my age, they are single again and have to deal with the liability of a child all on their own and yet are not financially independent as their spouse was the earning member until then.'

Misha's own groom-hunting process commenced around 2015, before Diwali, as she signed up on matchmaking portals like *Footloose No More* and met a few eligible men over lunches and dinners, discovering soon enough that most didn't really have a concrete marriage mindset. Also, since she lives independently in Mumbai, they were plain curious of her lifestyle and assumed she would be hooking up with multiple guys. The majority of men she met through matrimonial sites came armed with standard invasive questions like, 'What would you do if my friends come unannounced to our place?'

'There are loads of fake profiles too, and I'm always fighting with my mother on the authenticity and need for background checks. Some guys vanish the second you ask for concrete details, while others are perverts, like a guy I was talking to, who belonged to a reputed management school who just wouldn't stop sending me double-meaning texts on WhatsApp! Being sexually open is viewed as an asset nowadays, thanks to a new trend of dating apps that I have also tried out. There again, most men desire one-night stands and no-strings-attached affairs, vacations and weekend stayovers,' observes Misha, citing an example of a guy who directly messaged her saying, 'You look hot! Let's make out.'

While a changing socio-cultural milieu has rendered chastity irrelevant as a virtue, where a single woman wanting to wait till she knows a man well before getting sexually involved is most often bracketed as boring and backward, almost every one of us reaches the familiar roadblock of having to deal with so-called modern men, demonstrating an age-old patriarchal pre-conditioning. Like the time when Misha brought up her PCOS issues frankly with a man she'd been conversing with until then regularly, casually telling him that she might need assisted reproductive help in the future. He immediately blurted out how he needed some time to think about their blossoming relationship and disappeared shortly afterwards, claiming later that his practical mind wasn't allowing him to take their association any further.

Procreation is still seen as one of the greatest duties of an Indian wife, with very little said or written about male fertility issues, for a change. A June 2016 report in *Hindustan Times*, however, claimed infertility—the inability to conceive after one year of unprotected intercourse (six months if the woman is over 35 years old) or the inability to carry a pregnancy to live birth—has been on a steady rise among Indian men over the last few years. Doctors at the American Urological Association (AUA) claim that misconceptions about infertility abound and that it's invariably attributed to women, which is not the case. Men can be infertile too, and they are, in nearly 30% of all infertility cases, finds the Society for the Study of Male Reproduction.

'In India, guys have the option of marrying a much younger girl. In fact, that's what they all prefer too—since marriage and motherhood are synonymous and the younger the catch, the more virginal and more likely to reproduce faster formulae. But women, as they get older, are seen as rejected/defective pieces in the marriage market that operates on a kind of primitive perfection. It's like a fish market, and a nubile, young bride happens to be the most prized catch,' Misha sums up her state of mind.

Rabri Devi, wife of former CM Lalu Prasad Yadav, recently stated, 'I don't want girls who go to the malls and watch movies at theaters, I want girls who can look after the household, respect their elders and can manage outside work as well. I want girls who are just like I am,' in response to a media query as to what kind of brides she was looking for, for her two unmarried sons—Tej Pratap Yadav and Tejashwi Prasad Yadav. And while social media may be up in arms against the regressive mentality of Rabri Devi, how many of us, as single women have been humiliated by to-be mothers-in-law whose first questions are usually centred around whether we can cook, what time we return from office, whether we wish to continue working post marriage, and whether we love kids.

Once Bitten, Twice Shy

It's not just unmarried women, but also newly singled/divorced women who suffer the rollercoaster ride while looking for a second chance at love. Having had an arranged marriage at 21 to an NRI guy, who was a decade older, via an alliance forged by her mother's best friend, Rhiti Bose, founder and editor of ezine Incredible Women Of India, feels she was then way too young and immature to get to know her would-be hubby, not batting an eyelid before saying yes, therefore. What followed, however, was sheer horror.

'The guy was not interested in me as a person. I was more like a polished English-speaking maid from India, and he forced me into having sex, mostly without my consent, hitting me if I refused him. Today I know it is called "marital rape",' recounts Rhiti who took 3 years to amass the courage to move out and file for a divorce. 'I packed my bags and ran away one day, literally. I didn't ask for alimony or did not seek to send him to prison for what he had done, simply because I wanted to be out of England as quickly as possible. My freedom was more important to me than his punishment,' adds Rhiti, whose parents were extremely supportive of her decision, though soon enough the pressure of getting remarried began to hound her.

All of 25, she, too, was keen to find a partner who would cherish her for who she was, and naively enough agreed to newspaper ads in *The Times of India* and leading Bengali daily, *Anandabazar Patrika*, along with subscribing to popular *BharatMatrimony* services. Having met 17-18 guys during this period, she recalls how being a young divorcee, it was naturally assumed that something was wrong with her!

The questions ranged from, 'If I had any hidden sexual diseases? Was I bad in bed? Would I work after marriage? Was I willing to house a *gharjamai*? Can I open my hair and show them the quality and texture? Was it my real hair? Apart from cooking, what are my hobbies? Why didn't I have children from the first marriage? Does that mean I was unable to bear children, which resulted in the divorce? Do I plan to wear western clothes after marriage? Would

I take care of my parents after marriage? Wouldn't that be difficult when I get married and have my own family?'

'At 5 feet 7 inches, I was probably considered too tall for most Bengali guys. Along with that, my wheatish complexion was an impediment for Bong families who mostly preferred a fair bride. That I was the only daughter of a doctor seemed key to them and not my own soft skills or that I was a voice-process-training professional. There were a few good guys, who were nice and polite and apparently respectful, but we were somehow incompatible and nothing worked out. After a while, the process got really overwhelming, the feeling of being rejected. So I decided against it. Even thinking about those 2 years, 2005-2007, right now gives me the shivers,' she remarks with an air of forthrightness.

Keeping An Open Mind To Arranged Marriages Has Consequences

While most singles take the plunge into the arranged-marriage scene, fuelled by lack of natural choices or mounting family pressure, some like Delhi-based features reporter Shalini Singh, who recently turned 36 and is presently pursuing a journalism fellowship at Harvard University, says the key is to be open-minded at all times. 'Age, death everything suddenly became more imminent after I turned 30 and I was keen to find out what made me happy. I told myself I wanted to be flexible in terms of the avenues to meet someone and so I enrolled in Sycorian in 2009, coughing up around ₹30,000 along with A-Z marriage bureau. I also paid ₹40,000 to a professional matchmaker, and started attending her forums regularly from 2015. Though skeptical, I went through all of this mostly not to harbour regrets later. I subsequently enrolled onto *Floh*, a dating network, when I did a story on them and ended up making many new friends since. It seemed more like a socialising space. Also, of 700-800 members, I was told just about 1% end up actually getting married. I also got on to a similar forum called *A World Alike*.

'On both these forums, more women in their 20s were signing up. I don't think it's about the age factor anymore, because the good part about growing older is learning to transcend barriers, both conditioned and self-inflicted. Now it's become about meeting someone you can like, who, to begin with, doesn't bore you!' grins Shalini, who also created a profile on Tinder. Again, the idea was to chronicle the experience for the publication she wrote for, but she ended up staying out of sheer curiosity—and hope. She added firmly on her bio that she is clear about her priorities, 'Whether it's dating, friendship or a relationship, it's good to know what you want. I meet many men, but as one gets older, finding near-perfect chemistry is possibly harder. I know that I want tenderness, affection and a long-term partnership which includes marriage. I envision it as a shared emotional and intellectual space where we both comfortably express our sexuality as well. Growing up in a protected environment in Delhi, for the longest time I used to think most people in India have sex post marriage!'

Will Single Indian Women Ever Be Set Free From The Centrality Of Marriage As A Medium To Companionship?

With the sudden influx of dating apps that hold out the promise of easy intimacy—will the 30-plus single woman finally be set free from the traditional trap of arranged marriages, and the very centrality of the institution of marriage in a woman's life? Radio personality Priyanka Tewari, 37, who was raised in the US and returned 4 years ago analyses why it's cool to explore the best of both worlds—dating and arranged alliances. 'Finding a mate was on my personal agenda when I came back to India and I was looking for someone with international exposure, polished and articulate in English. I tried

Tinder after having gone down the route of marriage portals and I feel while it carries the reputation of being just a hook up site, it also makes sex an easy option for single women who want just that—you meet, talk, have drinks, go dancing and then if you want so, mutually, you get physical. If you want a guy to take a holiday with, there are options for that sort of companionship too or simply an intellectual chat, if that's your thing. However, if there is no potential, one can always instantly unmatch in the virtual world.'

According to Priyanka, a single woman's relationship with sex is complex in India, thanks to our staunch moral conditioning where we are taught to hold back, play hard to get, lest the guys presume we are too fast. We are scared of the question, 'Am I a whore for giving in to desire?'

Furthermore, 'There's a lot of external pressure to couple up—like everywhere I go, I am constantly probed how being smart, professionally successful, articulate, and funny, I still haven't found a life partner? So I begin to internalise what I am lacking, why I am still single and if there's something wrong with me. As we get older, we question the need for marriage, and yet, whether we admit it or not, every man we date, we can't help but size up as a future husband. Somewhere we still crave coming home to a significant someone to share our triumphs and insecurities with, and let's face it, to be touched by a man who makes us feel like a woman,' she summarises.

31-year-old singleton Sonal Jamuar, trainer with Enamor in Bengaluru, engineer by education, classical dancer by passion and writer by choice, in a telling online piece on *Womensweb.com* admits the arranged-marriage process that is full of humiliation at the hands of suitors, also includes a certain shaming by one's own parents. 'The difference begins when you are educated, and able to make choices. There comes a point when the same parents remind you that you are a girl,' writes Jamuar.

Jamuar's moment of truth began with the prospective's family arriving. 'The boy from London and his family were supposed to come down and meet me soon. I had been summoned to my hometown. I had to resign from the job in Mumbai because the prospective groom lived overseas, and it would not be possible for me to continue working. My mother had requested that I spend some time with them so I get some pre-marriage training, which I seemed to have been deprived of, having lived in a hostel for the last 10 years. Aunts and relatives advised her—and she in turn demanded that I be a *good* and *obedient* daughter for once in my life, and say goodbye to Mumbai where I'd been working for the last 4 years.

'My father welcomed the boy's family, and they, in a truly royal fashion, with the condescending attitude, sat down. Then I was ushered in for a probable meeting with the boy. But here the situation was a little different. The boy's mother wanted to do the initial screening. So the question and answer round started, and I, as advised by my mother, kept my head down, and answered only in monosyllables. The boy's mother seemed a little unhappy since I had been living in Mumbai for the last 4 years, that too in my own rented apartment. What made her uncomfortable was that I had hired a maid and a cook!' continues Jamuar, adding that the real bone of contention was when she asked her mother—'Does your daughter know how to cook?' (Since her son in London cannot afford a cook and usually does his own cooking.)

'My mother vehemently started defining my qualities and how, unlike other girls raised in the hostel, I have somehow learnt to cook as well. It was just due to my busy lifestyle that I had to hire a maid and a cook. I realised then that my mother was excellent in marketing. It took me 2 years to understand sales pitches and how to close the deal, but here, my mother—who has never worked in a corporate setup—excelled at the art of sales. The commodity being her own daughter,' her article states harshly.

The reasons for rejection given to her were as follows:
- Acne marks
- 5 feet 3 inches tall
- Reading glasses

'After being rejected thrice, each day I woke up and looked at myself in the mirror, and wondered—were they correct? That was 3 months ago. But better late than never! I realised in the right time, came back to my senses, and explained to my parents that their daughter is not what they are trying to portray. I am a beautiful woman. I refuse to subjugate myself to the insults and the emotional trauma, each time. I want a marriage, but not based on my colour, my height or my father's bank balance,' strongly states Jamuar.

STATUS SINGLE: *Almost all single women have suffered the arranged-marriage rigmarole and withstood the humiliation and the persecution, because sometimes there is no other option to finding a man to settle down with. Also it's a tad nauseating to be asked the constant question, 'why aren't you dating?' like it's a crime that a singleton is committing by not actively looking for a man. It's not that I am personally dating-averse. I would love to meet like-minded men, but like a lot of single women, I confess to being slightly fatigued to put myself out there repeatedly and be used as a guinea pig in the laboratory of relationships. And I don't see why my whole single life must revolve around unsingling in the first place?*

Dating, too, is a personal choice, and again like marriage, while the peer pressure is extreme, especially post-30s, don't do it if wanting to meet a man more naturally seems the go-to way for you. Also, stop entertaining questions on your sex life—your virginity is strictly your personal business and whether you choose to have casual sex with someone you've just swiped right on Tinder or want to wait till you are in a committed relationship to go the whole hog—there is no need to defend what you feel right about.

A lot of single women post 35 feel embarrassed or shy to admit they are still looking for marriage—the most common reason being perhaps a sense of past failure and the instant need on the part of those known to you to hook you up with all and sundry. A lot of the times, being single is circumstantial and doesn't denote the woman's mindset or her desires. But if you have no other way out of it, embrace it for all its worth. You control your personal choices.

Chapter Six

Sex in the City

I HAVEN'T HAD SEX IN an embarrassingly long time, and it's not because I turned frigid after 35 or something, or that my physical desires are any less potent than when I was in my early 20s. It's just that I probably belong to a generation where casual sex is morally uncomfortable and while making out is fun and as a married friend swears, the only cure I truly need for my raging insomnia, ironically, I've only been able to enjoy the experience with men I've been romantically involved with.

Sex is an extension of emotions—a vote of trust for me. But as fellow single women often joke, species such as us belong to an ancient dinosaur era, because now, more than ever, a lot more single women in India aren't inhibited by the premise and promise of marriage or a lasting commitment to demand physical gratification, just for themselves.

Sleeping Around Isn't A Cardinal Sin

So even as society continues to pressurise single women to marry and despite a lot of us being trapped in the 'is it too early to get intimate?' existential dilemma, there's a clear generational and socio-cultural shift—single women are increasingly uninhibited about getting sex on their own terms. In fact, a singleton's growing sexual freedom and experimentation, is today, in many ways, a reflection of her personal empowerment and liberation—where she's not necessarily waiting to be pleasured or pining away for an elusive ring on her finger.

The emergence of online dating, fuss-free hook ups, networking communities that meet over flirtatious and fun social events, financial independence of urban, professional singles who live alone or with liberated, free-thinking roommates as opposed to conservative, ageing parents, along with the heady influx of social media where relationships tend to be uncomplicated, minus the pressure of 'forever', have unanimously contributed to a delicious anonymity. And a culture of no-strings-attached free mixing, sometimes leading to sexual bliss between two consenting adults. One-night stands are now more of a personal choice that one isn't quite judging. The guilt, thus, of what was once regarded as illicit behaviour is more likely to be viewed as a license to lead life on one's own terms.

36-year-old event manager Purabi Sawant *(name changed on request)*, based in Hyderabad, who openly admits to 'sleeping around and loving it,' relates the reason for sex emerging out of the closet to more women remaining single by choice, well beyond their 20s and defying age-old conditioning taught to us as little girls that sex is something that should occur purely post marriage, being necessarily linked to love and making babies. The idea of sin is naturally synonymous with infidelity, and having sex outside a committed relationship is treated as dirty and against our cultural prudishness. However, according to Purabi, in the present climate of open-minded mixing, with more men and women working night shifts together and travelling out on work, the onslaught of mobile dating apps and websites has turned the idea of a woman looking for just sex, into a gender-neutral physical urge that is her choice as much as it is for the opposite sex.

Having recently had a one-night stand with a younger man she met at a do organised by a dating website, she's categorical that if sex is available easily, there's nothing wrong in a woman lusting after it, equally and unapologetically, not waiting around to first check out the quintessential emotional connect. Most times, Purabi is the first to leave the next morning and not the guy, as she can't bear to see him any longer, and with her physical needs having been satiated, she's clear that the man in bed is not someone with whom she can see herself having a cerebral conversation, or a second date later. 'Why waste time?' being her mantra. 'The whole notion of waking up next to the man or him cuddling after sex is a construct of mushy, western romantic movies, chick lit and Mills & Boon novels that stereotype women as sexually needy and clingy emotional creatures, when in reality, sometimes, it's me matter-of-factly asking the guy to leave my apartment, even refusing to serve him a cup of coffee. Sex is more transactional today, and with more single women owning up to this reality—hopefully, we will be saved a helluva lot of heartbreak in waiting for the prototypical Mr Right!' she adds defiantly.

Known to dress up provocatively, Purabi has often been the bane of sleazy office gossip and slut-shaming in her colony too, thanks to her frenzied social life, late-night drop backs, partying in her apartment with loud music, free-flowing drinks and men staying over. However, she feels that the tag of 'slut' that is unfairly attached only to a single woman society perceives as 'fast', and therefore assumes will never want to settle down and have kids, is something that members of our sex also do to each other. Purabi, on the other hand, often looks at her married women friends and feels sorry—to be stuck with snoring, pot-bellied men and bawling kids and painfully demanding in-laws. For her, causal sex offers a lot more variety and zilch emotional baggage where she owns both her physical and mental space. 'I am in complete control—of my body, my desires, my time and my side of the bed I chose to sleep on,' she sums up with confidence.

Married Men Not Strictly Off The Block

In a sexually evolving social milieu that is celebrating free choices for single women, married men, too, aren't totally off the market, and are often considered just as eligible as any other single man. Over the years, I have met a lot of single women, some in their mid-30s, openly dating married men. They harbour no guilt, nor view themselves as the quintessential 'other woman/*souten*/mistress,' both parties clear most of the times that there's no obligation to leave the legally married wife and kids. Some indulge in plain fun on the side—unbridled physical intimacy, romantic getaways with cell phones switched off and sex at any given time of the day or night, just about anywhere, while others commit to a lasting emotional connect—maybe a missing link in the man's claustrophobic, arranged marriage or one that has grown deadweight over time, sometimes post the arrival of children. Also, with marriage as an institution gradually ceasing to be a goal in India, thanks to a latent cynicism in the face of skyrocketing divorce rates, more ambitious, career-oriented women who prefer being choosy, and with more late marriages and live-ins in vogue, it's not just the opposite sex who singularly carry the tag of 'commitment-phobic'.

Or as a friend in the corporate sector puts it bluntly, 'Most men in India in the 35-plus age bracket are much-married with kids or are gay! So how long does a single woman keep waiting? I have cobwebs down there. I can either get the big, fat dream wedding that I now feel is not meant to be or hot sex in a swanky hotel room and just get on with my life. And honestly, I'd rather go with the flow than end up a dried old maid, with simply my fancy dildo and the TV remote for company!'

Trapped between casual dating and legitimised marriage are emerging a new brood of single women, openly taking their singlehood in their own hands or going with what they get, sans attaching the typical societal stigma to an interested suitor, never mind if he comes with a wedding band firmly attached, or his wife's picture as his Facebook profile photo.

So, are we single women actually running out of choices? Or is the moral fabric of our culture transforming itself to bridge the increasing loneliness that stares us in the face, despite the crowd of virtual friendships and frenzied professional lives? Why are eyebrows not raised any more when a girlfriend confesses to a steamy one-night stand with her boss on an overseas trip, or why is the perception of the 'other woman' in Bollywood no longer one of the slutty, wasted, homewrecker, an unstable, drunk, morally deviant single woman, in yesteryear movies like *Arth*, for instance? How come almost all television serials today revel in the one man and two women formula—the wife, and the mistress?

Priyashi Sen Chowdhury, 38, a divorcee now dating her married colleague, 10 years her senior and twice divorced, feels that maybe everyone is commitment-phobic at some level, and the millennials no longer harbour hope of being with that one true love for eternity, that she jokingly calls the '*saat janmo ka saath.*' 'Today most people's motto is live and let live. While I know my boyfriend is never going to leave his wife and family, he's there when I need him. I'm single and he fills a space, physically and mentally, which is like a breath of fresh air. I also don't intend to walk down the aisle again, so this arrangement works for me just perfectly,' she claims pragmatically.

What's interesting is the manner in which single women, even those who never married before, seem to be equally at ease with dating and sex with married men.

41-year-old Pramada Vasudevan (*name changed on request*), a Mumbai-based investment banker, currently planning her bi-annual sex vacation with her partner, also a married colleague, is bindaas about her love life for the past 8 years. She says, 'My family knows—and while my parents naturally don't approve and have called me a messed-up homewrecker, I know I did nothing to rock his boat. Besides, at 40, I have seen the whole tamasha of arranged marriages and single men who, in this country, are probably just getting hitched to lose their virginity. We keep breaking up intermittently, but then coming back—because physically he's so good and makes me hungry to have him all over again, besides emotionally also understanding me and my moods! Anyway, it's damn tiring to get on these dating sites and open up to complete strangers and keep test-driving on our chemistry. At my age, dating is kinda boring and been there, done that!

'Some of my friends, when they discovered that I was having an affair with a married man, distanced themselves—and these were, of course, from the married fraternity, who are probably aware of their own husbands looking outside for fun. Fidelity is a myth today and so after trying to make our friendships work, I realised I was being seen as a potential threat, so I said to hell with it. A lot of my single friends, however, are more liberated, and non-interfering and as long as I am fulfilled—how is my personal life anyone else's liability? I'd rather sleep with and date a hot married guy than a boring, middle-aged divorced man with kids and a helluva lot of emotional baggage or some loser still left behind at the bottom of the matrimonial food chain'.

The Tinder Tag

With sex being identified as an equal need for women, apps like Tinder have grown to become a massive hit amongst single women in India, with most having given it a go, at least once, despite its popular reputation of being largely a hook up site, even internationally. Being horny is not a big deal anymore!

Having downloaded the app on her smartphone post a bad break-up, all that 25-year-old PR professional Divya Abhilasha Mohanty remembers from her initial days was guys wanting to touch her in weird places or asking her if they could drop by at her home on the first date itself—a clear booty call. Some even passed overtly sexually loaded comments saying they dug her cleavage. Having played the field, Divya feels that life for single women today is way more complex thanks to the sexual openness that is in the air. 'Both men and women enjoy a lot more sexual options, and these dating apps are actually responsible for making meeting your soulmate akin to the experience of being in a crowded fish market. Life has become much more confusing, as mostly people are looking for uncomplicated hook ups and wanting to get into each other's pants, with romantic relationships more like commodities, and commitment an alien, demanding concept.

'I have plenty of friends just looking for one-night stands and even Tinder is filled with married women hunting for sex and ways to kill their boredom when their husbands travel or are away at work. A very close friend is clear that she only wants to date firangs, because they like to indulge in more foreplay, unlike Indian men who are usually skeptical, for instance, of going down on a woman, but demanding in selfishly asking for a blow job for themselves. Lots of single women for the same reason also seem to prefer and nurture a sexual kink for married men viewed as "experienced" and knowing how to perform in bed and sexually satisfy a woman vis-à-vis a completely virginal man, who may be a total novice, sexually frustrated and inept. Most of these flings that begin with a virtual swipe play out in hotel rooms or B&B setups, paid rooms, barely lasting more than a few months. Boredom sets in soon, and dating does not translate into marriage and *janam janam ka bandhan* any more,' Divya claims matter-of-factly. She then adds, 'There was a guy who once sent me a picture of his penis asking me if I wanted it for dessert! No one really dies of shock to hear or pass these comments that aren't viewed as dirty and derelict coz if you are uncomfortable you can always un-match and block—but what if you are not? It's fair game, right?'

Is India ready for the sexual unbridling it seems poised for? Are women like me who still shudder at the prospect of being a mistress understand that rules are being flexed, broken and crossed over without the leftover blame and hurt? Most young Indians are openly promiscuous and aren't afraid either to lose their highly overrated virginity. The hymen, simply a part of female anatomy, is no longer the stringent *Lakshman rekha* it once was.

As the Indian economy surges forward, with women earning and living independently, and not being reliant on the moral sanction from their families about their lifestyle and sexual openness; as they invest in homes and cars for themselves; drink, dope and smoke, and call for an Ola cab just the way they can casually look for a date, being sexually active is a sign of a larger being set free. Where one's conscience does not keep one sexually inactive and pleasure-starved.

Sapna Jha (*name changed on request*), who works for an NGO in Delhi, says her conservative mindset changed all thanks to Tinder, about which she first came to know of from a popular city guide. She had downloaded the app post a break-up, in the hope of connecting with new people. Till then, Sapna labels herself a quintessential 'bra-burning feminist', who'd be very stand-offish towards men approaching her randomly on the app. But as she went along, a whole new world opened up.

'The year before last in June, I hooked up with a French guy who pleasured me with 4 hours of foreplay, something which I think an Indian man will never ever do! In fact, swiping right I now realise is hugely empowering. You instantly feel a high and yes, I've even visited a hotel, to give vent to my raging sexual appetite,' she confesses.

Like scores of modern single women, Sapna admits to also having made out with men in existing relationships, something for which she harbours no regrets. 'I feel more like an equal actually, with the confidence to even stand naked in front of the mirror today. I have been able to forsake my psychological issues with regards to my negative body image,' she claims. As a rule, Sapna also splits bills with the boys whom she gets intimate with. And before you make assumptions about men being more desperate, she adds, 'There are loads of married women also wanting sexual gratification. In fact, my girlfriend hooked up with a bisexual married woman from Delhi whose husband wasn't satisfying her enough. I am not looking for marriage at this point, and don't want the emotional baggage of a long-standing relationship either. I'd rather focus on my career shaping up, and have fun being single!' she concludes tongue in cheek.

With sex a powerful tool for intimacy, and women not being as morally shy and staid, there are even start-ups catering to the country's hormonal outrage. StayUncle, a Delhi-based start-up, is challenging the typical Indian mindset towards premarital sex with the tagline on their home page reading plainly: 'Couples need a Room, not a Judgement.' The StayUncle platform allows users to book rooms in the hotels that it's partnered with, and one need not book for an entire day either—it offers 2 time slots you can book for, between 10 am and 7 pm, or between 9 pm and 8 am. Hotels listed on StayUncle are upscale, high-class hotels ranging between 3-5 star—'Handpicked and rigorously checked in terms of security and hospitality,' the FAQ claims. The bootstrapped start-up currently supports bookings online and via WhatsApp. On the website, searches for hotels which are couple-friendly are demarcated with a graphic, and lists amenities and package inclusions, such as breakfast, car parking, Wi-Fi, and air conditioning. An app launch is on the cards, next.

Single Women And Sex Toys

On her 40th birthday, Smita Wadhawan, a marketing professional and single mother who confesses to being 'sexless' for over a decade and occasionally jokes about becoming 'revirginized' in the interim, was determined to break the jinxed 'men-o-pause', by pampering herself with a rabbit vibrator—something she'd only read about until then in magazines like *Cosmopolitan* and watched on her favourite soap, *Sex And The City*. The vibrator is known to offer dual stimulation, to both the G spot and the clitoris. Curious but skeptical to ask her friends about its availability, she found encouragement through a recently married junior colleague who asked her to check out sex toys being sold online. 'My colleague had a kinky hen party where she was gifted a naughty hamper with everything from handcuffs, arousal oils, erotic lingerie, adult games, delay gels and edible body paints by her girlfriends, and soon getting hooked to them, she told me all about buying the products online regularly. In fact, on their first month anniversary, her husband had gifted her a roleplay costume of a nurse. While she had surprised him with a penis pump to spice things up in their sex life!' blushes Smita, who accompanied her colleague to Palika Bazaar, before she decided to venture online.

'I just couldn't stomach the intrusive stares and the salesmen sleazily suggesting that I invest in breast-enhancing products, ranging between ₹200 to ₹300, pointing at my fitted top. One of them specifically asked me if my *"pati"* needed lubricants. With a wink, he added that I should try sexy gum—the newest aphrodisiacal high. The experience was akin to a woman buying a condom or sanitary napkins over the counter, or asking for an intimate vaginal wash in a departmental store! I was self-conscious and felt dirty in a primitively, puritanical way. Like I was a "bad" girl... *gandi khayalaton wali*...' she recalls.

Broaching the subject of sex, outside its cloistered, 'normal' (read narrow) confines only to be shunned as an untouchable or be branded a 'loose, perverse woman', is not uncommon in India. However, the current e-commerce boom in India has witnessed a quantum leap in the sex toys market now expected to touch ₹8,700 crore by 2020, claim industry watchers. The trend, initially started by e-tailers specialising in adult toys, witnessed key players like Amazon and Flipkart dominate the same space. Today, sites like *ThatsPersonal, IMbesharam* (endorsed by none other than Sunny Leone), *Oh My Secrets* and *Lovetreats* which focus on erotic, adult products, are seeing a 600% growth in terms of visitors and an annual sales jump of 400%.

'India is in the throes of a sexual revolution,' believes Ute Pauline Wiemer, who co-founded *Lovetreats* in October 2016 with her husband. This Bengaluru-based sexual wellness start-up is growing at 50% month on month, and places Bengaluru, Mumbai, Hyderabad, Delhi NCR and Chennai as its top markets, with vibrators, flesh lights, body paints and spunky wedding hampers among its highest selling items—half of its buyers being women. 'A significant portion of the Indian sexual wellness market consists of products like gels, sprays and creams, advertised to change or "enhance" a woman's body parts. Condom ads are never quite about promoting safe sex or a healthy partnership; instead, they depict a woman as a seductress or a lame sexual prop, playing along to a man's fancies,' observes Ute, who believed setting up *Lovetreats* would add the missing female perspective in the Indian sexual wellness market story.

Samir Saraiya, founder of India's first adult online store *ThatsPersonal.com*, points to a survey conducted by the site that discovered that 59% of women who've bought from them wanted to know about upcoming innovative products. And 41% of the queries and feedback received from women revolved around new product suggestions. 'From vibrators, lubricants to arousal oils—there's a huge demand for products that fall under the category of self-pleasure. Today our research shows that women, especially in the 25-35 age group, are keen to show confidence and expertise in the bedroom, and are very open about their sexual needs, and more actively participatory—a far cry from the coy, conservative generation where men primarily initiated sex, and women were always shy and inhibited. These days we get mails from women saying that they don't want the products delivered to their home address, since even if a woman is single here, her home is always infested with either visiting parents, a cook, a part-time cleaning lady or a masseuse,' says Saraiya who has recently launched a 'customer pickup' innovation where the customer gets to collect products discretely from the courier office rather than getting them delivered at home or office. 16-17% of the customers opt for this service.

Raj Armani, co-founder of adult online lifestyle store site *IMbesharam* corroborates, 'In the past one year, we've seen more female customers making purchases for themselves and their partners. We also see their average cart value between ₹4-12k which is much higher than what men shop for. This means they look for quality and branded options. We also see more sales of LGBT products, toys, lingerie, etc., which indicates a greater audience in that community is getting to know of our brand and discussing it internally, hence the word of mouth that drives more shoppers to our site.'

Dating Apps Driven Mainly By Sex, Or The Promise Of Marriage, Still?

With women selfishly reclaiming the right to pleasure, is sex, therefore, driving the dating game in India? Or is the promise of matrimony in a culture pre-conditioned to companionship for the sake of advancing its progeny still the modus operandi of the prevalent dating app culture, with some apps like *Woo*, for instance, that especially prides itself in not being 'Tinder-like'? However, like its international rival, it requires users to sign up with Facebook.

Woo's CEO Sumesh Menon looks back on the gestation phase before *Woo* actually came into being, 'There is a preconceived notion that dating apps are just a means to get laid, but our intention was always on meaningful relationships, rather than a casual date or a hook up. We believe in connecting like-minded people. Before we started, we did a lot of preliminary research and spoke to focus groups of single women above 25. The main problem they faced was their social setup didn't extend beyond school, college or their work cubicle and where does one meet an eligible person was the biggest challenge, since the social community dries up after a point with most friends getting married, moving out of the hometown, losing contact with others, etc. What women wanted is predominantly meaningful relationships and their own safety since online there always lurks the danger of stalkers and creeps. We, thus, included LinkedIn integration so people can search for partners of a particular profession. Also, for safety and privacy, we only display the initials of the person till they are matched. We have approximately 4 million users across India now, with the numbers escalating daily.'

And while the app can't guarantee wedding bells, it prides itself on lending a secure meeting environment where the highlight is on the user's personality. Some interesting trends the app has witnessed are that more single women prefer entrepreneurs as a suitable match. They also tend to ask men a lot of questions about their hobbies and interests.

While most of these online dating apps operate on customisation of what a user wants, a lot of single women, like me for instance, are somewhat skeptical and prefer to do the good old-fashioned thing—wait for destiny to usher in Mr Right. Or Mr Right Now, as one can say.

Smita Sharma, a 34-year-old model based in Mumbai, shares the same vibes, 'Finding a trustworthy companion online is to me a tough call, and I will need time to know someone before I say I do. When I was in my early 20s, my parents did the usual groom-hunting, but now they understand that in my mid-30s I need someone with a similar mindset and I'd rather meet a person naturally, than this paying for dating someone system. I'd rather be alone or adopt an orphan than date in haste and marry and end up in a messy divorce or be embroiled in domestic violence.'

Varsha Agnihotri Vadhyar, who helped set up *Footloose No More* in 2009, claims her website with over 8,000 members across India as well as NRIs, isn't a traditional matrimonial platform while being clear to specify that it isn't a dating site either. 'We clearly say no hook ups and the members are also hand-picked with care and caution,' says Varsha. Regarding single women users, she adds, 'Women are much more open about wanting to be married and having someone to complete them. In India, while there is all this talk of causal dating, mentally we still picture marriage because the whole notion of dating is extremely raw and exists in a nascent stage still. Single women in India desire to be in serious relationships because no one wants to be the quintessential ageing party girl, after a certain point in life. In the last one year, we have observed not just women but even single men aspire to tie the knot. The perspective is changing and instead of random swipes and vanilla conversations, singles are seeking lasting commitment. With women being more financially stable and living independently, more aware of their biological clock, they aren't willing to play the damsel in distress of the past. They are being more serious about their goals and know their bodies and their minds. Of course, women in their 30s are way more cautious than 20-somethings.'

Has more single women knowing themselves intimately and being more confident in their own skin made sex no longer a taboo—or does it still carry the risk of heartbreak and the excess baggage of a frustrated, failed relationship? Will the current sexual openness bring men and women closer or just make relationships more transient? And finally, will the darkness between our thighs be dispelled by this uninhibited and unbridled, sexual awakening that we are witnessing?

'Dating for sex and dating for marriage are two diverse entities and women are pursuing them separately. Also, married people are now in the available category, since whether we discuss it openly or accept it or not, cheating is now commonplace. The change that we see is that single women are now in the driver's seat of their sexual destiny, and even if they ultimately want to marry and have kids, a lot of them aren't hell-bent on celibacy till death!' rationalises Pramada.

My Sexuality, My Choice.

45-year-old Arundhati Ghosh, executive director of an arts foundation in Bengaluru, calls herself not single or double, but 'multiple', as she believes in polyamory, and not in prefixing labels on relationships. She says her sexual delineation allows her the freedom to love and care for as many people as she would like and is drawn to. 'Some relationships are fleeting, while others starting off as long-term sometimes tend to transform with distance or life-changing circumstances and environments and unless one has been abused or exploited, the end of a relationship isn't quite a full stop, but a semicolon, as in, you can't stop loving someone once you start to love them. There is always a possibility of a connect again, as relationships are not finite,' believes Arundhati, while quoting John Berger, '"Never again shall a single story be told as though it was the only one."' Polyamory to Arundhati, is consequently the extension of a deep political and life belief where she has abiding faith in collective diversity and the possibility of myriad voices being heard in a poly world.

Arundhati, however, confesses that she grew up feeling that she was 'too fickle' and a 'misfit,' since she didn't fit the overarching narrative created by books, films, social conditioning and popular culture that harped on the ideal of heteronormative, viz. 'one true love.' 'I told myself I need to fix myself—and was unclear why I was liking multiple people. Conventionally, a woman like me would be bracketed alongside sex workers and be labelled a slut/whore, with terms in my mother tongue like *barowari*, implying a woman who slept with many people,' reasons Arundhati who was in love with two men by the end of college and couldn't stop loving one, as both were uncomfortable and jealous with the idea of she sharing her affections.

'A choice had to be made,' reminisces Arundhati who took time to own her sexuality, an intense 8 to 10 years, that involved her reading books like *Ethical Slut*, which lent her an understanding of alternate possibilities before she 'came out' as a polyamorous person, in her late 30s. She says that her ex-husband, who remains a good friend even now and is very close to her widowed mother, 'worries about my emotional security even to this day telling me that I might be lonely and finally all my lovers will marry or settle down with someone, leaving me in the lurch.'

Arundhati chose to celebrate her 40th birthday in Goa where

she invited all her friends, current lovers and exes. 'After coming back from the holiday my ex-husband said to me that he had finally understood this is who I want to be and the life I choose to lead,' she adds.

Dispelling the popular perception that polyamory means the license to sleep around with a lot of people, Arundhati emphasises on the word 'amor,' meaning love. Currently involved with multiple people in different cities and time zones, she says there is a huge amount of time and emotion invested in each relationship that is equally deep and desirous. She says, 'I always tell a person right at the start that I'm a polyamorous person as I think the key is to act with emotional responsibility and curb one's greed knowing that hearts may get broken. And when I am told that the person I am interested in is strictly monogamous, I have to deal with it, too.

'Also, just like there are multiple variables with a couple who could be constantly pushing boundaries, for instance, sexually, like enjoying a threesome, in polyamorous relationships, too, there are diverse approaches to living. For example, if one of my lovers has a new lover now and he naturally wants to spend more time with his new partner who may not want his past creeping between them, I have to make peace with us spending less time these days and also not having sex anymore. Some polyamorus relationships are based on one primary partner, but I don't live that way. I have never felt that'. She feels that men being assumed to be 'naturally polygamous' are more socially acceptable than a woman owning up to being polyamorus since we naturally assume that men being men are born to sow their seed wherever they desire. So while adjectives like 'horny' and 'flirty' are used commonly to describe a man with a roving eye, a woman who does the same is viewed as a cultural and moral affront and immediately slut-shamed and seen as a 'dangerous' influence on society. 'My mother once asked me: "If you give your heart away so many times, won't it get over one day?" I gave her the example of the Kalpataru tree, a wish-fulfilling, eternally giving tree in Hindu mythology... the heart is capable of loving infinitely.'

In a culture where being open about one's sexual identity remains a struggle, 30-year-old Naina Sharma (*name changed on request*), a corporate lawyer from Mumbai, confesses that it may take a long time before she, too, can own up to her innermost fetishes. 'Understanding my own instincts took time because I was raised in a very straight environment where I hardly ever saw any intimacy between my parents, let alone being comfortable with self-pleasure or loving my body. I grew up hearing I had to settle down by 30, so one naturally keeps looking forward to a man noticing, loving, marrying and touching you. But as I entered college and had my first sexual experience and subsequently started having sex more frequently, I seemed to only enjoy it when I was tied, or being beaten—when there was a certain degree of submissiveness involved. I felt a tremendous sense of fulfillment, having been liberated from sexual ennui and my closeted childhood filled with stern instructions of how a woman has to cover her cleavage, shouldn't undress openly or how my bra strap couldn't accidentally peek out and how I was banned entry into the kitchen while I had my periods.

'In fact, not just my family, some of my closest women friends could not get it when I confessed that I was turned on by rape scenes in movies or saw the heroine being slapped hard or tied to a pillar. The sight of blood made me orgasm. I was branded a pervert. My first boyfriend in law school couldn't handle my kinks and bitched about me to my friends saying I was a closet lesbian. Most people feel that BDSM involves extreme pain and it's an abnormal, cruel sexual alienation. Now, while that is surely a high for me, it's also about the ecstasy in being controlled mentally, the chase and being able to surrender to my sexual master,' says Naina, who discovered her bisexuality when after her first break-up she had a torrid affair with her senior in the same law school.

Active today on countless virtual communities, such as the Indian BDSM Community on Facebook, she adds, 'Contrary to popular perception in India, male submissives searching for mistresses and those who love being dominated also exist, but seldom emerge out of the woodwork, thanks to the stereotypical, strict codes of masculinity that society creates to preserve its own gender biases. They are scared of being blackmailed in case they are looking for marriage, and live in fear, never opening up about their sexuality. No wonder most Indian men prefer the missionary position while having sex. Playing safe. The women, too, are silent pleasure recipients. I remember switching roles once during a session with a guy I met in a chat room, making him lick all my high-heeled shoes, till his lips bled. Before massaging my feet with his penis. I even whipped his buttocks. Everytime he would cringe in pain, I'd scream in pleasure. It's like a drug. This is who I am inside out. Why should I live my life in denial of my sexual orientation?'

The Risk Behind Risqué

As singletons opt for the sexual gratification that best suits them, Dr Shyam Bhat, psychiatrist and founder of Seraniti.com, points out the hazardous implications of technology on modern relationships. He says, 'With over 250 million singles aged between 18 and 34 and 235 million smartphone users currently, India is one of the largest dating markets in the world. According to digital data resource Mindshift Interactive, nearly 33% couples now meet online and 67% of singles know someone who has met or romanced online. One of the world's most popular dating apps, the usage of Tinder in India supposedly jumped 400% in 2015 with India being among its top 5 growing markets, the largest in

Asia, attracting over 14 million swipes each day in the age bracket of 19-25. Tinder promises "hook ups", millennial slang for no-strings-attached sex—implying sex sans emotional expectation, physical intimacy without emotional intimacy, mingling of body fluids, the souls hermetically separate. But even as "hook ups" are the promise of Tinder, it's not clear how people are actually using it for that purpose in India.

'Millions of young men and women these days leave their homes and move to cities for academic and career opportunities—this mass migration and displacement naturally leads to a sort of new-age isolation. Loneliness is a toxic condition, afflicting people in urban societies all over the world, and known to cause depression, stress and an increased risk of physical diseases like diabetes and heart disease. People longing for a real connection with another human being turn to social media and apps to address the overwhelming loneliness, but these apps further intensify the feelings you seek to relieve, each superficial and unsatisfactory encounter depletes us further, worsening feelings of emptiness and lonesomeness. For those battling low self-esteem, such online apps can be dangerous because one becomes dependent on love, attention and appreciation to feel a high about themselves. Going from one casual fling after the next results in a more gnawing loneliness, one that can cause depression, and in the vulnerable, even suicide.'

From Sexual Prudishness To Sexual Openness: Has The Average Indian Man Actually Changed?

38-year-old Gujarati American Avani Parekh, a trained counselor specialising in domestic violence, moved to Delhi at the age of 35, after her divorce and on the threshold of launching her chat site *Lovedoctor* (presently acquired by Sheroes) which helped women to connect with counselors and sexuality and sexual health experts.

'I was curious to know what would become of me and wondered would I be celibate, aware that at my age most Indian women are married with children, since youth is at a premium here,' says Avani who found a relationship within her first week itself in India, via Tinder. 'Being raised in the US, I lost my virginity in high school which is typical of most American teenagers, and had naturally undergone a sexual awakening much before an average Indian girl. I was told by the men I dated that they found me more "experienced", than most *desi* girls, and thus their "best sexual partner",' adds Avani who, however, went through her personal share of the rollercoaster ride. 'A surgeon I dated, who had discussed that he loved kids as I did, told me on the first date, "let's have a baby together," and while I let it pass, I know now that I should have realised he was a complete nutjob! Another time, he dropped by to my place past midnight, slightly drunk, supposedly on his way to his cousin's home and was in the mood for a quickie. While kissing passionately, he happened to put a *hajmola* inside my mouth!' adds Avani, calling it 'a unique Indian experience.'

It was exasperating when none of her dates turned out to be a dream match. Avani admits frankly, 'Every once in a while I go through this period of "F this shit" and I take myself off all the platforms and go on mancation—but the nagging voice in the back of my head tells me I should be trying. When you are 38, that voice tends to belong to the one egg that you have left, clinging on to dear life. My egg, let's call her Andi, is responsible for making a lot of the bad decisions in my dating life. Andi does not want to be washed away in a torrent of nutritious blood—she wants a chance at life. And hence, after a period of dating some flashy guys with sweet words, I put myself on a popular matrimonial website, probably the most well-known platform for brown matrimony in the world. The website lets you screen potential suitors, but also lets people interested in you contact you. Logging on to the site every day has been an exercise in patience. Premium members have an unprecedented access to me—they can see my information and pictures, send me texts indicating they think I am a good fit... basically everything but show up at my house with their biodata in tow. I noticed a pattern with these inbox inquiries. Everyone who likes me is an uncle. Now I have nothing against uncles, but I am a very young-looking 38, most people assume I am 26-27. My energy is bubbly. I have that joie de vivre—I know what I bring to the table. 30 to 60 "uncles" were landing in my inbox every day. Uncles from all walks of life. All shapes and sizes, and from all corners of the earth! A few things bound them together in a global brotherhood of uncles: bling, and a refusal to let people see their eyes,' claims Avani, who subsequently experienced a total shutdown when she faced physical assault on one of her dates.

'I was in Mumbai to meet up with people, and happened to meet a guy who was cosmopolitan on the face of it, and we had an instant connection, but we had only had phone chats until then. When I actually met him, he turned out to be supremely boring as all he did was go on blabbering about himself. Then I met another guy—never married, 40-year-old Gujarati—I was interacting with for a while, who had met my criterion of an Indian guy with a pluralistic breeding, and like me was exposed to the western world, being based in London. We met at a café. Over a pitcher of sangria I casually chatted with him, and mentioned meeting the first guy as I have always been very transparent. Soon he got extremely agitated and went on probing suspiciously. I was uncomfortable, and suddenly he said in response to something I had said, "Do you want me to slap you?" I was horrified and got up immediately when he roughly grabbed my arm. I asked him to let go and finally when he relented, I got inside an auto, but the guy wouldn't back off, despite even a waiter intervening. I was en route to the airport and he just sat with me for nearly 10 minutes, till I had to literally force him to get off the rick, saying I was done with him,' recounts Avani of her unpleasant experience, the price she paid for putting herself out there.

Having dated close to 35 men since she first came to India, Avani signs off with hopeful expectation, 'I believe I deserve some magic and a real connection. I want to meet someone and for everything to click—to feel that rush of possibility. Maybe, this is the next Mr Parekh.' Last heard, Avani was dating again, having met her match naturally through a friend. And the icing on the cake, he's also a fellow entrepreneur.

Like Avani, 29-year-old Pune-based content writer, Sudha (*name changed on request*) also dreams of meeting her 'companion' organically, one day. Sudha was born with a neurological disorder called Spina Bifida and today walks with the support of crutches, having had her first spinal surgery when she was all of 4 months. 'Till 25, my parents never broached the topic of my marriage. When I was a teenager, my father had told me how I may never get married and should rather focus on being self-reliant. But I was pretty certain that I wanted to settle down, and told my parents they should start looking. We attended a couple of open house meetings and *sammelans* organised within my community for disabled people, but I realised most urban, well-educated, independent men were keen on a "normal" life partner who didn't have their own shortcomings,' says Sudha, whose run-in with so-called 'normal' men is reflective of the deep regression prevalent in India.

'Someone told my father he needs to give the groom a lot of money failing which I will never get a "good guy". I was once chatting with a man for a while and finally we both met in Pune and he said to my face that after seeing me all he felt was sheer sympathy. Once, a normal guy, who was a colleague, and I came close to getting intimate, when he suddenly revealed he had a girlfriend. Thankfully, we had not had sex. One day, out of the blue, his girlfriend called me from his number and started abusing me, saying because I am disabled I was desperate, labelling me a slut. When you are disabled, like I am, no one sees you as just another single woman who dreams of companionship with dignity. You are expected to remain an object of sympathy. Luckily, my family is liberal. I know, I am probably expected to stop dreaming about finding love. But I believe in equal partnership and I don't see why I can't stake my claim to it,' she adds.

Shankar Srinivasan, co-founder of Inclov, the world's first matchmaking mobile application for people with disabilities and health disorders claims that within India's 26.8 million disabled people, 42% never marry. Started as an offline matchmaking agency, known as Wanted Umbrella, within 7 to 8 months, Shankar found a membership spilling to 2,000 men and women from all over the world. 'We soon realised we needed technology to scale this,' says Shankar, who in 2015, which was the year of start-ups in India, began work to build an app. A crowdfunding campaign sourced ₹6,15,000 from 143 people globally, leading to the recruitment of two developers, one of whom was visually impaired. Today, the membership of Inclov has globally grown to touch the 10,000 mark, with the age bracket spanning 18-60 years. 'Most single disabled women are reclusive as they are viewed as liabilities for their parents and larger society. Most of them don't socialise much either, so the idea was to make the matchmaking experience as mainstream as we could. Which is why the meet-ups that we organise aren't reserved exclusively for the disabled, and neither is membership on the app. In fact, 40% of our members don't have disabilities,' says Shankar. On dating apps, users either reject people with disabilities outright or ask questions like, 'Can you have sex and produce children?'

Sudha is a member of Inclov and has corresponded with some men, none of whom have volunteered to come and meet her in Pune yet. 'I will not settle for someone just because I am on crutches,' she concludes with hopeful determination.

I was discussing turning 40 at the end of the year with a single cousin while writing this chapter in my book, as she, too, is all set to turn 60 next year and much to my surprise, she remarked, 'After 40 you will see your desires will all go away!'

Her words were laced with a sense of cold stoicism, so I probed, 'Desires, as in?'

'You know, sex and all,' she added dismissively. Somehow, I can't stop hearing these words play out in my head, and ask myself, if in India, a single woman turning 40 means a graveyard shift, where she is supposed to lead the life of a sexless ascetic, while middle-aged men merrily advertise for 20-something brides in leading dailies? Why parents of a girl never celebrate her 40th birthday the way they would a marriage, per say? How the internet is agog currently with news of 52-year-old Milind Soman dating a woman half his age, as is Anurag Kashyap, both women in their mid-20s? I process the word sex and think why it should be limited to physical age alone. Why desire should only connote sex, in the first place? Why a woman can't dream of being desired, at any age, primarily by herself? And whether I have sex or not or believe in casual sex, why should I end up sans desire, minus any physical urges? Why we even have sex, to begin with, I am forced to examine, just to procreate after marriage, always with a man?

Who defines desire?

Why is a woman who claims the right to pleasure such a potent threat?

I am turning 40 in December. I still dream of my fat son. And a house facing the sea with a blue-and-white tiled kitchen. And the books that I will birth. I still dream of making love. Lying naked, all by myself.

I still dream of loving myself. Of saying yes.

STATUS SINGLE: *Thanks to the advent of convenient and online dating apps, and women being financially more independent and willing to take charge of their sex lives, indulging in casual sex is no longer looked upon with a harsh judgmental taboo. Also, married men aren't out of bounds either, with open marriages on the rise and many single women having affairs with married men, consciously, out of their own free will. Sex in India is now seen as an empowerment tool, and while as a single woman you are solely in charge for your own choices—be responsible and play safe.*

Chapter Seven

Parents, Privacy and Protectiveness

At 39, I LIVE with my parents, juggling between our lives in South Delhi and South Kolkata. As a single child, my greatest fears are quite honestly, what becomes of me after them. Because no matter how much you get irritated at your mom for asking you to bathe and eat your meals on time, or dad rolling his eyes when you return late, or the constant concerned calls to enquire if you have left a party because it's unsafe in Delhi, or my mother sneakily ringing the driver to find out if I have reached a particular destination, or the quintessential question just before I exit the front door, of whether I will be very late returning and come home and eat dinner—there is still a pervasive, human connect.

Someone to place hot food on the table, manage the maids, grocery shop on your behalf and carefully count and hand clothes out to the *dhobi*, clean up after your guests leave, accompany you to the doctor, tend to you when you are ailing, supervise your finances and remind you of bills and insurance premiums, apart from being with you through sickness and good health—in other words, create a general secure feeling of being loved and looked after. It's reassuring to know there is someone in the next room to watch your back.

Living with parents after a few years of being on my own and single didn't start off smooth though, and continues to be a work-in-progress.

I used to have my own two-bedroom apartment in South Delhi when I worked full-time as a journalist. Until about 10 years ago when my parents relocated to Delhi from Bengaluru, and my father took up a sprawling apartment in Kalkaji, a stone's throw away from mine in CR Park, in the hope that we could all live together again. There was no asking what I wanted and if I intended to move in with them again—it was taken for granted that as a close-knit and small family of three we would naturally live together. Not surprising since in India—the *'hum saath saath hain'* formula still holds strong!

Initially, I was reluctant to give up my own flat, one that I'd painstakingly decorated and maintained, along with the accompanying thought of once again playing a buffer when my parents squabbled and bickered as all couples do after years of being married. I knew that if I lived with them, I'd have to inevitably choose sides as an only child and follow strict 'house rules' even though my parents are extremely liberated. This meant I could probably not have a man stay the night over or be out till the wee hours of dawn. Also, entertaining would necessarily now translate into an extended family affair that sought permission and planning—my mother, for instance, always wanting to serve dinner by a certain time, when probably all I want is more drinking time with my peers. The generation gap between us is glaring during such instances—our sense of what is fun, stark in comparison. The way I have to fight for my solitude during my lengthy and unpredictable working hours as a full-time writer, the way I can't conform to strict meal timings or fit a normative discipline of bathing or sleep, streamlined to maid timings. The way Indian parents are supportive, but find it hard to understand the chaos in the life of a creative person.

But looking back now, I consciously signed up for this life, knowing this would be inevitable, especially after Dad, who is very close to me, seemed visibly heartbroken when I had shared my doubts about all of us living together. We did not speak for a while and so, dilly-dallying for a few weeks, I finally gave up the apartment that I had loved so much, and agreed to live with my parents.

Now, a decade later, honestly, I occasionally nurse mixed feelings about the decision that was taken a couple of years before I also happened to quit my full-time job, taking the plunge to be a writer. There are still days when I long for my own pad, when I fight bitterly with my mother, and wish we didn't have to meet at the breakfast table so soon again, hating the constant frenzy of one maid after the next, secretly envying women who are single and own their homes and can balance both their families and their personal time and space. Before the moment of realisation strikes, that being a self-employed person with no fixed salary at the end of the month—a roof over one's head and no monetary pressure, is nothing short of a blessing.

It's no cake walk living with ageing parents, but neither is living alone because even as single women are now more and more economically liberated, our society is still used to witch-hunting our species, with our character being easier to assassinate and our personal lives perennially under moral surveillance. Also, having a strong support system is a boon in an age when thanks to the frenzied pace of life—all of us confront a gnawing urban loneliness. Something that I realised last year when I was detected with fibromyalgia—an autoimmune disorder that as one of its symptoms, brought on major clinical depression. And while my parents, too, grappled with something they couldn't grasp—it was my 60-plus mother who dragged me to the psychoanalyst, constantly telling me on the way how I would be writing about it one day. That I would win.

Making The Best Of Both Worlds: In The Same City, But In Different Living Spaces.

Subs (*name changed on request*), 39-year-old corporate banker from Delhi, who took the decision to relocate closer to her roots, had left home soon after her post-graduation, returning to see her folks every 2 months, and calling them daily. Being self-sufficient and belonging to an independent family, she faced no pressure or nagging for living alone in various cities like Kolkata, Mumbai and Lucknow. Her sister, too, has been based away from Delhi for the past 15 years now.

In 2011, Subs was transferred back to Delhi and while she was certain about wanting to come back and live in her childhood South Delhi neighbourhood, this time she was bringing back a lot of luggage, which meant needing her own flat. There was no space in her parents' home and not being used to living frugally, Subs chose to discuss the option of living alone frankly and freely with her parents. While she expected a lot of stubborn opposition, they were extremely supportive of her decision to build her own nest. Subs ascribes her initial hesitation in bringing up the topic of staying separately to the typical Indian mindset where if a woman is single and in the same city as her parents, she's almost always expected to live under the same roof—because if she's not, there's either suspected family trouble or the girl is perceived as being too 'fast' and lacking family values and thus estranged from her parents. Another factor, she adds, that further influenced her resolve to live close but not 'with' family, was also the difference in their basic lifestyles—Subs's parents being early risers preferred sleeping early, for example.

A question that often confronts Subs, like any other single woman inevitably, centres about her so-called sex life with men she meets socially. She is often asked point-blank about how she is able to have sex, since living close to family implies a definitive and demanding curfew. She cites an example of once dating a man briefly, who had proposed they take a couple holiday, to which she had blurted out matter-of-factly that he would first have to ask her parents. To which the flabbergasted guy smirked, 'But you are 39!'

Subs clarifies at this point that her parents would never say no and neither are they rigid about her personal choices, especially if they see she's confident about the man in question. But to her, these situations are more a Catch 22 paradox, because she claims one does have to consider how parents will react to a proposition such as a vacation or a weekend away. 'I couldn't just have packed my bags and left without an explanation. Does that make me traditional, and thus boring, to a certain extent? Or suggest to men that I am off limits since the first question a guy inevitably asks is if I live alone? Do I miss casual sex or telling a man after a few drinks, "Wanna grab coffee at my place?" Maybe yes, but most of these scenarios are hypothetical, since I hardly meet interesting, eligible single men anymore! And have never been the type to enjoy one-night stands and fleeting sex with strangers,' she adds bluntly.

Years of living alone in multiple cities has made sleeping alone a habit that Subs is now pretty much accustomed to. She is much happier reading a book or travelling solo, instead of hooking up and trying random dating apps to find a guy.

Subs has also gone through the rigmarole of looking for a match through the arranged marriage route. She did all the online matrimonial hunting in the past, which she feels was no less than a full-time job, where she was constantly doing background checks and investigating the authenticity of the boy's claims, besides being objectified herself and having to answer a long list of illogical questions. 'So at some point in 2011, I decided I'd gone through enough of this bullshit. I was tired of castigating myself and decided to regroup my priorities. That's when I took the call of making my own home in Delhi—a floor above my parents actually, in the same building, so that I had them in my life prominently, simultaneously also creating my own safe sanctuary, a second home whenever I wanted to take a breather. I spend a bomb on rent today and most of the time I am at my folks' place, but have become way more self-contained. My flat is my defense mechanism in many ways,' she decides.

Living In Your Parents' Pad: Boon Or Bane?

While some singletons like Subs walk a middle path, with the best of both worlds, so to speak, others like 33-year-old Sudesna Ghosh, a Kolkata-based author, and an only child, still lives in with her parents, and works from home. Sudesna feels that stereotypical parental restrictions along with the suffocation of always being around the same faces aren't the biggest challenges of sharing her living space. Having lived in the US for her higher studies, and battling clinical depression during her post-graduation, she chose to come back to stay with her family on her own free will, since the isolation of life overseas was mind-numbing. 'I missed my folks and my pets bitterly,' she confesses.

While Sudesna is content about her own life in the sheltered comfort of her family, she claims that turning 30 and being still single have been something of a reality check, with mortality and the slowly deteriorating health of her parents, the loss of friends' parents around making her realise how scary it is to be left alone in the end. Today, Sudesna craves for a man in her life and confesses of her insecurities, 'I've stayed up nights wanting a man to just hold me in his arms. It's really not so much about getting great sex or wanting to have kids because you are now well into your 30s, as it is about the reassurance a lover offers… something I also find discussing frankly with my mother of late, confiding in her about my loneliness. My parents, too, are keen that I seek and find companionship. When you see most of your girlfriends settling down, having kids, their priorities changing, one is bound to wonder at times if there is something wrong with you and why you are still unattached? There is, after all, a limit to the time friends can give you, since the nature of their commitments alter after they marry, and this is true more so for women,' she observes. Having tried Tinder and Shaadi.com briefly, Sudesna adds it's hard to find an eligible man from the same community, since she's also a vegetarian. Her criterion of wanting a man who has lived abroad considerably like her, and her disinterest in random hook ups makes finding a like-minded, long-term companion tough, more so in today's age of no-strings-attached sex and zero commitments.

Many of Sudesna's single women friends prefer staying alone, sometimes even relocating to other cities, just so that they can bring in men, without the constant nagging and need-to-answer their-family situation. But she, on the other hand, is pretty certain that she wants to be based in Kolkata, and even if she has to live in, for instance, she adds that it will have to be close to her folks. 'Living with parents is a dual responsibility for a single woman. They need you, as much as you need them. As for their anxiety, whenever I am out late, which is something I hardly do, my father calls up dutifully, asking if I have left, a bit hesitantly, instead of threateningly. This is not something that irritates me. Rather, I find it sweet that someone is concerned about my safety. As for maintaining my own space, I hit the gym daily as it is vital both for physical and mental health, do the groceries, work from a coffee shop occasionally for a change in scenario, and also make it a point to meet a friend once a week for a meal. But at the end of the day it's good coming home to someone you love deeply. My parents are totally cool with my life choices—so there is no real conflict of interest!'

As Sudesna rightly points out, a single woman feels most vulnerable when her parents get sick in their advancing years, and more so if you happen to be an only child—it's a sinking feel. And sometimes, it is the failing health and ultimate demise of parents that makes a single woman question her unconventional life choices.

Heera Nawaz, who teaches in Bengaluru, and is a feminist writer and poet, whose father Mohammed Khader Nawaz, a Muslim atheist, eloped with her mother Leela Yelavati, a Lingayat Hindu, and got married, says, 'I am single. Not enticingly single like Oprah Winfrey, but single nevertheless. When I was 19, I thought my decision to remain single for life would hold true forever. At that time, both my parents and a coterie of uncles and aunts and cousins were eager to get me married off to any of the many marriageable suitors who I thought were just out to make more than just hay when the sun shines. I adamantly refused. I kept saying, "Not now, maybe next year," and slowly, but steadily, the years rolled by, as I remained committed to my celibacy vows, through my 20s, 30s, and 40s. My sister and brother eventually got hitched; I was left in the lurch, since none of my friendships with the opposite gender crystallised into matrimonial alliances.'

Having been single most of her adult life, Heera, who is now in her 50s, adds positively, 'I can get up at 5 am to write a poem without a family member saying, "But that's when you should be doing your ADLs (activities of daily living) and getting the family up and ready for the day." I can read Zig Ziglar's *Over the Top* without a husband intruding into my space saying, "the only priority should be housework". In short, if one is single, nothing beats the space, freedom and independence one has. Since I am a Muslim and, therefore, have to pray 5 times a day, I can also do so at an unhurried pace, causing my nieces to call me "Heera Namaz" instead of Heera Nawaz!'

However, Heera's carefree singlehood and perspective to being on her own changed irrevocably in 1998. 'In December 1998, I got a rude shock to shake me out of my selfish cocoon of complacency. In a month, my father, who I thought would always be there for me, fell seriously ill. On 30 December, 1998, the doctors informed us that his life could not be saved even by the best treatment. The next day, he began violently vomiting blood and exactly 1.5 hours before the New Year, passed away. 1 January, 1999, stands out in my memory as the worst day of my life as I wept inconsolably at his funeral. Luckily for us, my mother remained a pillar of support. But, when 7 years down the line, she, too, developed health complications and was diagnosed with diabetes mellitus, we realised that we were suddenly on the verge of losing our mother too. I still remember 8 October, 2005, when my mother passed away due to a massive heart attack. How after her funeral, our huge ancestral apartment brimmed with a gnawing vacuum. Since my brother and sister were already settled, there was no choice but for me to live alone there. I realised that it was high time I took charge of my life and did a volte-face in my thinking. I decided to stop being such a choosy, supercilious wimp with a negative attitude and a misplaced "holier-than-thou" perspective and start thinking of myself as "marriageable". Being lonely and basically aloof is fine for a creative writer, but when it comes down to brass tacks and practicality in everyday living, joining in family get-togethers and having a bit of a social life, too, is not a bad deal.'

When Daughter Turns Doer: Identity Crisis Of Care-Giving

The pressure of care-giving for a single woman is an uphill and lonely road. Delhi-based Supriya Dhaliwal (*name changed on request*), a senior journalist in her 40s, has battled this lone crusade since 1998 and admits that for a long while she possessed no self-identity or life of her own, except being a daughter and primary caregiver to her ailing parents, both of whom have expired now.

Today, Supriya lives in a sprawling apartment in West Delhi that she has inherited and confesses that being 42, she's not too hopeful of finding a companion, though the idea of wanting to share her life with someone remains a strong priority, more so, as she lacks siblings. The interest in her single life remains constant, with her yoga teacher, who comes every morning, also not sparing her the sermon and asking her pointedly why she's still single. A guy in the visa office, too, remarked when she went to renew her passport, 'Kyun shaadi nahin ki aap ne, umar toh kaafi ho gayi hain aap ki?'

And yet, despite the nagging scrutiny, Supriya, who lives alone, is quick to add that she has to be selective in not exposing her vulnerability to the first person she meets as she could be seen as the quintessential golden goose. A lot of men, too, probe her asking her why she is still single followed by the eternal reprise—what does she do for sex? Most of them assume she's lying when she confesses that she's never been in a relationship. Since she is a journalist with long and late working hours, they can't seem to digest the fact that Supriya could still be a virgin!

Supriya claims her life changed drastically when in 1998 her mother, who was the rock of their family, suffered her first cerebral attack. Her father was shattered, and before she knew it, all the emotional and physical needs of care-giving descended on Supriya's shoulders. Initially, preoccupied with managing her parents and her gruelling day job, she barely had time to feel the vacuum of not having a partner. At the beginning of 2000, Supriya's mother's chemotherapy and radiation commenced and her father, unable to deal with the rising financial burden coupled with the emotional stress of running back and forth to hospitals, started smoking heavily again, which took a serious toll on his heart condition. In 2002, Supriya's mother suffered her second attack, post which she stopped recognising people or talking, with barely any eye movement, her downward spiral having begun. This was a phase of frequent hospitalisations when wanting a man, Supriya confesses, felt like a luxury as all she prayed for was that her own health remains perfect so that she could soldier on and look after her parents.

In 2004, Supriya's father suffered a massive heart attack. Having already undergone a bypass in 1984, with stents been inserted in his heart, he needed a pacemaker in 2007. 'At that time I operated like a machine—having to handle nurses, financial matters, rushing in and out of hospitals at any given moment, waiting for doctors and also managing long night shifts. I deliberately didn't opt for a reporter's portfolio, making do with a grinding desk job that ultimately affected my own health,' Supriya recalls. She adds that she often felt lonely and frustrated, occasionally spending a night with a friend, getting sloshed to relax and forget her worries, before once again dutifully rushing back home to resume her responsibilities robotically. On the verge of a nervous breakdown herself, Supriya's dream of a companion, many a time, made her feel selfish, given the trying circumstances.

Living with ageing and critically ailing parents is a daunting task compounded when confronted with their evenutal demise. Supriya poignantly says that one of the toughest decisions she had taken as a single child was to admit her mother in December 2009 to Shanti Avedna Sadan, a hospice which took care of cancer patients in the final stages of life. Her dad also suffered a nasty fall and had broken his ribs. At her wit's end, Supriya faced his ire since he was dead against the decision to hospitalise her mother.

'A doctor from the hospice came over to have a long chat and asked my father, "Are you aware your daughter is also on the brink of an emotional breakdown?"' she pauses with a tinge of sadness. Even in those last days of her mother's failing health, her final wish was to see Supriya settled, but relatives often visiting remarked insensitively that Supriya should not dare dream of marriage because after that who would take responsibility, adding that post marriage, a woman's first duty would naturally gravitate towards her in-laws.

On 16 January, 2010, Supriya's mother breathed her last. 'When I saw my mother's face after she'd passed away, she looked so alive. At that moment I realised that I must have done something right that she was peaceful at last,' recounts Supriya, who also lost her father in 2011.

Supriya's battle with the unexpected emptiness in her life and her struggles as a single woman soon escalated when she herself met with a fatal accident, a fortnight after her father's demise. A critical head injury landed her in hospital for 21 days. 'The wheel of the auto dislocated and I was flung outside and hit my head against a sharp object. Soon after the accident happened, a colleague had called to know where I was when the police picked up my phone and informed him about my condition. He then informed my friends and that set the chain of information in motion. After being discharged, I spent 15 days with my aunt and another 15 with a single friend.'

Reaching home after nearly 1.5 months was when the terrifying loneliness hit Supriya as she realised her parents were gone forever.

'I tried looking for marriage too, but most of these sites are jokes. I'm not into one-night stands either,' Supriya clarifies, having faced a lot of rejections earlier being the only daughter of critically ill parents—many families assumed that hers were looking for a *ghar-jamai* or a male nurse to take care of her bedridden parents. 'I'm living my life despite this loneliness and am happy. I've travelled in the country and outside in these past few years and plan to do so more often. Yes, I do still feel that I must get a life partner, but am looking for companionship, deep love and mutual respect—three elements I had seen in my parents, and I am not ready to settle for anything less,' she maintains with an air of self-assuredness.

Supriya's isolation isn't entirely new. I, too, have been rejected because of my 'only daughter' status, with a man on a matrimonial site once telling me on my face that he wasn't comfortable with the closeness I shared with my parents, one that he apprehended meant that I would want to visit my *maike* a lot—something his patriarchal mindset probably didn't permit. Funnily enough, he himself lived with his parents at 40. '*Mujhe Piku jaisi ladki aur usska baap nahin chahiye,*' he had smirked condescendingly.

That was the last interaction I had with him.

Ironically, a recent survey conducted by *Shaadi.com* claims that out of 3,952 single men who participated in the survey, 54.3% said they would like to stay with their parents post marriage. On the other hand, when 4,617 women were asked for their preferences, 64.1% said they would wish to live only with their husbands.

In a country where culture dictates that single daughters play the role of primary care-givers, most of them choosing to stay with parents, sometimes after years of being on their own, 37-year-old Aditi Rao (*name changed on request*) from Chennai feels being single in India is akin to a curse as the responsibility of taking care of your parents, medically and emotionally, is inevitably thrust on to you. Single women are naturally picked out, a sweeping assumption made on the premise that since they only have their parents to fall back on, the duty of staying and looking after them is also theirs alone.

'I am not a single child. But my brother and older sister who are married and live in the US naturally assumed I was going to stay back and look after my mom, who has been suffering from Parkinson's since 2009, and my father, who has been bedridden since the last 5 years, having suffered a cerebral stroke. Since I am unwed and was based in the same city as them, it was taken for granted that care-giving was my job, and mine alone. They keep asserting that they are sending dollars and paying for bills when I bring up the topic of sharing the responsibility. They always take me for granted, and never quite acknowledge the sacrifices I have made, giving up my cushy IT job that involved late hours and frequent travels, to working from home in a completely different domain.

'No man wants to marry me either—almost like the stigma you attach to a divorcee with kids. I always carry this excess baggage. I can't stay out late since I am nervously checking the phone to see if I have got any calls from home. I can't bring guys home or even plan long holidays, abandoning my sick parents. Everyday I battle mundane domestic issues—nurses, injections, doctors and medical bills. When my siblings visit once every couple of years, they travel through India with their kids, and insist on their duty to spend time with in-laws and how they deserve a break from their frenzied routine back home. *My* time or personal life is inevitably on hold. I wish I could run away at times. While I love my parents dearly and would always want to hold on to them, I simultaneously crave a life and a home of my own where accountabilities are equally shared. Just because I am single—is it my fault?

'My sister, a year older, who would earlier try for alliances overseas, nowadays seems disinterested and says after 30, getting an arranged match is hard anywhere and that I should ideally fall in love and choose my own companion. My brother claims he can't take such sick patients to the US, and tells me that it is my obligation as a single daughter to take care of my family since I live with them. I am honestly made to feel like an unpaid ayah— neglected and stuck with ailing people all day. My friends tell me

I should revolt, but relocating to another city means dumping my parents at this tender stage, and that is something my conscience doesn't allow.

'Does marriage give the woman a license to conveniently escape her daughterly duties? Or is it jumping from the frying pan into the fire? Why is a single woman taking care of her parents never given the respectability she deserves—similar to the one she always commands as a woman taking care of her in-laws and children or a son taking care of his parents. My parents are my children today, quite honestly, am I any less than any married daughter, then?' she questions strongly.

Perhaps the existence of these glaring inequalities in society led to the recent judgement upheld by the Bombay High Court that a married woman, too, is responsible for maintaining her parents. In a particular case of Vasant vs. Govindrao Upasrao Naik, Criminal Revision Application No. 172/2014, the High Court rejected the preconceived notion that a married daughter has obligations only towards her husband's family and not her own parents. This progressive decision questions the prevalent notion that a married woman's in-laws are supposed to be more important to her than her actual parents. Moreover, it contests the assumption that women cannot be providers, and puts them on an equal footing with men as far as financial responsibilities are concerned. Besides dispelling the patriarchal belief of daughters being *'paraya dhan'* (belonging to somebody else's family) and, thus, not taking money from them.

Living Alone Not Necessarily A Bed Of Roses

Pooja Sharma, a 39-year-old banker who has lost both her parents, and has no siblings, gives an alternate insight into what it means to live all by yourself, even in a so-called cosmopolitan city like Mumbai. The stigmatisation of a single woman runs deep, according to Pooja, in a culture conditioned to couplehood, as a sign of sacredness and stability for a woman.

Having lost her mom at 18 and dad at 22 and being cheated by her uncles of family property, Pooja didn't even possess a roof over her own head. Borrowing money from a lot of people, she finally invested in a 1 BHK, committed to rebuilding her life again, during which time she withdrew into a shell and socially isolated herself, mostly out of fear of being used and cheated by all and sundry again, with almost everyone wanting to take advantage of a woman who is an orphan. Starting to work at 18, Pooja today has worked up the corporate ladder and is presently a vice president at a reputed financial organisation.

During this phase of refusing wedding invites and social engagements, etc., Pooja confesses to losing out on many friends, as her main priority was her career and regaining her much-needed financial independence. Yet, society's curiosity in Pooja's life as an *akeli aurat* never receded. 'My maid was once asked by people living in the same building if I was a lesbian and even inane stuff, like what brand of milk I drank daily. I sacked her immediately, and did all the household work for nearly 3.5 years. Once a neighbour even rang my doorbell on a Sunday and asked me point-blank if I smoked? I said yes, and my reply was immediately communicated to the society members, to whom I was asked to give an explanation for my "lifestyle"—as my influence wasn't allegedly encouraging for the kids in the complex,' sardonically recalls Pooja, who was deliberately kept out of Holi functions or Ganpati festivals. Ostracised and unfairly judged, it was approximately just a decade back that she started to actually rebel, telling the same society members to take recourse to the legal route, since she wasn't going to start coming home early and live according to their convenience.

4 years ago, Pooja decided to buy her own apartment and with the site still under construction, she was left with no choice

but to rent a flat—once again facing the oppressive discrimination of being a single woman sans her parents or any concrete family support. Despite telling the broker that she just needed the place for a year, within which time her own building would be up and she'd move out, and that she wasn't 'single by choice,' on several occasions Pooja would be informed that landlords didn't want a woman 'like her'—though she was an associate director by then and would be taking the flat on a legitimate company lease. At least on twelve instances, Pooja asserts being shunned because of her 'single' status. Her broker also lied to most landlords, being primarily interested in getting a good commission, and left her to face the humiliation.

'Finally, I did manage a place, because the owner knew my cousin who was getting married to a relative from his family. But the minute he discovered I was single—this much-married man with a 14-year-old daughter, sends me a WhatsApp text the very next day, asking if he could come over for coffee? When a woman is past 35, she's naturally perceived as desperate for sex, children, and needing a man to complete her—and my case was no different, I suppose. I love solo travel with women's groups, and each time I returned home, I would be taunted by neighbours, "*Aur kya karegi tu* salary *le ke*? Who will you save for? No parents to think of. *Baccho ka koi* tension *nahin!*" It sounded accusatory...' she trails.

Even as more and more single women like Pooja live alone, either by choice or due to circumstances, their condition is mostly an exploitative one—with prospective suitors also being more often than not interested in moving in immediately, making the most of a free living space.

'Intimacy is a natural human craving, and I seek companionship. I think a lot of single women are scared to own up to their own deep-seated loneliness and because we live in an age where social media is an intrinsic part of our lives—there is this constant pressure to project ourselves as content all the time. I mean I have visited a psychologist, how many women even own up to depression?' questions Pooja, adding in the same breath that single women in India aren't trained to be alone—with parents of a single daughter always assuming somewhere that she will get married eventually.

'We have no clue of inheritance laws either, and aren't taught to manage money or even fix a light bulb. I'd be lying if I say there are still times when I am not petrified of opening the door for the courier guy, or of picking up a fight on the road. The watchman in my building keeps checking me out—a single woman is perennially on the scanner,' says Pooja, who is always running into men who conveniently want to live-in. 'Once they see you own your own apartment, most guys are only interested in a free fuck and sharing the living space, since Mumbai is super expensive. The majority of Indian men you meet for arranged marriage and their moms, on the other hand, are all looking more for someone working and also able to look after the guy's family. Aren't we sick of the same question, "Can you cook?"' she points out sharply.

Professionally, too, the perception is if a woman is single—she's naturally slept her way to the top! Or she's immediately slotted as being too ambitious—and rejecting marriage or kids, with marriage viewed mainly as a character certification, be it in the building one stays in or the boardroom one is a part of. Today, Pooja admits she has stopped attending girlfriends' weddings because she knows she'll inevitably be clubbed with a total stranger, thanks to a latent sense of pity in seeing a single woman in her mid-30s. Recently, a cousin, too, who she had always considered close, surprised her by saying her life goal was marriage as she's touched 30. Her family had also asked Pooja if she is a lesbian.

Singles Demand Space

Safety, scrutiny and security—does living as a single woman entail a mix of these three emotions, be it with parents or by yourself? Arpita Melhotra, 37-year-old advertising professional from Pune, puts it best, 'My dad once walked into my bedroom where I'd sneaked in my boss, a married man who they knew, for a quickie. He literally saw us making out, and the cold war that followed made me exit my home soon enough. However, after my affair soured, I realised maybe I had been too immature and taken a rushed decision. I craved home food and hated being sick and lonely. I wish my father realised I was in my mid-30s and gave me the emotional and physical space a single woman needs, living under the same roof. Maybe, if I had a separate entrance or something, and if they weren't so stuck up about men staying back or late-night drinking binges, we could have co-existed. The rules in India are different for men and women. My twin brother, also single, is allowed to bring home his numerous girlfriends with some of them staying over too, but questions aren't asked, if he's marrying any of them! My parents don't hound him about his personal life or keep tabs on his whereabouts, the way they still do with me. Parental affection is key to a single woman, but if she has to/wants to live with her parents, they should also realise that it's not just born out of an obligation on her part or that because she's still single and perhaps in the same city as them. They have a holy duty to house her, until her *doli* leaves the threshold. To create a mutually happy living space, both parties should be willing to compromise and respect each other's privacy.'

The concept of allowing your kids to just be as they are, thoroughly alien to a traditional Indian family, remains one of the primary deal-breakers.

Singleton, 33-year-old Jayapriya Menon (*name changed on*

request), who works in the HR department of a telecom company in Bengaluru, took the decision to live alone in the same city as her parents and married, younger sibling. 'My parents were posted in Abu Dhabi, when I chose to finish my 11th and 12th in Kerala, after which I moved alone to Bengaluru to pursue a B.Sc. in Biotechnology, staying in the hostel. Being keen to become financially independent at the earliest, I switched to an MBA degree in Human Resources, and when I was in the first year, my folks returned wanting to spend time with my sister and me before we got married. Despite moving in with them, I desperately missed my own "space", and would also end up spending more time with good friends, my social life at an all-time high,' looks back Jayapriya, who consequently took a shot at the arranged marriage market.

'That my ambition wasn't finding a boy was an alien concept to my parents, and I did meet guys just for their sake. My marriage was almost finalised with a Malayali who worked overseas. During our long-distance courtship, however, we soon came to the conclusion that we weren't compatible and that made us jittery to take the final plunge. Finally, I went up to my family and called off the impending nuptials and while my parents were supportive, they couldn't digest my fierce independence and stubborn refusal to just marry for society's sake, even suggesting I visit a shrink. Those were turbulent times,' reflects Jayapriya. She then adds, 'My sister was seeing someone and was keen to settle down and asked me if I was okay with the idea of her choosing to walk down the aisle before me—another common stereotype in Indian families. I gave her my blessings. I, too, had started courting a woman and wanted to strike out.'

Jayapriya, who was equally attracted to men and women, gradually discovered that she could only live together with a woman, as she experienced the strongest emotional connect with her own sex.

'I needed to stay by myself so that both my sexuality and I evolved equally. My parents, who initially wanted to move to their roots in Kerala, soon changed their mind and remained in Bengaluru and were perhaps slightly shocked by my decision to live on my own, their views somewhere coloured by an apprehension of what society and our relatives would say if an unmarried daughter stays separately, in the same city.' Jayapriya, who initially lived in with a friend, finally moved on to her own pad within the second year and has since found companionship with a woman.

'I have purchased my own apartment where my parents live today, whereas I live alone in a separate accommodation, my partner having recently relocated to Mumbai. My parents know about us as well. Though technically being single, I do sense in my parents a greater expectation of being more available than my sister. I am there for my parents. I know they're growing old. I'm also prepared for them to move in with me or me to move in with them some day… my sister, too, echoes the same feeling as me. We ensure that either of us are always available to our parents,' she adds pragmatically. At her workplace, where Jayapriya has been employed for the past 5 years and leads the Diversity and Inclusion practice, she is open about her bisexuality.

STATUS SINGLE: *I have lived alone, and now stay with my folks, and I think both have their own sets of pros and cons. So while living alone means you can bring in the boys, have wild parties and run your kingdom sans explanations, I'd say it's possible to do most of that with parents, too, if they are non-interfering and give you enough space to have your own life and make your own decisions. But be prepared to be called and asked what time you will be back, if you are out late; asked about dinner and lunch, and not having men in bed or at the breakfast table—since no matter how liberal they are, most parents still belong to another generation. However, weighing both sides, I'd say that it's nice to*

come home to people who care about you and not have to worry about groceries and maid management. One has to define clear boundaries, of course, have an extra set of keys and entertain freely—most of my friends adore my parents and love the warmth and pampering as well as the air of freedom. But if you'd rather maintain your own pad—do it for your own needs. There is no rule that single women must look after and always stay with ageing parents (especially if you have siblings), just like there is no shame in still going on holidays with family and living with mom and dad. Your life. Your rules.

Chapter Eight

The New Singles

At a get-together a few months ago, we were a group of mostly single women into our late 30s discussing men, matrimonial sites and mothers, when one of our friends actually raised her hand to make a point. 'Look, your being single at 39 and me being a divorcee at 46 is different. We are looked upon as two diverse identities. In fact, most men take us to be sexually active and available. And god help you if you are straddled with kids,' she almost sounded bitter.

I studied Reema's face. A successful professional with a leading media channel in the city, she didn't look her age at all, and because she had been single for as long as I was acquainted with her, I'd never really surmised our conditions to be quite so different. The 'single' state of being had seemed to cover us equally. But the truth is that the status single category isn't the sole preserve of unmarried women like me anymore, with it gradually getting populated by women who courageously or circumstantially had chosen to end their marital relationships, some with children, some on their own.

Single After Marriage Vs. Single Sans Marriage: What's Different?

How different could we be? I asked myself after that evening culminated. Did we share common fears, foes and fantasies? With skyrocketing divorce rates in India and women becoming increasingly financially stable and able to live in cities geographically distanced from their families, was the life of a single divorcee as challenging as that of a woman who was still unmarried? Was the stigmatisation more or less? Was being on your own after being seen with a man and his family a gnawing emotional and financial readjustment—a non-conformism creating both a physical and mental upheaval?

Are women in India ever really prepared to be alone? Does our cultural conditioning, juxtaposed on couple-hood, allow even the slightest window to imagine a phase in which a woman becomes single again? Is the pressure to remarry as potent as what we single women suffer? The questions on one's sex life, as direct and in your face? Are women on the eve of their marriages—touted as the biggest day of our lives and a social prestige issue for the girl's family—taught anything of the Indian Penal Code? How to react if you are abused mentally or physically violated? To know when to call it quits? What are the mental checklists and alarm bells that we must always look out for? To walk into a police station alone, or face a crowded family court proceeding? Is being a divorcee yet another forbidden label?

49-year-old Jhilmil Breckenridge, poet, activist and writer, who made a deeply personal transition to being single admits that as an only child, she expected a lot from her marriage and the life she was about to create as a young bride. Jhilmil thus consciously created a large family of 4 sons, loving the idea of a loud, happy home, perhaps something she'd missed out on in her childhood. However, life dealt her an ugly blow, with not just her divorce, but her 4 children being abducted by her ex, something she adds is common in international divorces. Her parents, too, sided with her former husband. Jhilmil consequently found herself isolated and claims it was frightening and lonely, but also in someway 'empowering'. Knowing how little one actually needs to survive and how happiness does not come from having people who actually make you feel lonelier and how the concept of family, especially in India, comes loaded with so many shackles and expectations, emboldened Jhilmil to thrive as a single woman, to find her feet again.

'With my divorce, initially there was disbelief. From a privileged wife of an expat, living in the poshest neighbourhood in Delhi, I was literally on the streets, at the mercy of a few friends,' recalls Jhilmil who was subsequently shunned by most friends and family till she finally found support from an American friend, Laura, who took her in and helped find a tiny room in a small shanty, paying her rent for three months. 'People who were all too willing to come and drink your best Scotch and eat your choicest desserts do not even want to take your calls. But you learn that the human spirit is resilient. Because when you are counting pennies and have to resort to picking up food from the streets (and I did this on one occasion), you discover that all that matters is to stay alive.'

Stronger and self-sufficient today, Jhilmil, however, subscribes to Reema's point of view that a woman sans a male protector, all of a sudden, is automatically perceived as an 'easy catch', similar to single women in India being considered sexual objects, desperate to 'get laid'. Like any other single woman, people have also outrightly offered Jhilmil sex like they were doing her a favour, taking liberties, that she is certain they'd never dreamt of when she was a 'happily married woman', carrying the legally sanctioned tag of a 'wife'. Once you are divorced, Jhilmil opines, people suddenly see a stamp of 'available' imprinted on a woman's forehead and say and do the most inappropriate things, like tucking a napkin with their phone number written on it into her pocket or into her bag!

Jhilmil is currently in London pursuing a Ph.D in creative writing and has also founded a mental health charity in India called Bhor Foundation. According to her, London and Delhi aren't really that different in the way a woman gets propositioned from unwelcome sources. On the flip side, she observes that it's probably easier to 'just date' overseas, should you want to. 'Apps like Tinder, OK Cupid, etc., make sex, relationships and hook ups as easy as ordering pizza! You decide what you want, and no one judges you,' claims Jhilmil, 'Another realisation that comes post a divorce is that women are your worst enemies. You are perceived as a threat.'

With most Indian women accustomed to living under a patriarchal umbrella and marriage largely an extension of just another overarching male protectiveness and validation, Jhilmil, who was once even forced into a mental asylum, says what makes becoming single again harder is our own mental make-up that subconsciously seeks male dependency. 'In India, sadly, a lot of people throw women into institutions, because they can, and often it's over property, divorce, to teach someone a lesson, etc. It is as easy as checking into a hospital/institution and telling them their wife is crazy. There are no checks and balances in place, and they simply admit you, drug you. You are labelled for life, your kids can be taken from you, your property seized. I was lucky that a lot of mental health activists and human rights campaigners and the media discovered my story and I was rescued. Else, who knows, I could have been languishing in some asylum for the rest of my life, as I know of several other women. The scariest stories happen not in the movies or books, but in real life.'

With our society thriving on male muscle power and women most often deliberately prevented from having the authority to make their own decisions, Jhilmil feels nothing is more dangerous to society than a woman in control of her own body, her own money and her own mind. 'In my case, as is with a lot of Indian women, you go from your father handling money to your husband managing it. In addition, I was extremely extravagant and would be continually shopping and filling the void in my life with buying things and other such mindless activities. Post my split, I had to completely change the way I live, the way I shop, survive within a budget, and in many ways, that has been a good thing. My property is still in the name of my ex husband and me, as he ran away from India without the court awarding custody/property. So I know one day, if and when I want to sell the house, it will be a problem.'

Divorced, Not Dukhi: How Society Sees A Divorced Woman Who Doesn't Wear Grief On Her Sleeve

With marriage projected as the highest validation of a woman's life, and most women entrusting their emotional and financial stability to the men they are betrothed to, who in a way replace their fathers, as we're always taught to look for fatherly qualities in our husbands—the biggest challenge post a divorce, apart from the struggles of being single again, is to rediscover your own voice. And learn at the same time to also turn a deaf ear to the slander and suspicions that surround a divorced woman's existence. The shock of a divorce is sometimes compounded with the lack of support a woman finds within her own sex. Sisters, friends and colleagues, start taking a microscopic view of your tough life choices, with the speculation growing more prominent, when a separated woman decides to co-parent, and share custody of her children with the same man whose home she left.

34-year-old Sunidhi Chopra (*name changed on request*), an aspiring writer who is active in the theatre circles of Delhi, married her childhood sweetheart at 20, buying into the notion of an archetypical fairytale romance—a staple diet young girls are fed on since childhood, thanks to popular culture and Bollywood, that all stories must end with forever and the appearance of a Prince Charming.

Like scores of women who either marry too young or sacrifice their careers after marriage and motherhood, Sunidhi lacked her own identity and allowed herself to be dominated. She was promised at the time of her marriage that she'd be pampered. Soon enough she began to lead a comfortable life, where she didn't know how to cook a simple meal, cutting herself off from her friends and surviving as an insular creature in a self-created bubble with her dream family. However, as time passed, Sunidhi and her spouse realised that they were incompatible, as the fights and abuses grew more vicious. As a mother, Sunidhi was certain she didn't want her only child, a daughter, to be raised in such a negative environment. Subsequently, she chose to consciously and amicably end her marital relationship, agreeing on balanced co-parenting.

'The biggest backlash I faced post my break-up was from women I knew personally, some belonging to my age bracket and social circles, who, I realised, represented the worst face of patriarchy in India. And maybe because a lot of them silently endured abusive and decadent marriages to simply maintain a public front, they couldn't stomach a gutsy woman wanting to live with dignity and ending her marriage for the same,' feels Sunidhi, who continues to maintain an amicable relationship with her ex, who, in turn, fulfills the duties of a father. This, she adds, had led to women often passing snide remarks on what is the exact status of her relationship with him, appearing startled at the healthy equation she has reached today. At family outings, too, Sunidhi dealt with a lot of hushed whispers probing why a single mother like her was invited. The result of a regressive moral and social conditioning, Sunidhi soon found the same-sex persecution to be harsher than the sexual threat from men.

Sunidhi, who is working on her debut novel now, is open to remarriage and has also dated some decent men in the past, even as her presently single status remains a subject of strict scrutiny in female circles. 'I attracted successful, good-looking men which turned into a topic of gossip and finger-pointing. Women are naturally jealous of other women and tend to pass judgemental comments as to how I could be so hot and sexy, perhaps referring to my physical appearance! And since my ex and I meet frequently for meals and take our daughter out, I'm told I could've tried to adjust and live with him, since he's an ideal father and doing all the things a husband would normally do. Learning to live as a single woman is a second birth—like starting from scratch...'

From Pampered Bahu To Sole Breadwinner: The Journey Of Uncoupling

Like Sunidhi, Bengaluru-based filmmaker, 40-plus Divya Ramesh (*name changed on request*), calls herself the 'credit card wife', who was completely unprepared for the collapse of her 16-year-old marriage. Never having been the breadwinner, despite being creatively inclined, Divya never pursued a full-time career that would provide her with financial freedom. Her husband gave her money, but she had no say in the financial decisions of the family—thus relegating herself to a secondary position. For Divya, her divorce was a colossal leap of faith where she had to not just take care of her son, but also ensure she didn't end up living a life of frugality.

One of the biggest mistakes, Divya says she made in the initial days of her split was to talk about her situation openly, realising soon enough that there existed a deep-seated layer of negativity and animosity amongst even her closest girlfriends who lent her a shoulder to cry on, but judged her for the personal choices she had made. 'Perhaps, courage by its very nature draws envy,' summarises

Divya, who had no option but to reinvent herself, starting from ground zero, and laying the foundation of her own company. Having been a pampered housewife for years, Divya had neither any training in finance nor had she been encouraged to develop a business acumen. Like many divorced women who flounder at the workplace after years of being homemakers, Divya also made myriad mistakes, often paying the price for her innate vulnerability, when people took advantage of her naivety. Having learnt the ropes the hard way, today, Divya makes people sign contracts right at the outset and claims she's also learnt the intricacies of accounting along the way. An ambitious, single woman is, however, always a soft target for Indian society used to obedient homemakers and yes-women, she agrees, looking back on her own learning curve.

From battling financial insecurities to beginning professional life afresh, to playing single mom—the road for a divorced woman isn't a bed of roses. 43-year-old Hyderabad-based Prabha Vasudevan (*name changed on request*) smiles, reflecting on her bitter divorce and the messy custody battle she fought, selling her last gold bangle to gain the rights to her only daughter who now lives with her. Married just after college, Prabha battled extreme family objection, going on to complete her Masters in IT, even as her husband suspected her of having an affair with any man she encountered. She confesses to never having had her personal bank account till she finished her studies, and expressed a keen interest to begin working. Ugly spats followed and her in-laws pressurised her to get pregnant instead, and at the age of 24, she became a mother.

Living with a sexually violent husband made Prabha want to end her fractured marriage many a time, but whenever she visited a marriage counsellor for advice, she'd be told that she was probably better off 'married', and needed to give time and compromise. Her parents, too, were ageing and she wasn't sure about the effect her divorce would have on them. Finally, after a decade of being married,

Prabha broke out of her abusive, dysfunctional relationship when she discovered her husband cheating on her with a female relative in the confines of their own bedroom!

Having always suspected his philandering, and reduced to a glorified, unemployed maid in the years of being married, primarily looking after her kid and ageing in-laws, not to mention cooking and managing maids, it was a shock for even Prabha when she walked out with nothing except her handbag.

Her husband's family being influential tried everything in the book to snatch her kid away, bringing false charges of adultery into the divorce proceedings, even alluding that she was sexually frigid and had refused to have sex with her husband for years after their daughter was born. The lawyers that she approached were also sexist and demeaning, till Prabha zeroed in on the right person, finally winning the court battle after 6 painful years. Today, Prabha is on the threshold of starting a mobile app, after having completed a couple of online courses in the digital space. It has been a road fraught with challenges, but Prabha has survived by sheer grit, taking a hefty bank loan, roughing it out in a mess, studying night and day to get up-to-date with technology and balancing a day job at an IT firm to earn her keep—a phase she describes as being back in school again.

'My daughter and I were distanced, thanks to the ugly courtroom dramas. She was also being fed many lies about my character by her paternal grandparents, but I was confident that with time our bond would strengthen. I was literally like an illiterate woman who was forced to begin from ground zero with barely any support from my widowed mother and my brother who made it clear he had his own family to look after,' Prabha says, adding that she knew it wasn't just about survival, but rebuilding her lost identity and self-worth. 'Ironically, I was tagged a "bitch" for demanding alimony and suggested by many so-called, well-wishers to make the case mutual and agree on a consensual, out-of-court separation instead. I was determined not to be the typical, soap-opera divorcee, shedding tears of regret. My heart and faith in marriage was shattered, but I knew I must live and fight this out to the end and reinvent my broken life.'

Prabha's app that is directed at helping out-of-work separated/divorced/widowed women find jobs and restart their careers is going to be launched soon, and presently she's working on getting funding, having recruited a marketing and tech person. She is determined not to look back at any cost. 'When my daughter asks what she should say in school about her father, I answer: "Speak only the truth, that my parents aren't together any longer, and that my mother is a first-generation entrepreneur. Women make the biggest mistake in compromising their freedom and respect for the sake of kids, parents and society. Live for those you love, but fight for yourself,' she concludes with a new-found confidence.

Practical Hassles In Being Single Again: Rent, Respect, Remarriage

For further insights, I call upon my friend Reema, who like many of the women featured in this chapter, also had a relatively early marriage at 28, divorced after a decade, as her husband happened to be a serial womanizer. After turning a blind eye to several of his flings, trying desperately to conceive, suffering a miscarriage and unable to get physical with him after a point, thanks to his recurrent cheating, she finally walked out.

Reema, who has since then tried to find a secure second innings, both in terms of work, living, and meeting a man, feels, 'There's a lot more respectability in being single at 39 or being a young, 20-something divorcee. At my age, you are the target of mostly married men, who perhaps earlier used to hit on younger single women.' Like a lot of single women, Reema also faced a roadblock when she sought to find an accommodation, running headlong into a prejudiced social system unwilling to rent out a flat to a divorcee, working in a media organisation with unpredictable working hours. Unable to afford more than ₹12,000-15,000 rent back in those days, and despite assuring the landlord that her parents would regularly visit and stay back too on certain days, it was tough to convince people of her character, Reema adds, especially because she was determined to build her separate existence, firmly believing that her parents had already fulfilled their parental duty of educating and getting her settled.

'There is a very real fear of being single again—since marriage in a way shuts up people and is seen as a valid social status. In fact, a cousin in the US who is highly qualified and 7 years younger is reluctant to leave her alcoholic and abusive husband fearing what people might say, despite her parents asking her to relocate. She's wary of *taana*. I shudder to think of women in backward areas! One of my cousins tells me, "*Aar biye hobena*," (you will not get married any more), while another says I should not be so picky. Ironically, both are women. I guess the centrality of marriage to our sex never ceases,' she says.

Reema, who hasn't stopped looking or believing in love, has suffered several heartbreaks, including an affair with a divorcee whose daughter tried to kill herself upon learning about her father's blossoming relationship. 'My female colleagues often probe if I get horny. But sex is an extension of emotional attachment. There is always a stigma that a woman, once she crosses the 30-year mark, is most likely to end up with a widower or a divorcee. No matter how many second marriages actualise or women gain the confidence to break out of faulty marriages, a divorced woman carries a lot of excess baggage. It's like everything you endured as a single woman in India and some more…' Reema points out with a dint of bitterness soaking her last words.

What Parents Don't Tell A Single Woman About Marriage: The Reality Of Divorce

With the boundary line between single and divorced getting smudged slowly, what with both categories facing similar stereotyping and stigmatisation, Delhi-based Henna Ahuja (*name changed on request*), who fell in love with a divorced man whom she married at 26, says, 'As a single woman, I looked at a divorcee as just a man battling a relationship failure... and these days we all have affairs pre-marriage, so what's there to judge?'

Henna battled an emotionally and physically abusive marriage. Her schizophrenic husband's adultery and violence took a toll on her soon enough. 'He was extremely emotional, wept like I'd never seen a grown man howl, was prone to violent mood swings and even lost his job, after which I was the sole earning member. He tried to hit me with a hot *tawa*, strangulated me on another instance, and yet I endured this torture for almost 2 years. Finally, I took him to a psychiatrist who asked me to be more lenient as a life partner, even though he was into adultery!' she recounts, going on to raise an extremely pertinent point that holds ground for any single woman looking at settling down today.

'When I separated and consulted a divorce lawyer, he questioned me as to why I hadn't come clean earlier, after the first instance of physical violence? It's an Indian woman's upbringing that teaches us to endure suffering in silence. We are taught to value marriage more than our lives, since as single women our whole growing up is goal-oriented, and while we are taught how to compromise and adjust into a new household, no one really guides us on domestic violence, legal provisions, or tells us what our rights in a marriage are, say, with regards to property, joint bank accounts or even the alarm bells a woman should be more attuned to. This also applies to parents.'

Today, while Henna's family is supportive, she lives alone in a rented accommodation close to them, primarily because her mother is skeptical of what people will comment if they see their married daughter lurking around in the *maike* for too long. The extended family hasn't been informed about her split yet. 'More than Dad, my mother is worried about the stigma the word divorce carries. She is anxious about my future, because for most Indian parents, settling down for a daughter is viewed and projected as the be all and end all of her life purpose. She keeps lamenting as to why this had to happen to us? I guess her fears are an extension of a larger mental conditioning that looks down on a single woman no matter how successful she may be professionally,' she rues.

Henna's insights are corroborated by leading advocate Sriparna Chatterjee, who ironically comments, 'One of my closest friends was in a physically abusive relationship, and after getting divorced with much difficulty, thanks to the constant coaxing of both sets of parents, remarried the same man. Within a short span, he reverted to his old ways—and she had to file for a divorce again. Just like child sex abuse where there is an increased incidence and parents now have no choice but to educate their children on good and bad touch and teach them to raise an alarm timely, if they feel something is out of place—Indian parents *must* accept that marriages breaking up is a reality staring us all in the face. And while domesticating your child and teaching her to be emotionally, socially and financially independent is viewed as normal, and something that is done as way of preparing her before she ties the knot, one must simultaneously educate the daughter on the law.'

She cites three broad laws that can help a woman struggling to escape the tyranny of a faulty marriage that she claims every Indian parent should talk to their daughters about:

- Section 498 (A) of the Indian Penal Code, punishment for dowry harassment with matrimonial cruelty in India is a cognizable, non-bailable and non-compoundable offence, along with Section 3 (if any person, after the commencement of this Act, gives or takes or abets the giving or taking of dowry, he shall be punishable with imprisonment for a term which shall not be less than 5 years, and with fine which shall not be less than ₹15,000 or the amount of the value of such dowry, whichever is more) and Section 4 (if any person demands, directly or indirectly, from the parents or other relatives or guardian of a bride or bridegroom, as the case may be, any dowry, he shall be punishable with imprisonment for a term which shall not be less than 6 months, but which may extend to 2 years and with fine which may extend to ₹10,000)of the Dowry Prohibition Act of 1861.

- Secondly, legislated as a tool for social justice, Section 125 of the Criminal Procedure Code, 1973, provides an effective remedy for neglected persons to seek maintenance. A follower of any religion can apply for maintenance under Section 125, without restriction. So, if a woman has filed a protection against domestic violence petition, in the interim, she can also seek maintenance so that her day-to-day financial expenses are taken care of or setting of a separate household is encouraged to help save a woman from daily harassment. Furthermore, a Hindu woman can avail of the Maintenance Pendelite provision under Section 24 of the Hindu Marriage Act where even if the husband files for divorce, the wife can file a Maintenance Pendelite and the Court is more likely to dispose this application so that the woman gets a financial cover while her case is on, beneficial to a large extent, in the case of a non-working woman.
- The Domestic Violence Act of 2005. The Act provides for the first time in Indian law a broad definition of 'domestic

violence', including not physical violence alone, but other forms of violence too, such as emotional verbal, sexual, and economic abuse. It is a civil law meant primarily for protection orders, and not to penalise criminally.

'Unlike Muslim women who are usually well-informed about *mehr* (a mandatory payment, in the form of money or possessions paid or promised to pay by the groom, or by the groom's father, to the bride at the time of her marriage that legally becomes her property. While the *mehr* is often money, it can also be anything agreed upon by the bride such as jewellery, home goods, furniture, a dwelling or land. *Mehr* is typically specified in the marriage contract signed during an Islamic marriage), very few Hindu women know anything about alimony and maintenance, even of their children, and this stems from the very sacrosanct nature of the Hindu Marriage Act itself, viewed as a holy sacrament, and not merely contractual in nature, but bound by the *Saptapadi* or the *saath pheras*, after which a marriage gets registered in the government records. Most parents of a single woman face social pressure to get their daughters settled and usually don't presume a thing about divorce, still largely regarded as a taboo. Indian parents need to keep evolving and make their stand and support clear that if their daughters suffer torture or harassment, they can come home and have the right to remedy. If this is encouraged, a lot more women will be confident of breaking out of their claustrophobic marriages, and being single again won't be perceived as a life threat,' she advises.

Teach Your Daughters To Be Self-Reliant; Not Sati Savitri, Pativrata, Dulhans!

If teaching your daughters about the law is the way forward, then strengthening her to face the actual system remains another cog in the wheel. 35-year-old marketing professional Aradhana Mehta, (*name changed on request*) battling a bitter domestic violence case for the past 4 years, highlights the harrowing harassment a woman faces once she decides to break out of her wrecked marriage.

Aradhana's ex used to always call her parents and complain about her and then request them never to tell her that he rang. Once he had even lied to them that she had fought at home and threatened suicide. The call came 4-5 days before he and his parents assaulted and dragged Aradhana forcefully from the bedroom to the living area, her mother-in-law all the while egging on her son, saying Aradhana should be thrashed more.

Sadly, as in the case of most single women, Aradhana feels most betrayed by women. 'One of my neighbours in the housing complex where my in-laws lived, shared a warm rapport with me and I always believed we were close. When I was being beaten and she heard my helpless screams being next door, she showed no interest in calling the police or rescuing me. When I asked her why she didn't stand by another woman, her diplomatic answer was that for her, both my husband and I were the same. Later, when I requested her to be my witness, she flatly refused to get involved,' reminisces Aradhana, adding that most women who see her today, living independently, question how she can be so 'normal' and continue to 'dress up and take care of her appearance' after what she has undergone. She's also often told that returning to an empty home is akin to a curse and that she should seek companionship. 'I think, the word divorce denotes a melodramatic tragedy and women like us should always be moping and weeping the absence of a man,' she observes.

Aradhana deliberately chose not to tell anyone about her single status at her workplace because in her earlier PR firm, when there was a whiff of her separation, she had sensed a clear change in the attitude of her female colleagues. Like any single woman of today, she, too, confesses battling acute loneliness, especially the year before last when she contracted dengue and found herself friendless. 'If I threw a party, my friends would all turn up, but in my ill health I only had my maid who I literally begged to be at home with me. Initially when I was married, my childhood best friend, also based in Delhi, used to invite me to her child's birthday celebrations, but stopped after the fourth year, since I was childless and there was a strong disconnect. Post my separation, she stopped inviting me to anniversary parties too, as I wasn't part of a couple anymore. Being single means realigning. You lose friends, you are banned from couple activities, you stick out like a sore thumb,' she claims.

Aradhana's run-in with the police and legal system, in a case like hers, also highlights murky areas where most Indian women are thoroughly ill-equipped. 'When I went to register my case as it had to be done at the nearest police station, the investigating male officer harassed me, posing humiliating questions like: "Did you have an affair?"; "Your husband doesn't look abusive, sure you were on the right track?"; "You are at the peak of your youth, how will you survive without sex?"; "You look desperate, am sure it's why you walked out on your husband!" I raised an objection with the ACP who later fired him for ill-treating a woman,' she recalls bitterly.

At the Crime Against Women's Cell, an officer took Aradhana's brother's number in Guwahati and rang him as he, too, happens to be a police officer, saying: 'Your sister's husband's character doesn't seem to be bad, I think you should investigate the matter more.' A woman's marriage certificate is akin to her character certification—once gone, leads her to be treated worse than a whore, in most cases.'

Single Mothers Soldier On, Despite Social Stigmatization

As more and more single women fight a lonely crusade, joining in are the divorced lot—our struggles, survival and stories almost the same. Among divorced Indian women, 68% are Hindus, 23.3% are Muslims, IndiaSpend.org claimed in a report quoting Census 2011 data on the marital status of Indians. Does a woman's fate solely rest on the vermillion smeared on her forehead? Or is it a more invasive darkness? Are second chances at love easy? Or is the judgement of being a marriage failure a veritable road block?

34-year-old Pratibha Behl, working in an NGO as chief accountant, single mother to Arpan, a 6-year-old suffering from cerebral palsy, says divorce is just the start of a lifelong survival race. 'Once the legal mess clears, and this could take years sometimes, though one hears constantly how the Indian legal system is skewed in favour of women—what is the actual percentage of women speaking up against their husbands and in-laws, and actually going the whole hog to be single again? The law may be pro-women, because today even an adopted single mother's name and signature is enough on a child's passport as his/her legal guardian—but playing dual roles of mother and father are challenging,' she pauses, before adding wisely, 'Never give up your job after marriage and kids, do something. And don't back on parental support or that from your siblings and friends, in the case of walking out. My child goes to special school and then day care for the specially abled, as I have to earn and have no choice but to be a full-time, working mother, though I would love to be there for my kid 24/7. My husband didn't give us a penny, blaming me for producing a retarded child. And I just wanted out as he used to torture us. Today, my focus is on being self-sufficient, so I have removed the word guilt from my dictionary. I know I am an absentee mom in some way, but someday when I raise my son well, I know my battle will be complete. Hopefully, he will never feel that he is only my son. And I, too, will never regret the absence of a man to complete our existence. That's the toughest call—I want to be a proud single woman again!'

Kolkata-born Monikanika Guha, a 33-year-old single mother working as a sales consultant in a leading IT firm, was pushed into an arranged marriage post the failure of a serious romantic relationship by her family who were concerned about her touching 30 and remaining single—a serious taboo, she claims, in a middle-class Bengali family, like hers. 'I chose to keep my dysfunctional marriage a secret from my ageing parents, primarily because my father had spent a fortune on my marriage and mine would be the first unsuccessful marriage in my family,' icily pauses Monikanika who was married for 2 years.

'I earned more than my ex and wasn't ever financially dependent on him, but still I remember removing the price tag from a new shoe I had purchased, because I feared being taunted by my in-laws and ex on spending too much on myself. Every time we went out socially, I was pressurised into wearing *sindoor*, *bindi*, traditional red and white bangles (*shaka* and *pola*) that symbolise marriage with my dress code always fixed on a sari. Even sexually, I remained unfulfilled as my husband literally tore into me, often tying my hands and feet up. It was akin to marital rape,' she recollects, adding poignantly, 'When I conceived, my husband disowned our child, telling me that since I travelled on work, he was certain I was carrying another man's child. He also texted my parents and relatives maligning my character. When I broke the news to my folks and told them that I didn't want to go back, my mother broke down as if all hell had broken loose, and tried counselling me. She even visited my ex's house where my parents were rudely told the child wasn't his and that if I wanted, I could return. That was when I decided I would never agree to a divorce by mutual consent, and would contest it, to reinstate my own dignity as a woman. I wasn't okay being the "*abala nari*".

'Even in my family circles, I was always in the news for being pregnant and calling off my marriage. Like I had committed a crime. The same prejudiced attitude also confronted me at the local police station when I brought up sexual abuse while filing a domestic rape case with the cops giving me stupid smiles, saying that a man has every right to demand sexual gratification from his wife,' grimaces Monikanika.

As a working, divorced woman, Monikanika often travels outside Kolkata for work. The upkeep of her 4-year-old child rests with her widowed mother. 'Mine is a transferable job and I have to be professionally engaged to keep my family running, pay my daughter's school and tuition fees and take care of her extracurricular activities. It's not the ideal scenario, but I don't want to feel guilty for continuing with my career. However, relatives fill my child's ears, telling her how I am an absentee mother, which is why initially whenever I returned home on breaks, my daughter treated me with an attitude that I wasn't her mother and had just come as a visiting guest. At family get-togethers, no one asks me how I am physically or mentally. The topic of conversation would naturally veer to my single status and how I must resettle, so as to ensure a secure future for my daughter. Most of the alliances our close relatives bring are that of divorced men, like finding a single man at my age is next to impossible—as if I am a social misfit.

'Be it at my job interview (Monikanika switched jobs 2 years back) or during my daughter's school admission, I was open about being a single mother, always reassuring my daughter too, that she's born from my heart. I even requested the school authorities to not keep asking about her father's identity. But despite the law being pro single mothers, the truth is that on-ground reality is starkly different. The school curriculum also paints the picture of a typical family with a father and a mother, so my daughter would keep asking who her father is. She would often refer to her imagined father as "Jack" from the nursery rhyme 'Jack and Jill'. These days she says her father's name is Moni. Other children in our colony also tease her saying *"baap ka naam bol"*.

Monikanika, who often finds interested suitors, adds realistically, 'I have desires just as any normal woman and have even had a relationship where I was physical, but long-term, I can't trust a man anymore. I am emotionally insecure, I guess.'

Leave Us Alone: A Divorced Young Woman Cries Foul About So Called Progressives

Chennai-born Jane Jeyakumar, a popular name in the world of radio and now working in Bengaluru, is extremely vocal about the agonising treatment meted out to divorced women by families of so-called progressive men. 'A week away from my 33rd birthday, I was divorced, and single. If that didn't have you tut-tut with disapproval and anxiety attacks, then swallow these words: Divorced. Single. And, mind-fucked. Yes, I said the F word. Because, that's exactly what your tut-tuts have done to me, and to a rising number of divorced 30-year-olds in India. "Oh, she must have slept around. Plus, of course, she can't cook, clean and consummate the marriage. How can she wear such short skirts and expect her husband to be fine? How will she ever find a husband again? She is going to die a crazy, old lady with a dozen cats,"' rants Jane.

She lashes out strongly, 'I've slept around. Because my body has needs. And you won't let me marry your precious, single sons. Because I have a disease called 'divorce'. So I sleep *with* them, because that seems like the only other available option to get closer to them, in the hope that something good will come out of it. He says, "I can't marry you, babe. You know, you are divorced. But you can be my dirty little secret. I will always take care of you." I'm his dirty, little (big in my case) secret. By the way, these are the same guys who want a 'virgin' bride. My last lover said, "I can't help but sleep with you. You are so curvy, so hot. But my mom and sis won't agree to marriage! You are just too open, too sexy and way too vocal."'

Jane points out to the innate double standards that a modern Indian single divorcee is confronted with and that adds to her 'bitch' avatar, 'I can't cook and clean because there's Swiggy, dammit! Also being a food blogger, I get enough free food, plus I work. I can afford a meal outside, and even a maid. I know exactly what I want on my plate and his, just that I don't have the time and inclination to do it myself. I do my laundry, though. And keep a decently clean house. But most men want me to be be a glorified maid, which is not my calling. I don't think prospective mothers-in-law have also ever heard of the word "choice," as most of them weren't allowed to go out and earn a living back in their time. But they should realise that their son isn't solely their pet project, or pet, anymore. He is a grown man. And he needs a wife, NOT another mother.'

Today, despite all the slut shaming and the battle with depression that Jane underwent after the failure of her last romance, she is adamant on finding a man to love, marry and cherish—who will hopefully treat her like an equal and isn't judgmental about her past. 'Isn't it ironic? That their hatred for me can only be answered by love?' she shrugs her shoulders.

STATUS SINGLE: *The most important thing for Indian parents to do is to prepare their daughters for the reality of marriage, instead of painting a rosy picture and sermonising on 'duty and sacrifice'—that is totally passé, given the skyrocketing rates of divorce in India. There is no way a woman should tolerate emotional, mental, verbal or physical violence.*

But before that we must ask ourselves the question that as we prepare and precondition single women to marry, are we on a parallel plane, also educating them on the Indian Penal Code and how they can seek legal recourse if they are violated. The stigma of divorce and the fear of being harassed for remarriage, coupled with the shame a woman dreads descending on her family, forces many women to rot in faulty, abusive marriages. Jumping from one kind of captivity to another. The nature of the cage, perhaps changing. Also, divorced women, like single women, face a staunch moral stereotyping as home-breakers and 'loose' characters. So be it renting a home or starting your own business—be prepared for a certain amount of social shunning and slut-shaming. You owe no one an explanation why your marriage failed, why you chose to now co-parent or why you wish to live away from your parents, sometimes even in the same city. You are divorced, not deranged.

Chapter Nine

Friend vs. Unfriend

One of my girlfriends was going through a rocky professional patch and I was helping her to move forward. On one weekend, as I invited her home for dinner, she asked me if she could get her husband along. Now, while I think her hubby is a great guy, I was somehow not in the mood for male company, not wishing to be formal and dress up. And honestly, he wasn't my buddy, just yet. Our past conversations had been formal and stilted. Yet, I wasn't sure how she would take my saying that while her husband's company was pleasing on several past occasions, an evening with a close friend sometimes meant just that. I discussed this with one of my other single girlfriends and asked her advice on how I could break the news gently or whether I should simply be blunt and say I was interested in a girly date or perhaps needed to infuse a dash of diplomacy or just call off the meeting. My single girl pal laughed saying, 'Dude, you should seriously stop hanging out with married women, coz in India weekends are strictly for *patidev* and potty training! There is no way in hell she's coming minus the hubby in tow. Be prepared and don't tell me I didn't warn you.'

To be fair to myself, my friend circle—that's been steadily waning since I turned 30—is presently a mix of married women *and* single ones, which is why I dissed her caution, and decided to tell the first friend exactly what I was feeling. 'Hey, think I can have hubby over next time when there are more men? Right now there will only be my dad at home and I am sure he will be bloody bored just by himself, with all our girl talk,' I made the first move over a WhatsApp text.

There were a few seconds of stupefied silence before my friend replied:

'No way, he's used to it all the time, and he is so looking forward to the evening, just like me.'

I gave up and texted my single friend, admitting self-defeat: 'You were right. The message failed. Have to deal with husband. Why can't she just get it?'

My friend sent a wink emoji, adding, 'Look, I told you. Married women operate like leaches, so if you entertain them, they usually land up in pairs. And frankly, sometimes even they are equally bored, like us, so perhaps she's also wanting a change of scene or is plain lazy to travel back and forth to your place, and needs a chauffeur cum male protector. Marriage is a habit, they aren't used to doing things separately. It's like a thumb rule. Wait till she has kids. You will have to endure them too. Does she have a dog? Lol.'

Can Single Women Be Friends With Married Women, Minus Husbands And Kids?

That night I just couldn't sleep. I actually thought of the number of times—in the past few years and in the cities I'd visited—I'd actually met a married woman friend, alone, sans the excess baggage of hubby, kids, in-laws, maids and pets. I asked myself if planning socialising with married gal pals was just as easy and effortless as hooking up with a fellow single is, and whether I had to always manipulate and manoeuvre my routine to fit in their busier-than-me schedules—kids' tuitions, karate or art classes, husband coming to pick them up post work by a certain prefixed time, mother-in-law's doctor's appointments and maids joining and leaving. Whether our conversation was boring and banal, and if like this time, I just couldn't say what I wanted or rather how I preferred to spend my Saturday evening.

With most Indian women in their mid-30s transitioning into wives and mothers, was our friendship difficult, often distant and even formal after a point? Was this the primary reason why after the 30s, every woman who remains in the 'missed the bus' category grapples with a gnawing aloneness and must choose to make peace with her own company on numerous occasions—the reason behind the rise of virtual connections on social media, meet-up groups and solo-women travel options.

Was this why I had personally also begun hating attending parties where I calculated I'd inevitably be the only single woman who, apart from being asked why I was still manless, would be fixed up with just about any man—the suggestions ranging from pure condescension, genuine sympathy to sugary warmth. Even if the truth was I had no interest in being hooked up so randomly or asked the dumbest question in the book—'How come a good-looking, successful, popular woman like you is still single?'

Beats me, duh!

35-year-old divorcee, Priyanka Chettri (*name changed on request*), who heads the digital media service in a PR firm based in Gurgaon, says that the tussle between married and single women is largely based on a sense of struggle on whose life is more 'complete', with women naturally prone to a same-sex competitiveness. She says, 'Married women are disposed to lecturing us on settling down and not spending our lives alone, while whining about their daily lives and the constant hustle-bustle of responsibilities that comes with raising kids; whereas, single women sometimes subconsciously try and prove their lot is better, as they have less baggage, wanting to assert how they are equally complete in themselves. I think what happens is that women who are single are so used to being picked on and probed on their singlehood, that they become sort of cagey about it—defending with the intensity of an alpha woman. It's like when I walk into a party, I can immediately sense roving eyes and women especially curious as to why I am unaccompanied by my ex or why I've suddenly stopped wearing my *mangalsutra* and *sindoor* that used to be my trademark style in some way, being married for 6 years. I haven't announced my single status on Facebook as yet, and so I think it does confuse a lot of people who are naturally inquisitive. While I am okay being asked about my separation, as it was mutually agreed upon, I am not okay with the underlying pity, as I am then viewed as a helpless, sad, recently single woman, who desperately needs to hook a man for marriage to escape being stigmatised by society.

'I, too, have recently distanced myself from a few of my women friends from my school days who just want to know how I plan to lead the rest of my life, if I want to remarry, crave a child, how my parents are dealing with my divorce and who inevitably start a conversation with the word "sorry". I admit that I miss a partner, but loneliness isn't something that a marriage or a child can necessarily solve. I think when we start respecting each other's choices and not judge superficially, more women can be sisters, and embrace each other's journeys without discrimination or labelling. Something every single woman hates.'

Are the worlds, life experiences and struggles of single and married women starkly different and is that the sole reason my core circle has visibly shrunk to mostly single women friends, divorcees, a couple of childless couples who, I must admit, have fewer hang-ups, and barely two odd married-and-with-kids couples? Would I in time also grow to nurture two distinctly diverse friend groups or would I have no single friends, soon? And what about guy friends—where have *they* all disappeared after marriage and kids? Were they actually no different from my girlfriends who got hitched and fell off the footloose-and-fancy-free category?

Do Singles Stick Out Like A Sore Thumb In A Sea Of Couples?

Hemchhaya De, single at 39, and editor of a leading regional magazine based in Kolkata, rakes up the clear discrimination that divides the two subsects, claiming the mindset of married people is cut off from the life journey of a single woman habituated to doing things independently.

Even the male glare is no different, she declares. 'My school gang comprised a lot of men and most of them today are well-placed in the IT or corporate sector with high-flying careers and hefty six-figure salaries,' says Hemchhaya, who first began noticing the differences in attitudes between them whenever they'd plan a holiday together. Being single, she was perennially dumped with the responsibility of ticket reservations, online hotel bookings, things that Hemchhaya feels should have ideally been a joint, shared responsibility, since she, too, has an equally high-pressure job. 'In no way do I think my life is any less busier or more hassle-free than that of a corporate biggie. Yet, I was always made to feel that since I was unmarried, I have no responsibilities and was something of a *vela*,' she looks back, ironically pointing out that the spouses of her male friends—educated women who were simply housewives, were conveniently kept out of this pressure of holiday planning.

'Being a wife bestows a woman with a certain kind of privilege in India—as though rearing kids is a novelty. And when I'd suggest they ask their better halves to also pitch in, I got the vibe I am belittling them. My men friends labelled me a headstrong, opinionated feminist and I have even heard the line, "You need to get laid" a million times, implying that as a single woman, since I am sexless by inference, I have become frustrated and ill-tempered.'

Hemchhaya's observations take me back to a time when a male colleague of mine said, sounding like my mother, 'Don't be so choosy about guys, soon you will feel like Cinderella minus her glass slippers.' Others have openly interrogated me on my sex life—the obvious assumption that good girls don't indulge in casual sex as they are tied down to morality and live with family, conveniently thrust on me, too. Probably one of the reasons over time I, too, have started trimming my Facebook friends list, frankly nauseated by suspiciously happy pictures of couple selfies and every intimate, incy-wincy, disgusting detail about kids—a constant live-streaming of engagement to marriage to pregnancy to delivery room to family holidays to birthday parties to anniversaries to second pregnancies.

'Actually, social media is a place where women seek validation of their existences, more like propaganda for your perfect little life that is so complete and that you need the world to watch and praise. I know of old friends who were just like me at one time, and who, after marrying and soon becoming mothers, do nothing other than post constant pictures and gooey updates about their child's day-to-day routine, an almost second-to-second progress report. It's tiring, and I really miss the same woman who once used to be so outgoing, cerebral and fun to hang out with and wonder, is she really this happy? Coordinating an outing with a married friend is like a rigorous workout... most women obligated first to serving the institution of marriage than hanging out with a single friend on her time.

'Also, there is this tacit implication that an unmarried spinster is probably a dried-up, old hag and that she's not getting any sexual pleasure, which is often viewed as an almost proud achievement amongst married woman. I really find it fatiguing at times to be in a party dominated by couples, which is what you'd mostly find in India after a certain age and point—where either you have to silently endure long hours of debate on maids, nursery admissions and swimming pools or be probed on your personal life and randomly hooked up, like everyone is doing you a massive favour. As if being single is a communicable disease that must not spread. The scope of socialising without being judged is rare. These days, either I just opt out of these occasions, or tell people off saying I'm not in a relationship, but have a whole lot of fuck buddies. It shuts them up. In this country, single women share the same socially deviant status as a gay or disabled person, and I can't help wonder, if there are active communities to support single mothers and for the LGBT community—how come there is none we know of for single women?' questions Hemchhaya.

I think of my married friends as I write this piece, especially one of my closest buddies from college, who I distanced myself from deliberately since all she ever did when I made an effort to reconnect with her in Kolkata was lecture me on how time was running out for marriage and how as a single child my life after my parents would be a disaster. She also made it a point to talk about having kids with an undercurrent of sympathy in her voice.

'What are your parents doing? Why don't you keep aside an hour daily to scrutinise profiles on *BharatMatrimony*? Are you interested in men at all?' she would pry, her eyebrows raised, a strange suffocation in her concern, like she was trapped herself.

Ironically, her own sister, 2 years older than us, is still single—something my friend conveniently never mentioned while sermonising me. I hated the way she'd always drag in my family—as if it was their fault I hadn't found a companion. Like she had a solid chip on her shoulders. Me deviating from the topic to my books would always be met with news of her husband's international postings and how rushed her life was—like we were suddenly competing. Looking at her on Facebook, too, started seeming arduous after a point, as she sported thick vermillion and the traditional white and red bangles a married Bengali woman is supposed to wear—her pictures mostly with women just like herself—married, sporting baby bumps, pot-bellied husbands or growing children, on international vacations. We started avoiding each other... slowly. Looking back, she was the first bleed—the first girlfriend I wanted to let go of because we had not just drifted away, but I had lost her to the vortex of marriage and motherhood. She was no longer the girl I knew. Her life had become someone else's story.

Making Do With Just Yourself: The Fear And Reality Of Adult Aloneness

Sowmya Iyer, 46, and originally from Bengaluru, who works as a freelance PR professional in Delhi—and someone who has been living alone for the past 17 years—says the constant insistence on companionship that most single women harp on, even if their priority isn't marriage after a certain age, tends to also limit us as a sex. With most of her friends getting married, Sowmya claims they started building up their own isolated islands where only friends of spouses and fellow couples with kids were permitted entry. There was no connect between them anymore, except nostalgia for a distant past that was soon overtaken by school timetables, holiday homework, in-law visits and packing for husband's tours and tiffin *dabbas*. It did take her time to adjust to this overwhelming adult aloneness that especially deepened during festivals, which in India are positioned and advertised as spending quality time with family. But today, from a movie, birthdays, hospital emergency, a music concert to the disco, Sowmya has pushed herself to go alone just about everywhere and is comfortable with herself. And, in an endeavour to meet like-minded people who may have the same interests as hers, she attended a few meet-ups in Delhi, but found the conversations restrictive. 'It was more of a casual and superficial timepass, rather than a platform to build a lasting friendship, or maybe it's hard to form enduring friendships after a certain age, especially in today's hectic urban maze where we are all grappling with a pervasive loneliness, despite juggling such frenzied paces of work and lives. Actually, the mystery of why we feel alone remains unclear to me because I sense this isolation even amongst my married friends,' she analyses.

Is Community-Building For Single Men And Women Possible Minus Sexual Hook-Ups?

With the loss of old friends, a constant striving to make peace with oneself and the emergence of networking communities to cope with this change in the social and psychological mind space, my thoughts veer back to a single girlfriend who is active in several meet-up communities and is always hooking up with new people. Is her constant reaching out for new experiences a sign of her own intrinsic loneliness or an indication of her youthfulness that makes her always seek greener pastures so as to preserve it? Or is she, as a lot of my other girlfriends speculate, looking for a guy to settle down with at any cost? Does a meet-up equal to a dating app—where the idea is to land yourself a hot date and a couple experience, after months of being single?

29-year-old entrepreneur Rohit Jain, who started his own meet-up called 'Single By Choice' in June 2014, that now stands at 64 members, says for 2 years he was seeking an experiential high, by participating in various meet-ups himself all over Delhi and NCR.

'Personally, I was done with dating and was simply seeking good company—a bunch of people who enjoyed literature, restaurant-hopping, travelling, theatre, and stand-up comedy. The idea behind 'Single by Choice' germinated from building a community of single men and women who met say once a month and hung out together in a largely public space that was both safe and fun,' claims Jain who admits that a lot of people primarily use these platforms for sexual hook ups.

He adds, 'While I do have strict filters and interested people need to answer a five-point questionnaire that helps me determine their intent behind joining us officially, one is occasionally bombarded with messages from men like: "Can we have sex?" or "Will you make friendship with me?" Or a pretty girl walks into an event and all the men straightaway start asking for her number and the next thing you know is she's being WhatsApped and hit upon—this, even after members are advised not to initiate any conversation until they have met the other person personally at an event, which is why we curate these events with utmost care.

'And while there is no membership fee per say, no friends of friends are allowed entry. We are clear that this meet-up is not for any lovey-dovey or hanky-panky affair, and while flirting is typical and harmless, so is a relationship if it culminates between people organically from the initial friendship forged on this platform. Our age bracket is above 25, with the oldest person in our group being in his mid-50s. While women should take care of their personal safety, I have never harboured any gender bias in the group and recently removed a woman, too, as she was reluctant to share her profile picture on the meet-up page.'

34-year-old Jasmine Bedi, an active member of the meet-up group, 'Single by Choice', lives with her parents who are not only supportive on the career front, but also liberal enough to allow her own marriage decision. Jasmine agrees that the frequency of friendship diminishes as women get married and have their own family obligations. With the couple circle being very different most of the time Jasmine finds her lifestyle and life choices often not matching her friends'. She cites the example of a recent friend's daughter's birthday party, where she felt like the odd one out because almost everyone present was a mother accompanied by a child and there was nothing in common among them. Jasmine has been trying to travel alone internationally—a practice she kicked off by going out with members of 'Single by Choice' on a trekking excursion to McLeod Ganj.

Meet-Ups For Single Women Rarely Find Takers

46-year-old divorcee Roli Sinha who has two grown-up children, aged 23 and 21 respectively, and is frequent on the same meet-up, says that she's lost most of her male friends thanks to their suspicious wives who always think a divorced woman is available sexually and comes with a hidden agenda. She adds that given the negative vibes, one is forced to stay away from nagging, married women friends who are perpetually trying to match-make, as if a woman's single status makes them more uncomfortable. 'There is a lot of emotional dishonesty and when you get hit on by married men, you realise how there is rampant infidelity and convenient open marriages, minus the honest admission that it is a boundary-less relationship,' observes Roli. She says that meet-ups just for single women are quite rare, find very little membership, with sometimes as little as 2 or 3 women actually surfacing at events and one also often witnesses men becoming members of these communities, with barely any screening by the coordinator.

Roli also highlights another common roadblock in these communities. 'Age is turning out to be one the hardest barriers to overcome. Counting on men from one's own age group to possess the intellectual and emotional maturity that any decent relationship demands is futile. Very often, the connect happens with men, either 10 years younger or 20 years older. And while we may enjoy each other's company, it seems impossible to ignore the elephant in the room—the looming age difference. Typically, such relationships, no matter how wonderful and lasting they might appear, are mostly relegated to "only friendships", and after safely friend-zoning the person who stimulates us emotionally and cerebrally and is a nice individual overall, the two parties continue to look for a person who will be age-wise more acceptable in society. And we all know that the search for perfection is endless,' she adds.

From Singlehood To Sisterhood: Can Women Bridge The Gap?

46-year-old, never married, Vibha Parekh (*name changed on request*), who created a successful, pan-Delhi group for women called 'Outdoorsy Single Women Companions' (age 30 to 50), says that after quitting a busy corporate career and now being involved in her family business and living with her parents, she realised over time that she had lost most of her girlfriends to marriage and motherhood, because of which loneliness inevitably crept in. 'Entering one's 40s in India and being single invites negative jeers. People don't ask if one is searching for a soulmate. Instead they probe on what could be wrong because of which one did not marry. Actually, Indian society looks down upon and disapproves of single, ageing women. Hence, there was a strong need to discover new companions who did not question our singlehood or mock at us for failing to find a life partner,' reasons Vibha.

Vibha, who earlier worked in a corporate setup in Chennai and lost her job when the company laid-off over 10,000 people, has an interesting personal experience to share. 'When one is single, others just assume you to be sexually deprived and desperate, and every man primarily wants to sleep with you. Also, if you are glamorous, like I coloured my hair, sported bright lip colours, dressed sharply, it meant I was pruning myself for attracting sexual attention. There exists a deep-rooted bias against single women who are somewhere expected to live the life of a nun/ascetic. So, if a woman wears a lot of make-up, drinks, smokes and parties, and is single, she's labelled a slut and perceived to be leading a promiscuous lifestyle; whereas, a married woman can get away even by sleeping around, as her *sindoor* and *mangalsutra* are her saviours,' she wryly observes.

Weary of being hit on by random men in her professional space, when Vibha landed this job in Chennai, she used the identity and name of her dad's cousin who was married with two grown-up children, as her virtual spouse. She also sported a huge (fake) diamond engagement ring and a *mangalsutra* on occasions like Karwa Chauth, and kept her nephew's picture on her desk just so that male colleagues backed off from investigating her personal life. And female colleagues stopped asking uncomfortable questions. Vibha even had a company health insurance made in her supposed husband's name. She also carried the same status on her Facebook and LinkedIn accounts, and deleted both when she was laid off. Today, however, she feels no guilt for what she did because at least she wasn't being hit on by men from 20 to 65 who just wanted sex, sex and more sex.

Vibha admits to wanting to live on her own, and says she has observed more and more single women comfortable with the idea of staying independently, not having kids and indulging in guilt-free one-night stands or no-strings-attached relationships and even polygamy.

Urban loneliness, losing friends to the frenzied pace of their own couple lives, a mechanical routine balance between work and home, making do with oneself, facing social and sexual discriminations and the pressure of looking pretty and perfect on social media is something that haunts every single woman in India—something a dating app or an online meet-up community merely proposes to solve—sometimes just filling up a deeper void.

STATUS SINGLE: *A lot of single women talk about their space being sacred to them, but the truth is it does get really lonely out there. And as a single friend recently put it, 'Once your girlfriends or male buddies or cousins or siblings get hitched, there is a palpable difference—your worlds are starkly different.' I get where she was coming from, being now the only single woman left in my friend circle that anyway diminishes with age and job commitments and people generally relocating and constantly shifting base, and of course the life changes and responsibilities that come post marriage.*

Over time and as you age, one has to let go of certain married friends whose lives solely revolve around their husbands and children, who have nothing else to discuss other than nannies, in-laws, summer camps and tuition classes. Also, single friends who are desperate for relationships and disappear the moment they manage to hook a guy, like they just won a jackpot or something.

Don't feel guilty if you want to deliberately excuse yourself from parties where you are aware that you may be the only single person in the room—it's thus perfectly okay to politely enquire about the guest list, before committing on your presence, because there are evenings you would rather surf the internet in your own bedroom, alone, than be hooked up with just about any random guy and asked the most inanely irritating question, 'How come you aren't seeing someone?' or the classic, 'So for how long have you been single?'

Learn to consciously make an effort to tell your married friends that while you may be genuinely fond of their spouses and kids—not every gathering, outing or movie date can include them. Couplehood isn't mandatory. While your social circle may have shrunk to an embarrassingly small number, saving your sanity could be more important. Follow a simple thumb rule—don't pretend to like someone in your friend's life or your own. So if your friend's wife and you don't have anything in common, there is no reason to go out of your way to accommodate that person in your life—notice and nurture the difference between politeness and compulsion. Growing up means taking certain hard people-decisions as well. Some relationships outgrow you, the others you may have to prune yourself and move on from buddies to acquaintances.

Chapter Ten

From 'I Quit' to 'I Do'

ONE OF MY FATHER'S favourite lines when I was employed full-time used to be, 'You're not cut out for a job,' which quite honestly made no sense to me. It's a line I've periodically heard ever since I quit my first job, post a gruelling 6-year stint, where I was paid a pittance, and mainly stuck on being idealistic about my profession, journalism. Before you draw conclusions, let me be upfront—my job karma is as faulty as my relationship karma, so even though I don't have a problem finding a man or a job, inevitably they turn out to be not quite right for me. Or maybe turning 30 had to do with my inner revolution that started off when I quit a high-flying PR job minus a substantial life plan, except writing a book that I'd carried within me for years, staring as I was at a meagre bank balance that I subsequently chose to exhaust on a month-long Australian vacation, hoping to 'find myself'.

Today, 4 years and 5 book deals later, I can safely conclude that 'finding myself' is a never-ending, thankless, nerve-wracking process involving a lot more than travelling solo, reflective meditation sessions or keeping a gratitude journal. It's a lot like being single, in a way—constant regrouping and battling real-life challenges.

'You sure you just want to write?' my first editor posed an existential question, sounding oddly maternal, her words soaked with the same sense of foreboding my mother demonstrated. Actually, turning entrepreneur of any kind, giving up a real day job that pays your bills to start or pursue a long-standing dream, flying solo and managing to survive in a mostly male-dominated professional space, relying on just your talent, negotiating your future as a singleton in a couple-crowded space, constantly explaining what you do to others, or why you needed a sabbatical, remains, for me, an everyday, uphill struggle. I often wonder how women who conceive, for instance, are never probed on why they chose to take a career break—even as single women are typically placed under a radar?

Let's face it, in India, women are groomed primarily for marriage. Businesses are largely handed over to the boys in the *khandaan*. Single women are never actually seen or portrayed in popular culture as fighting tooth and nail for their inheritance, scared to severe sacred family ties, conditioned as we all are to sacrifice and surrender to the will of patriarchy. Despite a 2005 ruling wherein the Government of India amended its inheritance laws to ensure daughters enjoyed equal rights to inherit their parent's land and property—on-ground reality remains starkly different.

A 2014 study released by United Nations Women India and Landesa, a US-headquartered non-profit working to improve land rights for women and men, claimed that despite their time spent working in orchards, cotton fields, and rice paddies, and changes to inheritance laws, women rarely inherited the land that has sustained them and that they have sustained. The survey of more than 1,400 women and 360 men in agricultural districts with a large number of women farmers in 3 Indian states—Andhra Pradesh, Bihar, and Madhya Pradesh—found that just 1 in 8 women whose parents own agricultural land inherit any of it. This, despite, nearly 80% of all rural women labouring in fields.

Is the urban, single young woman any different when she has the courage to dare, takes the plunge to start a new enterprise, take over an existing family business or demand an equal slice of the pie, surpassing the men of the household while acting as her own boss? Is she likely to confront the same, deep-rooted sexism that one faces when trying to rent a flat alone or walk into a bar on a Friday night minus a male companion? Why single women must work harder at social acceptance and even professionally, how it's an uphill battle for more legroom and a sense of propriety? How is starting something new more of a challenge for single women?

Kolkata-based Ruchhita Kazaria, single at 35, and born to a Marwari family, started her own advertising agency, Arcee Enterprises in 2004. She has since faced the backlash of trying to conduct business ethically, sans the lofty backing of a husband's surname or the validation of a male partner. Running her own firm for the past 12 years single-handedly has led to Ruchhita believing that 'women in general, unfortunately, are still predominantly perceived as designers, backoffice assistants, PR coordinators, anything but the founder-owner of an entity.'

To validate her cynicism, she cites the example of a meeting in 2014 at a five-star hotel's coffee shop with a renowned city-based industrialist. 'We smiled briefly. His eyes, however, remained restless. Tired of his darting glances, when I finally asked him point-blank what was on his mind, he replied with a sheepish grin: "Arey! I'm waiting for your husband." I smiled back politely, updating him that the company belonged to me alone; and that I was single. We proceeded to have green tea before biding adieu,' she concludes.

Single Women Entrepreneurs Face Deep-Seated Moral Prejudice And Sexism

In professions like Ruchhita's, where client engagement is optimum, the baggage of being a single woman often camouflages a deep-seated societal and sexist prejudice. Ruchhita claims that while married women are also propositioned in nearly every job field, single women are more easily perceived as being available, and sexually frustrated, and hence willing to compromise for achieving professional success. 'Almost all men within my circle—social and business acquaintances alike—have taken a chance and probed into my alleged "loneliness" and "bodily requirements" at some point.'

Initially, to save herself the horror of being hit upon and asked out by random strangers, Ruchhita confesses how she'd blatantly lie saying she was in an existing relationship and that her lover didn't appreciate her night-outs. Her firm, that also boasts of a vertical of event management, is into organising fashion shows, after-parties and allied events, and here, Ruchhita highlights, the misplaced stereotyping that occurs daily, thanks to her clothes that don't reveal her cleavage or aren't above her knees. Pegged as 'boring', she's often told what a complete misfit she is for the glamour industry. 'The industry probably needs to take the blame for such derogatory comments, since single women are easily stereotyped.'

Needing to socialise for the sake of healthy business networking, Ruchhita, who mostly attends parties alone, looks back on the myriad experiences of arriving and leaving solo. 'In October 2014, I was approached by a friend who asked me if I was "secretly" dating someone, probably finding it difficult to digest that a single woman could head a company minus a male counterpart and even socialise sans an arm candy.' Within the next fifteen minutes, the same friend sought to fill Ruchhita in with details on Marwari couples and a gang that indulged in swapping, threesomes and orgies, encouraging her emphatically to be a part of this 'discreet' group, to loosen herself and maintain a healthy hormonal balance.

Lately, Ruchhita adds that she finds a lot of married, ageing men interested in her. On many an occasion, she's even been sheepishly told to 'arrange' and 'supply' eye-candies and arm-candies by many a client. Initially uncomfortable with the out-of-line requests, over time, she mustered enough courage to speak back.

Offbeat, Creative Professions Meet Larger Familial Resistance

Be it family, society or even within one's own sex—finding a solo professional path is a tough call for a singleton and more so if your background is conservative and tradition-oriented. Mumbai based top fashion photographer, 37-year-old Sarika Gangwal, who belongs to an obscure village in Madhya Pradesh, quit her job as a successful gaming designer to pursue her passion—photography. Initially, Sarika's mother would be extremely anxious about her career path, her only exposure to the medium being in the form of male photographers who would shoot weddings in Singhana, from where the family hails.

Sarika says, 'She also saw a lot of boys, hoping to get me married off, but when nothing clicked, I told her to search for my sisters instead. Today, my older and younger sisters are happily married, but I know my path is different and somewhere I thank my single status that has made it possible for me to pursue a challenging career like photography, as I don't have kids or a husband to look after and be answerable to. I can come and go as I please. Thanks to me breaking free, a lot of young girls from my native place have been allowed to go out and seek professional employment, and when my name is taken in this regard, being a first, it now makes my mother proud. Personally, however, I find women to be more negative and they can't seem to support or digest the idea of a single, successful woman. Even amongst my clients, it's the women who haggle unprofessionally and try to make life miserable.'

Like Sarika, Kolkata-based cinematographer, 38-year-old Sonali Sarkar, an only child born and raised in the US, relocated back to her roots after her father's untimely demise. 'I hated the idea of returning to India as to me the US was "my" country until then. Back home, I was often the odd one, since I wasn't well-versed with the culture and was teased for my foreign accent. What made it worse was my mother being ill-treated as a widow, her condition no better than a social outcast, back in those days. She would be denied entry during auspicious occasions, a discriminatory attitude inflicted upon us, even within our own family. All these experiences infused a negative feeling in her till she put her foot down and insisted on snapping ties with her extended family.'

Sonali, who has been passionate about photography since childhood, chose to pursue the unconventional stream of cinematography at the prestigious Film and Television Institute of India (FTII), Pune, post her Mass Communication college degree, moving to Mumbai shortly after passing out. 'It was hard to sustain myself there and I was sure television wasn't my thing, which I would have had to join to survive, so I returned to Kolkata in 2006,' adds Sonali, who was in again for another culture shock of sorts.

'Many women fall prey to the notion that cinematography is a man's job. You have to put in labour, which a lot of women think is not possible for us to achieve. But in reality, cinematography is a mental job. Even if a woman is unable to do the camera work herself, she could appoint others for the same, but the creation part is what she's solely responsible for. As a cinematographer, I had to mostly man a crew of electricians and lightmen and I discovered a rigid resistance to taking instructions from a woman boss. One of the directors I was in talks with for a film, sent me to meet the producer, where I immediately sensed the need to grant him a sexual favour. Thankfully, I fled the scene. Another time upon a friend's recommendation, I engaged in talks with a woman boss at an agency, who refused to give me the project despite favourably receiving my portfolio, telling my friend in a sexist manner that a woman DOP means she will suffer period pain.

'Having lived abroad, people easily embrace change, unlike India, where there is little acceptance to what we consider new or rare. Marriage is thus seen as a sort of face-saver that grants a woman the legal license to get away from the fierce social and moral glare. But being single after a certain age immediately sends out a signal that she's the type who's not settled down, as she wants to have 'fun'. As an Indian-American, today, I love this country and hold my head high as a single woman,' grittily remarks Sonali, who's keen to diversify and is soon planning on setting up a café as well as start an agency of her own, given her varied copywriting, filmmaking and designing experience.

Singles Seen As Sex Objects Even Professionally

With marriage largely seen as a woman's character certificate, sadly even in the professional ambit, Bengaluru-based Shanthala Mruthyunjaya, a single mother to two college-goers, recalls how as a young widow in her early 20s, her life was tumultuously transformed when from leading the luxurious life of a wife, she was unexpectedly catapulted into the real world, forced by unfortunate circumstances to earn a livelihood on her own. Married off at 18, Shanthala survived an abusive marriage straddled with two kids, and played the role of a co-sister, wife, mother and daughter-in-law for over a decade. Her in-laws being extremely conservative never encouraged her further education and though she struggled with finishing college, she'd always be dumped with housework before and after classes, with zilch support even from her spouse. Belonging to the cloistered Lingayat community, she would be told girls from families such as hers don't go outside and seek work.

Life took a sudden U-turn for Shanthala, when at 28, she lost her husband in a car accident and faced a sudden question mark on the way forward in life and supporting her children's education. She joined the job ranks as a recruitment consultant and crossed over to a team lead in a new company within a year-and-a-half. But the ill health of both her parents led to yet another drastic career shift. 'Initially, I started after-school English classes to keep afloat, slowly diversifying into soft skills training for companies and the government, in partnership with a female friend,' recounts Shanthala, who is today the director of a private limited company that only hires female employees, except hired external male consultants, and is also a part of the prestigious Skill India Project.

As a widow and single woman, Shanthala says, 'I've been forced to dress in a particular fashion, especially while interacting with government officials whose first stare is invariably fixated on my cleavage followed by my toes—to gauge whether I am wearing the traditional *mangalsutra* and silver toe rings. The moment they arrive at the conclusion that I am a single woman entrepreneur, I immediately sense a change in their body language.

'It's not easy at home either. In my case, for instance, my parents were unhappy that I used to stay out for long hours and attend client calls and meetings in faraway places that were mostly male dominated. I was often interrogated as soon as I returned home late and made to feel guilty for being an absentee parent,' she admits.

Surviving in a male-dominated professional space has meant a lot of single women like Shanthala having no choice but to learn to think and operate like a man—and yet, she adds, the moment she walks in through the front door, the emotional focus instantly shifts as she is immediately expected to be a typical mother or an obedient daughter. 'The fact that you are running your own home, paying bills and taking care of an entire family's emotional and financial needs, together with managing a full-fledged business empire is conveniently forgotten, even by your kids who hold you accountable for the smallest thing being out of place,' Shanthala rues.

Listening to stories of these gutsy single women entrepreneurs made me recall a personal experience. My father has recently started a manufacturing business and every time I ask him to involve me in the same, he says selling weighing equipment isn't something a creative person will enjoy. The fact that I am also bad at handling finances is perhaps another sore spot and yet, I can't wonder why certain professions are automatically ticked off the list as something a woman can't handle on her own? I have asked myself if I were a boy or was married by now, would my dad be comfortable handing over the reins of the business, sans second thoughts? The thought that at 39, I could still have a slim chance of getting married—is that another mental deterrent? Or is it the dealing with men, largely, that he is wary off—a protective parent to an only daughter?

Failure Of Marriage And Learning The Math: Single Women Start From Scratch

Bengaluru-based 41-year-old Ishita Agarwal (*name changed on request*) points out to the harsh lessons about money and shareholding that her marriage and impending separation taught her. 'It's easy to fall in love at 22, even easier for Marwari girls to get married at 23, especially if the other side belongs to the same caste. This was 1999, in Kolkata, when I also co-founded a technology company with my husband. I worked as hard or possibly harder, completely dedicated myself to the organisation, and left my last leg of CA to focus on the business. However, something didn't sit right. From the day of formally founding the company, to getting investors into the business, I was never once made a shareholder of the company. I asked why and was told that it's all in the family. In fact, for the 12 years of my working in the company in India, I wasn't paid a fair wage. Sometimes, I brought up the unfair pay, to which my husband responded that I could go work elsewhere,' says Ishita. She adds ironically, 'My husband was paid a fair salary, as was his father who was helping run the accounts team and calling all financial shots. The business did fairly well, too. However, my salary didn't come close to my husband's at any point. And, of course, no shareholding. In the meantime, I launched an events business as an interest, which also had my husband as the shareholder and not me. He played no role in running the business, except discourage me multiple times. At one point, my husband agreed to transfer the shareholding to me. Papers were signed, and never seen again.'

In the midst of a crumbling marriage and a move overseas, Ishita looks back, 'My husband shuttled between Kolkata and the US. I had no choice as my daughter was giving a local Board exam. So I spent time on myself, began getting fit (I weighed 106 kgs back then) and travelling as well. My husband didn't like me reclaiming my freedom. "You are no longer scared as you don't have any elders sitting on your head", "why are you losing weight?", "your emails are not written properly", were some of the comments I heard. In 2016, I went on a reconciliatory trip with him where he turned physically violent. Twice he threatened me with separation on that trip, even accusing me of an affair. He also gave me a list of men not to speak to. I was confused because I was fine with the idea of a separation. When we returned, my husband threatened me again. This time I calmly retorted: "Let's do it." Much drama ensued. I resigned from the company I was working in. Anyways, there was a lot of money due to me from them.'

Ishita's children today are in their teens. 'My husband wanted to take my son's custody, and grant me custody of my daughter. The first term's document was drafted after a discussion with his parents, his brother-in-law and him. I did not bring in any representation from my side. My father was 80, a third stage cancer survivor, and that was the immediate family I had. I didn't think it wise to involve him. My father-in-law called him, accusing me of having an affair with a golfer. On two separate occasions, my father-in-law called me a "bad woman". My mother-in-law mouthed lines like, "*Puchho, kabhi humne isse mara hai kya?*" and "*Humare baad sab tumhara hain.*" Not only did I not have my rightful shareholding in a company I'd built, I soon had no job or income security and found myself in a new city, too. I was given tempting offers to return to Kolkata, where all my expenses would be paid, I would get a separate house, etc. My husband even offered to put the kids in full boarding. Currently, they are in a weekly one which gives me almost 3 days of the week to be together. I won't agree to this,' says Ishita who moved base to Bengaluru 6 months ago.

'I'd like to tell women reading this story to always keep finances separate and never work for a spouse or a family business where you do not get compensated fairly and equally. Patriarchy is a slow mental poison. Today, I know a lot of amazing people in Bengaluru and live in a lovely house. I am slowly building up work. I look forward to my weekends with my teens and meeting my friends. Divorce is yet to be filed. I am probably a non-category right now. Separated, I guess. It has also been a year since I've been financially supporting myself,' Ishita sums up.

Single Women and Sexual Predators

Single women who work in male-dominated sectors are still, even as we exist in the 21st century, exposed to typical male chauvinism. They are considered easy prey for married men who often think that they are doing the women a great favour by helping them satisfy basic sexual urges. Comments like, 'Why is an attractive woman like you still unmarried?' or 'Come with me and your company will benefit financially' are commonplace, and fending off unwanted suitors is an art that has to be developed very early if you want to keep them at a safe distance.

Negotiating lecherous males and their over-suspicious wives, and simultaneously getting your work done, is like walking a tight rope! Delhi-based Tarini Singh (*name changed on request*) was in her 40s when her father's sudden death 15 years back catapulted her into the position of heading his engineering company that worked mainly with the government. Exposed to an environment with very few single women, she had a difficult time managing to survive, with her morals intact. Thankfully today, the stringent 'sexual harassment laws' have made it easier for Tarini, as officers are wary of meeting her alone. She agrees that the scales are heavily tipped against single women working in male-dominated sectors, but confidently claims that if you stick to your moral values you can succeed on your own terms.

Women Are Women's Worst Enemies: In Life And Work

28-year-old Apsara Reddy, party spokesperson for AIADMK, based in Chennai, has undergone a trial by fire to claim her position as a proud, independent transgender woman today. She draws attention to the glaring discriminatory treatment that a woman with an alternate sexuality faces from both the sexes. 'As a single, transgender woman I've faced scathing remarks from women. A former minister of women's welfare and social development told me on my face that I should tie my hair or move to the back of the party office where I was less visible, as I'd be bringing bad luck to the political party otherwise. I refused to budge. Why is a woman's character always picked on by other women? A transgender woman is relegated to the streets, mostly. We don't want pity, but equal opportunities and mainstreaming.'

Apsara, who underwent a sex change surgery in the US, came back to India to find her own place under the sun. She reflects, 'A lot of people said cruel and baseless things—from my mental state to allegations of how I was treated when I was a child and none of it was true! My mother was supportive, but it was a hard journey, because she was in the city for many years. She had friends and people knew her. If I walked in, people would giggle or turn the other way. At parties, they would be nice to me, but said things behind my back that would inevitably reach my mom's ears. People would come home, planning their times of visit when I would either not be at home or would be sleeping. I realised that the only thing that could help me was becoming successful.'

Apsara found her wings as a features editor of a popular daily, where she penned a successful column. But the road ahead was rough. 'I would walk into the canteen and people would walk out. I'd pitch a story and my peers would dismiss it. There would be situations where I'd submit an error-free copy, but in the final stage, they would introduce errors. My car tyres were punctured on the premises. I was subsequently offered a very senior position at another newspaper, where I was finally promoted to senior editor. Even there, when the staff celebrated someone's birthday, I was not invited. While working there, I used the female toilet. Women were okay with it. Men, however, made nasty comments. I looked very much like a woman when I started working there; I had long hair since I was transitioning. For me, it was the most natural thing. I could never go into a male toilet,' she pauses on an icy note.

Like any other single woman striking out on her own and a first generation political figure, Apsara adds, 'It's a constant fight to shatter the stereotypes that singlehood throws up. Even while getting a US visa, for instance, a single woman is made to feel she's looking for a meal ticket and will settle down there with the first man she meets. A woman on her own turf, financially and emotionally sorted, is a threat to the patriarchal system, be it in politics or business. I am clear with my priorities, I am not looking for a provider.'

Start-Ups, Stereotyping, Slander And Survival

If it's pressure of sexual politics single women fight against at work, there are also equally demanding family obligations. Divorced and single mother, Mumbai-based Nidhu Kapoor, who is professionally practising energy medicine and is the force behind *mysticlotus.com*, quit a high-flying corporate career to pursue a career in spirituality. Nidhu admits the toughest part of being an entrepreneur *and* single is managing the haunting loneliness. 'Today, my driver, maid and plumber are my support system and while I salute the power of a single woman, it's hard taking care of one's own financial, emotional and physical health and if, like me, you have a child, your hands are perennially full; juggling diverse roles in a single day. Also, as is the case with single women engaged in offbeat professions like mine, there is a tendency to demand free services because one is conditioned for years in India to view spirituality as dependent on *daan dakshina* and hocus-pocus. It's not a cash-rich or organised and developed sector as yet. Because there's an exploitative side to spirituality, one views my career with suspicion, with more *babas* than *devis*!' she laments.

Have changing times led to a significant change in mindset? And is the fight for professional acceptance somewhere intrinsically linked to the race to respect a single woman's overall life choices? Delhi-based, 43-year-old Anupamaa Dayal, one of India's leading fashion designers, who started her garment business 13.5 years ago, began operations from her basement. 'I'd travel to a masjid in Maharani Bagh where I was printing just three to four pieces of the garments I'd designed. I used to wear my own designs and when I'd go to pick up my son from school, I'd get a lot of queries as to who the designer was for what I was wearing and these school moms became my first clients, in a sense. Over time, when my husband travelled to Mumbai, he carried some pieces with him, and Melange, one of the top stores in the city, offered to stock them, and ended up scoring record sales. So, in that sense, there was no struggle. By the time I started participating in Fashion Week, mine was already an established brand outside India,' recalls Anupamaa, whose marriage collapsed 7 years ago. 'Professionally, though, I was doing everything, and, also paying for my children's school fees. However, while I was still in the marriage, my tall, fair, light-eyed ex was generally treated as the boss by my workers—thanks to their latent conditioning.

'Till then I had not really taken any credit for my accomplishments. I asked myself: what would I do next? And that's when I started a women's empowerment initiative, filling up the void inside by providing others financial independence and happiness. Bigger breaks followed, as did larger, international orders. But I was also exposed to the seamy underbelly of the industry. Vendors would often be hostile, possibly sensing I didn't have a man by my side. As a woman at the helm of a business empire, I also felt a latent abuse towards our sex with people like the Labour Inspector openly asking for bribes. Often, I'd be probed suspiciously on what my husband does and in every scenario, like even while buying property, I heard comments like, "*Apne* husband *se nahin milwaya aap ne!*"' she looks back.

Anupamaa, who has a built a resort called Anupamaa Mangar in Faridabad, admits that while doing the rounds of the courts, she preferred to dress conservatively, so as to befriend the cops and know more about the legal rights. 'I had six, shapeless *kurta pajamas*. I never showed any skin on purpose, chose to keep my hair out of sight, and was apprehensive of looking back into the eyes of a man,' she says.

Anupamaa's personal struggle of surviving as a successful, single woman entrepreneur has been a gritty journey to gain inclusive self-respect, where today, she claims, she's privileged to not just map her own career, but also look after her children and many women from privileged as well as underprivileged backgrounds. 'I was pressurised into marriage as I was in my 20s which is why I chose the man I finally married, and in a bid to be the dutiful daughter to my wonderful parents I later struggled with coming clean to them about my separation. I approached a clinical psychologist who finally gave me the courage to tell them everything, post which I found wholehearted support towards me and my children. It took a lot of gumption to be who I am now,' she concludes on an introspective note.

Like her, 33-year-old Neha Arora took the entrepreneurial plunge when she quit a high-paying job at Adobe in November 2015, to officially launch Planet Abled on 1 January 2016. Planet Abled was founded to grant people with disabilities the freedom to travel by overcoming their limitations, and be included into mainstream leisure and travel.

Born to a blind father and a wheelchair-bound mother, Neha's personal travel experiences were the reason she formed Planet Abled. 'As kids we never travelled much and it was mainly for school picnics and grandparents' houses. When we grew up and started to travel as a family, we'd face many issues in terms of accessibility and the kind of leisure activities available. There came a point when our parents stopped travelling, citing that they were not able to enjoy the trips. Having faced this hurdle and being immensely fond of travel myself, I began looking for solutions, but sadly, there were none,' says this gutsy singleton, whose personal struggle was far from over.

'The first resistance was from my parents who were regular service-class people in government jobs. And maybe because they had been at the receiving end of dealing with disabilities, they dreamt of a safe space for me. They felt it was already difficult for me to manage just the two of them, and now my entrepreneurial journey would include many others. Plus, I had no tourism business experience either,' recalls Neha, who still stuck it out.

'A blind professor in a university whose help I sought in disabled student outreach, asked me questions like: "Who else is there with you in this? There must be a male person?" He wanted to know if I had a boyfriend who would help me—before telling me how I can't start this venture alone! He went on to lecture me on how this project would take up much of my time, probing on what I did in my free time as well. "Do you drink? Smoke?" he went on, adding that I could be candid with him since he prided himself on being "open minded". Another person with disability asked me to organise a solo holiday, specifying how he would come only if I tagged along,' adds Neha, who has since then faced the last statement several times, by various disabled and influential people she's met and sought help from.

Being single further adds to Neha's work woes. 'Once a person with disability asked me to let him take me for a ride in his jeep to his village and treat it as a date where we could talk about my questions, while having fun on the side. I had no choice but to just cut such people off totally. Another prospective traveller called us wanting to book a rafting tour, but insisted that his travel buddy had to be a female who'd stay with him 24x7 in his room. I had to ask my team to tell him directly that Planet Abled is not an escort company!'

While Neha has found a lot of support, not just in the disability space, but even in the tourism industry, she continues to face navigational dilemmas—thanks to her marital status. 'Once I asked a government tourism official about a destination I was going to visit in a couple of days and he immediately retorted how he was going there, too, on that day itself, and how I could join him so that we could have a nice time. Even older men don't shy away from hitting on you assuming that being single, you must be vulnerable,' Neha lashes out.

As more and more single women break out of convention, their professional lives are a reflection of their tough personal choices—one is forced to re-examine not just the existing gender gap, but also the role of a woman in the family, vis-a-vis the position of a woman in our society. And how we still encounter the same demons—sexual prejudice, persecution by the same sex, a slanted, moral judgment for standing tall. Alone.

STATUS SINGLE: *Being a single woman entrepreneur is every bit as hard as living alone in a city—the most inevitable question being of male validation and why and how you are still unmarried. Today, a woman can not just claim equal inheritance within a family, but also sue a company for sexually discriminatory policies, or if she faces sexual harassment. So don't compromise on your dreams and instead of being a man in a woman's skin, be your own woman.*

Epilogue

Single, Not Sorry

I WAS RECENTLY INVITED TO speak at a networking summit in Kolkata, organised by a leading women's outfit that believes in building communities and sharing stories and journeys of incredible strength and hope. My session was post lunch, and before me was another speaker, a disabled woman in her mid-30s, head of a reputed multinational company. She stunned us all by her inspiring sojourn of overcoming her disability, of today being in a position to lead the inclusion and diversity practice of her organisation, and how she is a role model of sorts, actively encouraging women in that space. We got talking after the summit, and discovered an easy camaraderie. I told her about *Status Single* and how I wished I had met her before I submitted the manuscript, as I strongly felt we need more change-makers in the single-women community, women just like her, not restricted by a pair of crutches or a wheelchair or a speech defect, or anything at all. During the course of our warm interaction, she opened up on how challenging her life had been, and how in a conservative South Indian family, she had to work doubly hard to carve a space unique to herself. I asked if she wanted to be a part of the book, already overflowing with the experiences and voices of so many diverse single women from myriad walks of life and parts of India. She was keen to be included, and so I wrote urgently to my editor, asking if we could perhaps include one more testimonial, which I personally believed would act as an inspiration to an entire gender, especially disabled women whose battle was twice as harder.

We mutually fixed a time for a lengthy telephonic interview, and later, after fervently making my notes, I painstakingly transcribed her story, mailing it to her to cross-check for facts and asking her if it was good to go. I also explained my tight deadline and that the book was closed for all practical purposes. Suddenly, an uncomfortable silence ensued. The cheery camaraderie of our first interaction that had effused with informal and heart-to-heart banter now turned into an icy, cold wall of unreturned calls and WhatsApp messages that waited for the double blue tick. Finally, after several attempts at contacting her, she answered, her tone strangely distant, informing me how her parents weren't okay with what she had disclosed and how she was nursing second thoughts.

I listened to her patiently, respectful of her familial concerns, before she blurted that she wanted her name to be changed. She wanted to know if that was a possibility, given that she herself felt that the sensational parts of her telling were critical to a book such as this. She added that she'd rather use an anonymous identity than a sanitised version of her life, especially parts where she had shared forthrightly about how despite her stellar academic achievements, whopping six-figure salary (she was pretty confident a man her age wasn't earning the same) and fancy corporate designation, she still faced humiliating rejections at the hands of prospective grooms and their nosy, insensitive mothers whose biggest concern remained her physical deformities and whether she could tie a sari or comb her hair on her own.

In the past, and because by then I had recorded the seething stories of close to 3,000 women, I could have easily agreed that we could change her name, the way a lot of the women in the book had requested earlier. But the truth is, something felt wrong. Something was wrong. Grossly wrong.

How a woman of the world, whose profile is flaunted on every professional networking site, whose overcoming of her disability is being marketed as motivation in conferences and summits that intend to forge worthy role models, where she's heading the diversity division of a reputed international conglomerate, being a leader and a public speaker—why a woman like this, is still so scared?

What exactly was she afraid of losing? The support of her parents? The respect of her peers? Friends who may now see her as vulnerable and broken and not the jet-setter, one would assume she is? The loss of lucrative opportunities to be recognised as the face of change in her community—when in reality, she sounded weak, vacillating and trapped. Or was it the men who had not given her a second glance or shuddered seeing her physical deformity that she had been defeated from within? Whose reciprocity and love she still craved for, perhaps—imprisoned, like millions of single women all over the world, in the promise of forever and fairy-tale endings?

I remember reading out to her a passage from a book I was then reading. *Spinster: Making a Life of One's Own* by Kate Bolick. 'Feminism is going to make it possible for the first time for men to be free. At present the ordinary man has the choice between being a slave and being a scoundrel. For the ordinary man is prone to fall in love and marry and have children.... He wants to see them all taken care of, since they are unable to take care of themselves. Yet, if he has them to think about, he is not free.... The bravest things will not be done in the world until women do not have to look to men for support.... [But] men don't want the freedom that women are thrusting on them. They don't want a chance to be brave…. They want to give food and clothes and a little home with lace curtains to some woman. Men want the sense of power more than they want the sense of freedom…. They want someone dependent on them more than they want a comrade. As long as they can be lords in a thirty-dollar flat, they are willing enough to be slaves in the great world outside…. In short, they are afraid that they will cease to be sultans in little monogamic harems. But the world doesn't want sultans. It wants men who can call their souls their own. And that is what feminism is going to do for men—give them back their souls, so that they can risk them fearlessly in the adventure of life,' I paused momentously, hoping she would have had a change of heart. See the larger picture, of how she was more than a solitary, single woman, but part of a movement that needed ownership.

'I'll have to run this by my parents. I will get back to you. I know your timeline,' she retorted curtly. I consented to give her a chance, a second shot at maybe changing her mind, convincing her family that talking about male rejection forthrightly isn't a measure of a woman's self-worth or her place in the world, that being the part she seemed most unsure of, the rest of her life and struggles already openly publicised. I recognised the value of her breaking free and how this exercise was perhaps more critical than simply agreeing to share her experiences with me. How, to me, she represented an entire generation of women like us—singletons, still hemmed in by staunch societal chains, unable to reclaim their truest self, for whom marriage and motherhood was a sort of playing safe, the way projecting professional success mattered more than claiming their own story. Their voice.

As I waited patiently for her response, I remember recalling a married boss, from many years ago in Mumbai when I worked as a journalist. She was a stunning woman and a mother of two almost perfect-looking boys, a high-profile editor with a fancy foreign degree from an Ivy League college. But she was treated shabbily by her husband and in-laws, physically abused for years. She deceptively camouflaged her pain behind oversized Gucci glares, acting like a diva at work, ordering her subordinates around like minions, being mean to almost everyone, enjoying her social status as the toast of the cocktail circuit, openly wooed by film stars, cricketers and socialites, before going home in a gleaming black Mercedes to a sprawling, sea-facing South Mumbai address, where after kicking off her fancy Jimmy Choos and flinging her expensive Gucci bag into a plush leather sofa, she would meekly ask, '*Chawal ya chapatti?*' Saying the same line, everyday, for the rest of her life.

To me, that was her life state, in more ways than one. Standing, as she still is, balanced precariously on a thin, red line, caught between being an overachiever outside and an underachiever inside. How our trajectories as single women, as opposed to married women, was strangely, and ironically if I may add, not starkly as different as I imagined when I'd first set off to write *Status Single*. How breaking free remains our biggest and most challenging fight, and flight.

Coming back to my unfinished conversation…

'I'm sorry I don't want to be a part of the book. Call me when you can,' read the last line of her text. I held the phone to my chest for a few seconds, my thoughts oscillating between disappointment and anger. There was a part of me that was irked at how she had literally led me on, wasted the time which I, as a professional had invested in holding my book edits, just for her sake, and also displayed what I felt was nothing more than a fake bravado, her confidence on stage and on the telephone, a flimsy farce.

But later and just before I deleted her message, I realised what her rejection meant for me. How deep our insecurities ran. 'Be it a normal single woman or a disabled single woman—we are all treated in the same way, seen through the same lens, in the end…' was one of the last things she had said to me before we ended the call.

I was haunted by her choice of words, the irony soaking them, as I am now asking myself even as I write this, while reaching closure in a book of this magnitude, if marriage will ever stop being fundamental to a woman's existence—so much so that she would grow to blossom as an individual and choose a life partner on her own free will and at a time she was most comfortable in.

Where her parents wouldn't treat her like *paraya dhan* from the day she was born, where *kanyadaan* wouldn't necessarily translate into a daughter never being able to step back inside her own home, without being made to feel she lost out on something, the chance to be something, bigger, better. To conform to a silent and tacit conditioning where women play a part, where feeling whole is delegated to outward appearance and one's reproduction abilities, where she can tell her mother to back off from dragging her to an astrologer, the same way she can refuse to grow her hair long or apply fairness creams or wear a stone ring or be asked to marry a peepal tree first. Where a woman could be more than her mother. Or all those before her. Not gutted by the failure of a romance, a marriage, the death of a spouse, parents, the lack of friends or siblings, job changes, infertility. Where she could demand an abortion, the same way she could insist on her inheritance—minus the unfair labelling and humiliation.

A fraction. A flesh. A fairy.

Not too long ago, one of my readers, and a self-professed fan, inboxed me saying how after *Status Single* releases, she thought I may find it hard to actually find a man, given that I'd be publicly labelled a 'single woman', something she forewarned wasn't going to go down well in a country like ours, where aloneness is equivalent to dull spinsterhood, sex to birthing children and happiness to being someone's wife. I mull on her comments now, asking myself if it echoed the same sentiments of one of my male friends who joked on how after the book is out, I would possibly be hit upon by women now—single, like me, sexually frustrated and available. 'Maybe, you should get a book out on single men, next. You'd get lucky, perhaps...hook up with one of the guys, for a change,' he laughed cheekily on a long-distance call. I hung up, citing a poor connection. The last three words of our conversation not leaving me easily.

'For a change...'

Let me be frank here. I chose to consciously not pen the last chapter of *Status Single* in a hurry because I wasn't sure how one concludes a book with so many possibilities and dimensions. Where every story—brave, brazen, beautiful—is my story. Each woman's trajectory in this book is uniquely different. But somewhere I feel they collectively send out the same, overarching message—of how we must learn to separate being single from not being married, because singlehood is so much deeper and richer. It encompasses so many other things, too, than not just having a man or a child by one's side: people and experiences, victories and wars. And we can only be more, if we want more. And expect nothing else. Nothing lesser.

Where women, like me, the only daughters, too, must quit being scared of being left alone after their parents pass away, because most marriages and partnerships also camouflage dark, soulless, empty, sexless pits. The same way, we can't keep hiding behind lofty professional achievements and being successful or rich or sexy or good-looking just for the world, so that we aren't being 'fixed' to a spot we think is reserved for the one who 'missed the bus' was 'too choosy/overqualified for her own good/too arrogant/never listened to her parents', 'unlucky/failed in love', 'couldn't make a marriage click/compromise enough', 'was a *baanjh*/barren womb', 'too dark/fat/thin/too anything/too everything', 'fast/slut/selfish/ shallow/self-absorbed in her career/passion,' 'too horny/too frigid.'

All of us love being called a 'feminist' because the tag makes us feel strong and protected, but the truth is we often lack the courage and conviction to own what just being a woman means, sans the fancy labels and the packaging we are conditioned to believe our sex relies on, to actually stand up to men, parents, bosses, organisations, doctors, grandparents, lovers. The list is endless.

Also companionship isn't to be confused with couplehood. It can be found in leading meaningful, richer lives, therefore diminishing the centrality of 'settling down,' and thus 'settling for', in our life. And with that we can finally get rid of the notion of needing another to complete oneself; when not having a child biologically will cease to be an earth-shattering verdict on our womb, an all-consuming regret we are told that we will have to suffer till we die. When we can savour solitude as a precious gift, and not perceive as an imprisonment, or colossal self-defeat.

And if we can manage to look at our lives with a little less of regret, and more of love for ourselves and our decisions, we will in turn be truly empowered, so much stronger than just being emancipated. When being self-reliant doesn't stop at a fancy designation or a separate cubicle or pulling off a hefty home loan, but expands itself, daily, as we reach our highest potential as people. When we can stop shrinking into our lowest common denominator only because we got rejected or hurt or humiliated by the opposite sex. Stop being equally affected by name-calling by our own sex. When slut-shaming doesn't force us to lie about being in a relationship, or fake a wedding ring or a *mangalsutra* while trying to get a place on rent. Or have to ask one of our male friends or colleagues to be a proxy as a husband or father while requesting a gynaecologist to perform an abortion, which is legally sanctioned in this country. When we don't apologise for who we love and lust after or leave behind, saying no with dignity and clarity, the way we want to say yes and can pronounce the word 'spinster' as nonchalantly as a man pronounces 'bachelor'. Where commitment is synonymous with contentment, where the new 'normal' is a woman who chooses to remain single because she won't be pressured into marriage or motherhood, where her sexuality is a birthright, and not a squeamish, sullen compromise. Something that she must camouflage constantly and convert from to please and placate others.

Where we learn to make peace with ourselves.

The path never easy, always alone.

The way I felt one night, when Facebook unexpectedly threw me an option of befriending the man who had hurt me the deepest. I was 24 when I fell in love. He was a MSN chat friend who graduated to become the love of my life in the months that followed. I had just moved from Delhi to Bengaluru and hated my new workplace, the staid locality my parents chose to rent a home in, the restrictiveness of not speaking the local language, of constantly hearing the adage 'Narth Indian', just because I spoke fluent Hindi and dressed a certain way.

We belonged to contrasting economic backgrounds. He promised marriage and children, luring me into his hotel room in Bengaluru for an afternoon of quick, clumsy sex, that I wasn't even sure of having, wanting instead to be loved, touched, preserved. Every time he left for Mumbai, he committed to speak to his conservative Malayali parents, weaving a new plan about our future. He would take me to furniture shops, show me diamond rings at jewellers and make me promise I would quit journalism after getting married. He would constantly cite monetary problems every time my father asked him what his intentions were. I had then asked my father to back off from interfering. My father and I didn't speak for months afterwards.

It was easy to give in, I suppose. To want so bad to be happy, a blushing bride-to-be, who everyone fusses over and every 20-something young woman on the unbridling of her sexual journey fantasizes about. To think your future is 'settled', so to speak. To be like the others: a perfect family, body, job, and a man who loves you back—this time, for real. The idea of completion and being a conquest, which we are all conditioned and trained to believe in as young girls.

'Our lifestyles are different,' his one-line text declared. His cell phone turned off. His mother, his best friend, his sister... all said they didn't want me calling him. 'I'm telling you in plain English, don't disturb me,' was our last proper conversation as I howled sitting huddled in an airless telephone booth at the corner of a busy thoroughfare, my heart shattered, my hopes turned to dust. Not knowing where I would go from there. Doing what every woman does at some point: beg, plead, apologise for things she's not even sure of. Panic, act desperate, try and cling on to a fractured verdict.

All these thoughts came flooding by suddenly as I scanned his Facebook timeline. A fancy foreign posting, twin boys, a petite, pretty wife belonging to the same community—a life I had been promised. My eyes welled up as I read his posts: birthdays, anniversaries, vacations...a world that had eluded me. All my strength and feminism melting away into flesh and blood. It was easy to shrink into self-pity, and I almost did, when a text from my best friend in Australia, a mother of three, shook me out of my stupor. 'Your life path was never meant to be just a wife. Your pain and emotional breakdown, and the fact that you picked up the pieces... that you are still single doesn't mean he's moved on, and you are stuck in a rut. It means you were meant to write a different story. He was a chapter. Not the ending.'

Every woman in this book hopes for love and commitment, and has at some point been in a serious relationship, been married or has attempted to settle down. And yet, despite us remaining single, the biggest takeaway has been knowing that what matters in the end is waiting for a partner, regardless of gender, who respects us as a person, willing to walk beside us, and not behind us, who will not look after us, not as his property, but look out for us as a well-wisher, as a true friend, be a part of our tribe. Because finding love is about finding what makes us truly happy. Just as the path to surviving being single is not turning cynical, but opening our hearts instead to the infinite possibilities of strength, sexuality and survival.

The way I felt sometime ago in Shahpur Jat, a high-end trousseau destination in the Capital, on a shopping jaunt for my cousin brother's wedding. While trying out some jewellery, the shop attendant probed incessantly on whether I was the 'bride.' I dismissively shrugged my shoulders, not answering her directly. After a few times, I snapped, a tad aggressively, 'Why is that important for you to know, may I please ask?'

She was perhaps a bit taken aback at being spoken to forthrightly, and replied, almost sounding apologetic, 'Actually, madam, you are only looking at all the heavy sets, these are mostly bridal.' I walked closer and asked in a cold tone, 'If I can afford them, then why not? Who is to decide if a bride alone can wear these, huh?'

'Actually, I can show you some sets for the other ladies… I mean, other functions… I mean pretty, but not bridal,' she interjected, genuinely startled by my bluntness.

Another buyer, a blushing young bride, I presumed, eyed me with curiosity, especially as I tried out ornate *polki* sets, accompanied as she was by a motley crowd of women, maybe her mother or mother-in-law-to-be and a few other grouchy lot, who could hardly stop themselves from commenting on her every choice. How the *nath* was way too big. The *pasha* not coordinated with her choker. The *chandbaalis* too small.

Our glances met.

'How do I look?' she asked in a soft voice, holding an emerald *mangtika* over her forehead.

'How do you feel?' I quizzed gently.

'Happy,' she eased into a reticent smile.

I flashed a victory sign, watching as she negotiated what she wanted with those buying her the jewellery, how she had to literally justify what made her happy, days before she walked into another home. Finally persuaded to select a ruby one instead.

Her smile, lost.

As I paid the bill after a while, watching her leave, her footsteps dragging, I felt a strange tug at my heart. How I always shopped alone. How I selected this set, too, by myself. Paid the hefty bill silently from my own credit card. How I immediately calculated that I could not buy the Mac mascara I had been intending to. A part of me, I must admit, wistfully longed to time travel. Be the young, bashful, 24-year-old, back in Bengaluru, who spontaneously spun dreams of fairy-tale endings, *haldi* ceremonies, pre-bridal parlour dates, wedding spoils, and eventually, fancy foreign postings and baby showers. Who called her lover every hour, always to tell him what she wore and how she looked, taking a picture instantly, and rushing back to a desktop to mail him. While imagining her parents as doting grandparents who'd be happy with their daughter's life choices, of her kids being called Vignesh and Vinaya. I thought of who we become when we allow ourselves to be loved fully. The way it destroys parts of us, forever.

'Ma'am…' the girl called out from behind, just as I was leaving, adding urgently, 'Can I take a picture? For our shop catalogue?'

'Why? Me?' I questioned, startled.

'You are the first single woman who has ever come here and bought a bridal set. All by herself, that too…' she was breathless. Her face flushed.

I opened my hair, put on a fresh coat of lipstick, and wore the set, as I was told to.

The mellow February sunlight inviting. Intimate. Falling carelessly over my shoulders. A tender reassurance as its tiny, gold specks settled all over my face.

'Cheese!' the girl announced in a shrill tone.

I took a deep breath.
And widened my eyes.
It was time.
I was more.
We are more.
Single is not a state of life. But a state of mind.

uOs explit doluptas etur solupta voleste stemquis ut lam quia vella diorem. Ciae non conem faccae volorib uscieni magnis iur?

Nam, sanis as mosseria voluptas experem quam re, ventio. Itatem consequate nestin rerata consequat vollatio que pe dolo volorit liatus, alique volupta quunduciam ius asimos ditio optatur, conseque odictumquo et que pora pa dissunt, aut harum aut volorro ratist ducit lab imolut del iusae

Acknowledgments

In 2014, I had the rare chance to meet and interact with a woman from Jaipur, who I call Neeti, as I am not allowed to disclose her name. An inspiration behind my bestselling erotic novel, *Sita's Curse*, Neeti was a victim of marital rape by her husband, almost a decade-and-a-half older than her who suffered from erectile dysfunction and whose family paraded her to an ageing godman who veritably raped her on the pretext of 'blessing' her womb.

Neeti's son from him is now 10.

'I want you to share my story with the world—I know you can see me—someday I want to tell my son that he is mine, mine alone. That my womb is nothing compared to my heart. Someday, I shall break free. I shall have the courage. I want to start a pickle and *papad* business. Be more than this, you know,' was how my interview with her culminated. Her eyes moistened. Mine, burning, as if I had a fever.

Over the years, Neeti and I have forged an unlikely, almost uncanny camaraderie. We have both changed a lot since our first meeting. Our only meeting. But, if there is one thing that I can proudly claim, it is this. Neeti is today single. Having walked out of her abusive and dysfunctional marriage, earlier in 2017, today she's found shelter with an NGO and has started making *papads* as she always dreamt of. Her son is not with her. As she prepares to fight a long-drawn-out legal battle—to me it is women like Neeti who symbolise the strength of singlehood, whose courageous battle to stand tall as a single woman defies the patriarchal shackles that suffocate our sex—that associates our self-worth with a surname.

As I discuss this book with Neeti, and tell her to say a prayer that it is well-received, she pauses at the end of a lengthy phone call. 'I was scared to be single at first. Ashamed. But I think of you. Women like you. Who face the world alone. Who fight for what they deserve. I want to be like you all. I want to work. Have my own home. I want to have a lover, be touched, be seen as a woman… a real life person, and not just a body, a womb to produce kids…' her words trail.

I think of the time my literary agent Kanishka Gupta convinced me that my own struggle of being single was a journey that would find many takers—and how I could have never imagined how right he was. Or how similar Neeti and I actually are. Of how as women we all fight the same demons—how we ache to be desired. Dream of being free, feminine, feisty. At the same time.

As I feel overwhelmed thinking of how far Neeti has come today, I am convinced that we—all of us single women—have so much farther to traverse. How my mother, a young widow, who was single for over a decade after I lost my biological father, was possibly carrying a legacy forward—how she was a veritable role model for her only daughter. How each of us are important. How the bridges we cross and build will help one another. To get stronger.

I owe my thanks for this book to my parents, as I do with any book I write. To my editor Rashmi Menon for being patient and a natural empath. To my first editor and life coach, Nandita Aggarwal, who tells me that single is sacred and who is my go-to person for advice, sanctuary and scoldings. To all the wonderful single women friends I have whose life and lessons are valuable to me. Just the way this book couldn't have been possible sans the brave telling of so many women, who shared so much of themselves.

Who, like Neeti, are such resilient crusaders.

Finally, single doesn't mean averse to marriage and motherhood and men, but neither is our life defined by the latter.

It is what I hope *Status Single* will make you understand. Feel. And own.

'I want to fly. To be enough,' Neeti signs off.